APPLIED ECONOMETRICS

MEGHNAD DESAI
London School of Economics and Political Science

APPLIED ECONOMETRICS

Philip Allan

First published 1976 by

PHILIP ALLAN PUBLISHERS LIMITED
RED LION COTTAGE
MARKET PLACE
DEDDINGTON
OXFORD OX5 4SE

0 86003 012 1

Typeset by E.W.C. Wilkins Ltd, London and Northampton
Printed in Great Britain by
The Camelot Press Limited, Southampton

Contents

Preface *vii*

1 The nature of econometrics *1*

2 Estimation *39*

3 Static single equations: demand analysis *71*

4 Static multiple equations: production function *105*

5 Measurement problems in econometric analysis: technical change *137*

6 Dynamic single equation models: investment behaviour *168*

7 Dynamic simultaneous equation models: wages and prices *205*

8 Macroeconomic models: simulation and policy applications *233*

References *269*

Index *276*

Preface

There has been a tremendous growth in the use of econometric techniques in universities as well as government bodies, national and international, and private industries. The notion of an equation and a curve has been imparted to their readers by the 'quality' newspapers and journals. Such a tremendous growth has been by no means problem free. In a sense, the respect for econometric techniques and faith in the infallibility of model builders passed its high point in the mid sixties. The debacle of the Phillips Curve and the whole notion of a stable empirical trade-off between inflation and unemployment has shown how tenuous the great constant relationships of our subject are. The forecasting record of model builders in the recent recession did nothing to enhance the confidence of the decision maker in econometrics.

Even within the academic profession, one is sensing a doubt as to whether the generation of more numbers for their own sake is fruitful. The ad hoc approach of many practising econometricians to the problem of hypothesis testing and of inference is illustrated by the popular image of much econometrics as a high R^2 in search of a theory. Garbage in–garbage out is how many describe their own activity.

It is necessary therefore to look again at the thorny problem involved in practising econometrics. In recent years econometric theory has been established on a sound foundation of mathematical statistics and many textbooks are available which expound the subject in a rigorous manner. There is therefore no longer any excuse for a student not to be thoroughly familiar with econometric theory. Indeed, in the course of writing this book, I have assumed that the reader has had such a course or can easily equip himself with the required knowledge. Thus while Chapters 1 and 2 sketch out the current state of theory and techniques they are no substitute for a course in econometric theory as a prerequisite for reading this book or to practising econometrics.

The gap between theory and application is still wide in econometrics; with a few exceptions – those who excel in econometric theory keep away from the messy contact with data. In applied econometrics, one is often encouraged to employ techniques known to be inefficient or even inappropriate on the grounds of simplicity or ease of computation. Thus a reliance on multiple regression analysis is often justified by appeal to such criteria or a scepticism in the efficacy of better methods. On the other hand, many go for 'high powered techniques' because they sound complicated and perhaps earn a temporary quasi-rent for the user.

The approach taken in this book is that good econometric research must combine economic theory with econometric theory in as systematic a fashion as possible. The econometrician must take his theory seriously and follow through the consequences of adopting a theoretical approach. This means that he should be interested not so much in the explanatory power of his equation (R^2) but in testing the validity of restrictions imposed by economic theory. But, in addition, since much economic theory is deterministic and we operate in a stochastic context, as much care should be taken to specify the stochastic aspects of our equations and here again the consequent action in the form of the use of appropriate estimating techniques must be taken.

The plan of the book reflects this. Two introductory chapters rapidly survey the theoretical background. Here no proofs are given for the many propositions made but attempt has been made to cover those techniques which are going to be of use. Special emphasis is put on indicating how restrictions can be tested and on adequate specification of the stochastic terms.

After that, Chapters 3 and 4 take up the problems of estimating static models. The single equation situation is illustrated with demand analysis. Here the available economic theory is rich in providing restrictions and itself indicates that the single equation approach is wrong in terms of economic theory. Sets of demand equations are discussed along with the problem of testing restrictions. Wherever possible actual econometric works are taken as examples, though our approach is not one of 'case studies'. Chapter 4 deals with sets of simultaneous static equations in the context of production functions. As will be clear, we have excluded no aspect of the problems that arise, be they in terms of non-linearities or in the use of maximum likelihood methods on the grounds of difficulty.

The next chapter deals with the problem of approximating the concepts of economic theory from statistical data. As an example, the concept of technical change is taken and the interaction of theory and measurement is discussed. The next two chapters deal with dynamic models. Chapter 6 deals with single equation models in the context of investment demand functions and Chapter 7 with multiple equation dynamic models. A major problem here is the specification of the error term, and special attention is paid to autoregressive influences in the error terms.

The last chapter illustrates the logic of large macroeconomic models and takes up the topics of simulation and policy making.

This book evolved steadily over many years. I have participated in the design and teaching of applied econometrics courses at the undergraduate and graduate level at the LSE for ten years. The book was started in 1970/1971 when I was on leave from LSE at the Delhi School of Economics. It has since been revised and updated annually. There is no guarantee that I have converged after several iterations to the correct approach but the criterion adopted for stopping at this stage is limited patience on the part of the author.

Many people have helped over many years in making this book possible. My first acknowledgement should be to my teacher Lawrence Klein who spared a lot of his valuable time to teach me econometrics literally from the beginning. Working in the Economic Research Unit at the University of Pennsylvannia under his supervision, with the comradely help of my fellow students, gave me a taste and addiction for applied econometrics. At the LSE, I have had the benefit of an ongoing seminar in which colleagues have tried to instil in me habits of rigorous thought. Above all I am grateful to Dennis Sargan who has done much to inculcate an analytical approach to problems of practical econometrics. I have learnt much from him and as well from David Hendry and Ken Wallis who have been my tutors in many areas of econometric theory. I thank them for the patience they have shown with my shortcomings. In addition they read several drafts of each chapter and made detailed comments. Franklin Fisher of MIT has also taken an interest in my work over many years and he made some searching criticisms of the first two chapters which led to drastic revisions. Donald Hester (Wisconsin), Grayham Mizon (LSE), Steven Pudney (LSE) and Michael Wickens (Essex) also read complete drafts and made many suggestions. At an earlier stage and for another publisher, Gordon Fisher (Southampton) acted in an editorial capacity. Martin Lewin was a patient and speedy editor at the final stage.

An army of talented and charming secretaries typed various drafts of this book. Early drafts were typed at the Delhi School of Economics and the University of Wisconsin. At LSE, Geraldinge Preece did the bulk of the second draft. Sharon Goode, Marianna Tappas, Christine Moll and Raija Thompson escorted the manuscript to its final stage. I am grateful to all of them.

MEGHNAD DESAI

1
The nature of econometrics

Most readers will have encountered by now some examples of econometric work in journal articles, textbooks or monographs, or even perhaps in newspapers. The first encounter is usually with an econometric equation with a variable on the left-hand side and one or several variables on the right-hand side, each with a coefficient attached to it. A modicum of numeracy has to be acquired to read and interpret such numbers and the related additional information (such as R^2 means 'R squared') that is usually quoted. We begin our introduction to applied econometrics in this familiar territory.

Equation (1.1) below is such a typical example of an econometric equation relating world demand for coffee (DC) for the years 1951–1969 (*Annual Data*) to income (Y) and price of coffee (PC).

$$\begin{array}{rcl} DC_t & = & 261.0 + 2.79 Y_t - 1.23\, PC_t \\ & & (3.2) \quad\; (5.4) \quad\;\; (1.76) \end{array} \qquad (1.1)$$

$\bar{R}^2 = 0.792 \quad DW = 2.35 \quad \bar{S} = 27.28 \quad N = 19$
$F(2.16) = 35.3$

In table 1.1, we have defined all the variables and also the statistical measures ($\bar{R}^2$, DW, etc.). For the present, we can see that equation 1.1 is a 'good result'. The $\bar{R}^2$ is 'high' explaining 79% of the total variance in DC; $\bar{S}$, the standard error of the regression is about 5% of the mean value of the dependent variable. If we wanted to comment further on equation 1.1, we could remark that the Durbin–Watson (DW) statistic is in the 'indecisive' range and so we cannot say much about the presence or absence of positive serial correlation in the errors.

A second set of conclusions usually drawn about equation 1.1 concerns the signs of the coefficients of income (Y) and price (PC). We say that the signs are 'correct', i.e. agree with prior expectations. Looking at the t-ratios given in parentheses below each coefficient estimate, we can see that a rule of thumb which says that if the t-ratio is higher than 2, then the coefficient is 'significant' (i.e. significantly different from zero at 5% confidence level) is satisfied for two of the three coefficients.

Notice carefully that some of the numbers on which we have commented (e.g. $\bar{R}^2$, t-ratios) are said to be 'good' because they are 'high', whereas others (e.g. $\bar{S}$) are 'good' because they are 'low'. Then, to confuse the picture still further, the statistic called DW happens to have a value which is neither good nor bad; indeed, its value is not really of much help to us. Such a description of the estimates obtained from an econometric equation, while useful in some respects, is undoubtedly informal and mechanical, and it does not get to the heart of the matter. When, for example is a number judged to be 'high' rather than 'low' or vice-versa? Can we be so definite as to say that we have a 'good'—as opposed to a 'bad'—result?

In trying to provide answers to questions of this kind, we must immediately face up to two fundamental restraints upon econometric enquiry. First of all, as the term implies, an econometric analysis is a *statistical* analysis of an *economic* problem. Consequently, the criteria by which success should be judged ought to be both statistical and economic, and there may be conflict between them. Moreover, the purpose of an analysis may be, at one time, more statistical than economic (e.g. developing a statistical forecasting equation for an economic variable) and, at another, more economic than statistical (e.g. an analysis of economic policy). Second, the data used in econometric research are typically not data originally collected for this

Table 1.1

Variables		*Mean*
DC_t	Demand for coffee all varieties in thousands of bags. Agricultural year 50/51 being treated as 1951. (Data from International Coffee Organisation.)	53,707
Y_t	World income; UN Statistical Year Book. Index Numbers 1959 = 100.	110.2
PC_t	Price in New York in cents per lb for unwashed Arabicas. (Data from International Coffee Organisation.)	46.9

Dependent variable DC_t

Independent variable	*Estimated coefficient*	*Standard error*	*T-statistic*
C	261.000802	81.909679	3.19
Y	2.793271	.520950	5.36
PC	−1.225944	.695918	−1.76

$R^2 = 0.8152$ corrected $R^2 = 0.7921$
$F-$ statistic (2,16) = 35.295645
Durbin–Watson statistic (adj. for 0 gaps) = 2.3546
Number of observations = 19
Sum of squared residuals = 11816.251545
Standard error of the regression = 27.175646

R^2 Variance of dependent variable (DC_t) explained by the equation as proportion of total variance. If $\hat{DC}_t$ is the value of DC_t computed from equation 1.1, then R^2 = variance of $\hat{DC}$/variance of DC.

$\bar{R}^2$ R^2 adjusted for degrees of freedom.

DW Durbin–Watson statistic used for testing hypothesis about auto-correlation in residuals from a regression equation. Define residual as $e_t = DC_t - \hat{DC}_t$. Then

$$DW = \sum_{t=2}^{19} (e_t - e_{t-1})^2 / \sum_{t=2}^{19} e_{t-1}^2$$ (See Chapter 2 for details)

$\bar{S}$ Standard error of the regression—a measure of the unexplained portion of the dependent variable. Taken as square root of the unexplained variance adjusted for degrees of freedom $\sqrt{\text{var } DC(1-\bar{R}^2)}$

F value of the F-statistic computed as $\dfrac{R^2/(k-1)}{(1-R^2)/(N-k)}$

k is the number of coefficients estimated in (1.1)—three in this case—and N is the number of observations. The values in parentheses beside F in the text are $k-1$ and $N-k$. If there were no relationship between DC and the independent variables in 95% of the cases we would obtain a value of F of 3.63. The probability of getting a value of 35.3 when there is truly no relationship is extremely small.

purpose; the data do not, for example, correspond to the measurements made in a controlled experiment under laboratory conditions. Consequently, econometricians must often work with very imperfect measurements and judgements of the success of results must then take this into account. What looks unsuccessful in a particular situation may nevertheless be 'good' in the circumstances.

More generally, econometric work must compromise between the type of economic problem to be examined (e.g. the world coffee market or the demand for coffee in the UK), the purpose of the analysis (e.g. whether it is a forecasting exercise or a policy analysis) and the availability of data. And, remembering that compromise is inevitable, we proceed to build the analysis and judge the results by posing questions at each stage of the enquiry: for example, in respect of equation 1.1:

(i) *Aims.* What was the purpose of the original exercise as part of which equation 1.1 was estimated? What are the aims of an econometric researcher?

(ii) *Specification.* Is the form of the equation arbitrary or is there a logic behind the particular variables chosen and the mathematical form (linear equation) in which they appear? How is the econometric relationship specified?

(iii) *Measurement.* Are the chosen variables measured as one would wish them to be measured? Do they correspond to their economic definition and are they free of measurement errors? Are they, on the other hand, arbitrary statistical constructs?

(iv) *Identifiability.* Is the equation meaningful in terms of economic theory? Is it a meaningful numerical representation of an economic relationship or just a 'bunch of numbers' without any economic interpretation?

(v) *Estimation.* Given the nature of the data and the considerations in (ii) to (iv), is the multiple regression method employed in arriving at 1.1 (i.e. ordinary least squares–OLS) the best method for our purpose?

(vi) *Verification.* Having completed the enquiry up to and including (v), do the estimates conform with the theory which underlies (iii) and/or the restrictions imposed under (iv), or are they at variance with either? Do we need to make any revisions of the theory in the light of the estimates? This is the area of testing hypotheses by which we attempt to substantiate or deny the theory on which the original equation was constructed.

(vii) *Application.* Having satisfied questions under (ii) to (vi), how do we make further use of 1.1 to accomplish the purpose set out in (i), that is the end use to which econometric results may be put and their limitations?

We now take up the discussion of each of these topics in general and with particular reference to equation 1.1. In the course of our discussion, we may be led to suggest alternative forms of the relationship that 1.1 purports to measure and even add other complementary relationships (e.g. a supply relationship). Details of estimation techniques used in 1.1 and many subsequent equations are surveyed in the next chapter which should be read in conjunction with this one.

The Aims of Econometric Research

Econometric research has usually a practical aim—forecasting the course of one or many economic variables or analysing means by which their future course may be controlled. Sometimes the aim may be purely scientific—e.g. testing hypotheses arising out of economic theory for discriminating between rival economic theories which may lead to a further growth of knowledge. In a sense, we are really searching for stable patterns of cause and effect in economic phenomena and we are seeking to quantify them in an adequate way. The only checks we have of the adequacy of our quantification and of the stability of any causal pattern are their agreements with past facts and their value as guides to the future course of events. We summarise this in one word—prediction, i.e. the predictive ability of our findings. We try to estimate a structure of economic relations (a system of structural relations) which embody a stable causal mechanism and this enables us, we hope, to analyse the likely behaviour of the variables which are affected and which we are studying when any of the causal variables actually *or hypothetically* changes.

Prediction is often thought to be synonymous with forecasting but we should make a distinction. Forecasting is concerned with the course of a variable over some future time period while prediction is concerned with its course in response to changes in causal–exogenous–variables. Accurate forecasting involves discovery of inertial patterns of movement in a variable but such inertia *need not* involve stable causal patterns. In a way, better predictive ability of an econometric finding about a variable ought to help us forecast the variable better. This is because information about causal patterns tells us more than the finding that a variable is likely to move in the future as it has moved in the past (inertia). By concentrating on the discovery of stable causal patterns between exogenous causal variables and the variables whose course the theory seeks to analyse (the endogenous variables), prediction also embodies a way of testing whether such causal patterns are those posited by economic theory. In a sense two rival theories may explain the same phenomenon by positing two different causal patterns. If one of them can be shown to have superior predictive ability, then it is judged to be preferable.

In our example above, we are studying the demand for coffee. One of the causal variables is income. (For reasons to be outlined below the other variable–price–is not a truly causal variable since it can in turn be influenced by quantity.) We may wish to forecast the quantity of coffee to be consumed in year 1984. We may on the other hand wish to predict the effect on the quantity demanded of a likely rise in income. The latter does not necessarily involve any accurate knowledge about the level of income in 1984, the former must. The latter can be accomplished by using the coefficient of Y along with its standard error to provide a range of changes in quantity of coffee demanded for possible changes in income. We can go further and compare two rival theories of demand curves by their predictive powers. For example, one theory might be based on a constant *slope* demand curve (such as the one we have used above) and another on a constant *elasticity* demand curve. The latter takes the form of ln (DC) as a function of ln (Y_t) and ln (PC_t), the coefficients then being the (constant) elasticities. We can compare the relative predictive abilities of these two rival theories but this topic must be postponed until later in this chapter.

Another objective of econometric research can be as an aid to decision making and to provide a means of evaluating the effects of potential action designed to control a system. Some of the exogenous causal variables may be under the control of the decision maker and one task of econometric research may be as an aid to better decision making by the individual or corporate decision maker. Imagine, for the time being, that equation 1.1 represents the demand curve facing a monopolist seller of coffee (as may be formed by a commodity agreement or by a producers' cartel). The monopolist wants to set a price so as to maximise total revenue (which illustrates the point and avoids the problem of introducing cost curves which a profit maximising exercise would involve). In our example this is given by rewriting (1.1) without a residual error as

$$\widehat{DC_t} = \hat{\beta}_0 + \hat{\beta}_1 Y_t - \hat{\beta}_2 PC_t \qquad (1.2)$$

where $\hat{\beta}_0$, $\hat{\beta}_1$ and $\hat{\beta}_2$ are the estimates as listed in 1.1. Then the revenue maximising price (PC_t^*) is given as

$$PC_t^* = [(\hat{\beta}_0 + \hat{\beta}_1 Y_t)/2\hat{\beta}_2]$$

Our equation thus enables the monopolist to set the price at the optimal level since by our assumption he controls the price. In a realistic setting, we also need to take care of uncertainty and of random errors and problems are rarely as simple as the one above. A decent econometric estimate of the causal structure is an essential but only a first step in any optimal decision making exercise.

Some Definitions

Before we go any further, we need to set out the definitions of some terms we have already used. We shall be studying not only single equations such as 1.1 but a set of equations. This is because in economics, the mutual interdependence of economic quantities plays a large part. The most familiar example is the simultaneous determination of price and quantity in the Marshallian demand–supply (scissors) diagram.

We shall therefore first talk about *models*, not equations. A model is a hypothesis or a set of hypotheses concerning the mutual causal relations among a set of variables. At this stage, we keep the definition fairly empty. A model should consist of at least as many equations as we have unknown quantities. The total number of quantities or variables in a model will be frequently larger than the total number of equations. This is because we assume that some of the variables act as data for our model, i.e. they affect the unknown variables but are not affected by them. These variables we have called above *causal* or *exogenous* variables; the unknown variables are called *endogenous* variables.

This breakdown is not entirely satisfactory because causality is, in general, time dependent: a cause must precede an effect in time, and some causes take a long time to work themeselves out. Consequently, some of the endogenous variables may appear with lags and a lagged endogenous may be regarded as causal in the same way as a simple exogenous variable. Variables which are lagged are often referred to as *predetermined variables* since, as an example, x_{t-1}, x_{t-2}, . . . , etc. have already been determined at time t, one way or another. On the other hand, all exogenous variables get determined by a means outside the scope of the model and, in this sense, are always predetermined. Thus the class of predetermined variables more generally includes all exogenous variables *and* all lagged variables: all exogenous variables are consequently predetermined but all predetermined variables are not exogenous.

The course of the endogenous variables is determined by their mutual interaction and by the effect on them of the exogenous and the predetermined variables. These interactions and effects are embodied in the *parameters* which are the constants in the model. For example, $\hat{\beta}_0$, $\hat{\beta}_1$, $\hat{\beta}_2$ in equation 1.2 may be thought of as estimates of the underlying parameters β_0, β_1, and β_2 respectively, whose numerical values are given in equation 1.1. When we give the model a certain explicit form, we embody a *structure* or a set of structural relations. Many rival structures can be subsumed by a model. We will, for example, deal with linear structural relations for convenience, but a model can be much more general than this. This said, in what follows, we shall frequently use the word 'model' in its narrower sense of a structure. The set of structural equations is called *the structural form of the model*; if the equations were rewritten in such a way that the mutual interaction of the endogenous variables was 'solved out' and each endogenous variable was expressed as a function of the exogenous and predetermined variables alone, then we have a *reduced form* of the model.

All the structures we shall investigate will be probabilistic or stochastic in nature. Instead of relationships and variables being deterministic, we shall assume that variables will contain random errors either because of inadequate measurement or because of imperfections of knowledge or behaviour. Relations, too, shall be subject to random errors. Our structure will embody the population values (in a statistical sense) of the variables, the parameters and the random elements. We may have some prior knowledge about the structure or about the probability distributions of the random elements. This we obtain from experience or introspection and embody as an assumption of the structure. Thus it will, of necessity, be only an estimate, an approximation to reality. We shall draw inferences about the population parameters from the information available and we may even test some hypotheses about them but we shall never know with certainty what are the values of the population parameters.

Let us apply the definitions to our example. We have in 1.1 an equation expressing the demand for coffee as a linear function of price and income. At the back of our mind is a model of the coffee market. The nature of relations comprising that model will be drawn from our theoretical knowledge of commodity markets. If we confine ourselves to the market for coffee, we can clearly take income as a datum since while income influences the market for coffee, the influence in the opposite direction is likely to be small. Income is therefore treated as an exogenous variable. But we still have to say how many equations are in our model and in the particular structure of which 1.1 is one estimated equation. Clearly, economic theory suggests that we need a supply equation for coffee together with a market clearing price determining equation. Since coffee is storable, supply for coffee (*SC*) consists of the output of coffee (QC_t) and the stocks of coffee (*STC*). We set up a *model* as follows

$DC_t = D(PC_t, Y_t, U_{1t})$	demand for coffee	(1.3)
$SC_t = QC_t + STC_{t-1}$	supply of coffee	(1.4)
$QC_t = Q(PC_t, U_{2t})$	output of coffee	(1.5)
$PC_t = P(SC_t, DC_t, U_{3t})$	market clearing equation	(1.6)
$STC_t = STC_{t-1} + (QC_t - DC_t)$	stocks level	(1.7)

Our model consists of five equations with five endogenous variables, *DC, PC, SC, QC,* and *STC*, one exogenous variable, *Y*, and one variable which is lagged endogenous and hence predetermined: STC_{t-1}. In the model above, we have three *stochastic equations* 1.3, 1.5 and 1.6; they are in implicit function form and include the random error terms U_1, U_2 and U_3 in their arguments. The two other equations are definitional *identities* for supply and stocks.

We can write the model of our coffee market in a much more general framework than that in 1.3 to 1.7. For example, as Marschak writes it (Marschak 1950, p. 19),

$$\phi_g [\chi, u; \alpha(g)] = 0 \quad (1.8)$$

where χ denotes all our variables, endogenous and predetermined, u the disturbances and $\alpha(g)$ the set of parameters for the gth equation. g goes from 1 . . . G and in our case $G = 5$. ϕ_g are general functions. We can specialise this general model to a more particular structure. We do this by saying that the functions *D, Q* and *P* are linear equations and the error terms are additive. We could say more about the way in which variables enter the equations and this takes us into a discussion of the second question we raised regarding specification of econometric relationships.

Specification

Specification of econometric relationships is a crucial step in any applied econometric work. By specification, we mean *at least* the following three things.

1. *Choice of the variable to be explained and the explanatory variables*: Some of the explanatory variables will be endogenous and others exogenous. This is because we shall not be specifying any one relationship in isolation from others but in the context of an overall model. In our example above, in the first equation, we are interested in explaining the quantity of coffee demanded. Economic theory tells us that demand for a commodity is a function of income and relative prices. We include some of these in our equation. At any point of time, our choice of what variables to specify is, of course, limited by what data series are available. Econometricians are mainly data users and this has interesting consequences for econometric methodology, as we shall see later. We also have a subsidiary problem that economic theory is not always clear on the choice of independent variables. We may be led to search empirically for some suitable combination of independent variables to include. Common practice is to do this by trying out alternative specifications in multiple regression analysis, estimating the parameters by OLS and choosing among the specifications on some simple criterion such as highest R^2, or high t values, etc. Though common, this is not in general a good practice. As we shall see later in this chapter and in more detail in Chapter 2, the appropriateness of OLS depends very much on the validity of the specification and cannot always be used as a device to discriminate between specifications without leading to erroneous conclusions.

2. *Choice of functional form*, especially whether the equation should be linear or non-linear: Ideally this choice should be

dictated by economic theory, but in practice linear specifications are usually chosen. We must make clear here that by 'linear' we mean linear in the *parameters* rather than in variables. Thus a log-linear specification with the dependent and independent variables in logarithmic form but otherwise of the form of 1.2 is linear in parameters but non-linear in variables since we have:

$$\ln (DC_t) = \beta_0' + \beta_1' \ln Y_t - \beta_2' \ln (PC_t) + u_t' \qquad (1.2a)$$

The reason for specifying 1.2a as against 1.2 may be preference for a constant elasticity relation rather than a constant slope one. A specification which is non-linear in parameters as well as in variables can be concocted (purely as an illustration) by writing the demand equation as

$$DC_t = A[\alpha_1 Y_t^{-\rho} + \alpha_2 PC_t^{-\rho}]^{-1/\rho} + u_t'' \qquad (1.9)$$

Linear specifications are adopted partly for computational convenience, since then OLS is directly applicable to them, but also as a *reasonable first approximation* to the 'true' relationship. As we shall see, more and more cases of non-linear specifications are occurring nowadays since they are more rigorously derivable from economic theory and because the computational problems have been tackled successfully. Linear specification needs therefore to be justified on theoretical grounds if it is the preferred alternative.

3. *Specification of the stochastic process*: It is extremely important to specify the nature of the random error term at the same time as developing the specification of the deterministic part of the equation. Since much of economic theory is non-stochastic, economists take great care to explain the theoretical background to the deterministic part of the equation and attach an error term without any explanation and just before discussing their estimates. Most studies also begin by (and many go no further than) assuming that the error term satisfies all the OLS properties (see Chapter 2 for details). Recently it has become common practice to extend this somewhat by assuming a first-order autoregressive error. This still does not explain the logic for any of the assumptions made. It is often realised that a dynamic

specification in the deterministic part, e.g. by hypothesizing a distributed lag mechanism, has direct implication for the dynamics of the error term. We shall try and show as far as possible the advantages of specifying the stochastic term as a part of the overall specification problem.

Correct specification is very important in econometric work since the choice of the estimation procedure depends on the specification. As we shall see in Chapter 2, our analysis of the consequences of mis-specification also starts by positing a 'true' specification from which we work out the direction of the bias in the actual (mis-specified) equation. In a sense, the 'true' specification can never be known but only better approximated each time. The role of economic theory in providing *a priori* information concerning specification cannot be overestimated. Frequently, e.g. in demand analysis, theory provides us with detailed information not only with respect to what variables to include but also with respect to signs of the parameters and also the size (see Chapter 3 for a further elaboration). In other areas, such as investment functions as we shall see in Chapter 6, rival specifications abound and it is not always possible to discriminate between them from available information.

To go back to our example, equation 1.2 or 1.2a is not fully satisfactory from the point of view of demand theory. We have not included the price of any substitute or complements, nor have we imposed the restriction that the demand function be homogeneous of degree zero in income and prices. But again we take up these issues in Chapter 3.

Measurement

Questions of measurement of economic variables are frequently cast as problems of error specification. Thus we know in estimation theory of the case of measurement errors or errors in variables and separate it from the case of errors in equations. Let us, however, raise the question of proper measurement in a larger context. In experimental sciences, the experimenter generates his own data according to a well-designed experiment. Hypothesis formation and design precede the conduct of the experiment, data collection and analysis. Economists work with data already collected and these data are the result of undesigned experiments in real-life situations carried out by consumers, producers, workers, civil servants, etc. In econometric work, there is a tendency to use published data that are readily available without looking carefully into the definitions used or the method of collection, though these can be frequently shown to lead to biases in the estimated parameters.

Errors in data collection due either to faulty statistical design or to mistakes in definition or plain human error are frequent and serious. There is also the delay in data publication and many subsequent revisions which plague any data-user. Non-availability of certain types of information or a small sample often forces the exclusion of certain relations from econometric study.

But there is also the much more serious problem that published data often do not measure variables that are economically meaningful. Thus, depreciation of capital stock either at the level of the firm or of the economy is measured by accounting conventions and does not approximate to the rate of physical or economic obsolescense. Economists are forced to use these statistics due to lack of any alternative series, but the testing of hypotheses is rendered difficult because the empirically measured variables do not correspond (though they may be similarly labelled) to economic concepts. Let us take the example of our demand functions. We have used observations on the quantity of coffee though frequently we have to use the money value of coffee sales. This, too, is for all varieties of coffee and does not permit us to make qualitative distinctions, unless we are very lucky and have detailed information. In the absence of quantity information, we may have to construct a 'price' index and deflate the money value of sales by this index to obtain a quantity measure. These problems are all the more complex when we seek to measure the quantity of a more aggregate variable such as fixed investment, consumption or real labour input. This is often known as the index-number problem. We take this up in Chapter 5 in some detail.

The problem of measurement is also connected with

specification. Our specification may dictate a certain way of measuring a particular variable. This problem occurs most frequently in the context of stock-flow discussions. A durable good, such as a house, is a stock which yields a flow of services over its lifetime. It would be more appropriate to seek a flow price rather than use the stock price when studying the demand for housing since the demand for housing is a demand for the flow of housing services. It is easier, however, to state this requirement than to meet it. An index of imputed rent on owner-occupied houses is one measure of the flow price but it is an aggregate measure; besides, ownership may of itself confer additional utility or return as an asset in the individual's portfolio. If the house purchase has been financed by borrowing then the flow of instalments paid per unit time after deduction of expected rate of inflation (as a measure of expected capital gain) is a measure of flow price of an owner-occupied house. Another measure will be the rent on an equivalent house and the latter is taken as a measure of the former. In investment demand functions, the rental on capital per unit time is approximated by the price of the capital good times the rate of interest plus depreciation rate, as is true in competitive equilibrium under certain restrictive assumptions. Such measures make it difficult to test theoretical propositions about the demand for durable goods in a disequilibrium context.

The stock-flow problem points to the problem of the time unit of observations. Economic theory is cast in terms of continuous time and instantaneous rates of change. Most available data are in discrete time very often with a high level of time aggregation. Thus data on the quantity of coffee demanded may be available only monthly, quarterly or on an annual basis. The quantity demanded as measured corresponds to a much longer unit of time than the theoretical model requires. In measuring the quarterly percentage rate of change in, say, money wages the problem is to decide where the change is centred.

If M_t is the percent change in money wages in quarter t, then we have the following alternatives:

$$M_t = \frac{W_t - W_{t-1}}{W_{t-1}} \qquad (1.10a)$$

$$M_t = \frac{W_t - W_{t-1}}{(W_t + W_{t-1})/2} \qquad (1.10b)$$

$$M_t = \frac{\frac{1}{2}(W_{t+1} - W_{t-1})}{W_t} \qquad (1.10c)$$

$$M_t = \frac{W_{t+1} - W_{t-1}}{\frac{1}{2}(W_{t+1} + W_{t-1})} \qquad (1.10d)$$

$$M_t = \ln W_t - \ln W_{t-1} \qquad (1.10e)$$

These are several attempts to measure an instantaneous change in a variable when the available data are observed at large discrete 'instants'. An alternative recently proposed has been to formulate the model in instantaneous time, i.e. in differential equation form, and then take a discrete approximation to suit measurement problems. The problem of measurement thus points towards a specification problem.

The problem of measurement is thus not only that of errors of measurement. It may also arise due to conceptual problems either in the nature of data collection or in the formulation of economic theory. These render the task of estimating economic relationships difficult. There is an additional problem, however, that the relationships we want to estimate are not directly observable in data. This is known as the identification problem and it has been at the heart of econometric discussion for many years.

The Identification Problem

As we have discussed above, in economics we cannot conduct controlled experiments to measure our relationships. We do not generate data from experiments designed to test hypotheses. We get our data already generated in non-experimental real-life situations. We observe many of the economic variables moving together in a highly correlated fashion. But as economists, we are interested in not just observing and recording high correlations but in providing a causal explanation for these movements. In fact, models whether derived from theory or by 'letting facts speak for themselves' are abstract mental constructs we seek to impose on these observed movements. Thus we observe prices and quantity moving in a correlated fashion; but the model of demand–supply interaction is an *a priori* mental construct which we hope will make sense out of these movements.

Another way of putting this is to invoke the correlation–causation problem. No amount of correlations, *of itself*, proves causation, since correlation is symmetric and reversible whereas causation is asymmetric (y is a function of x but not vice versa) and irreversible. If our *a priori* causal model 'fits' the data when imposed upon them, we are satisfied until either it fails to predict future movements of data or a logically more adequate model fits the facts equally well if not better. The task of the econometrician is then to make sure that the imposed model is a logically satisfactory construct derived from economic theory rather than a set of *ad hoc* relationships put together for a particular occasion, to see that in fitting the model to the data adequate care is taken so that the resulting numerical model structure corresponds to the prior causal model, to see that the model fits the data and to enable discrimination between the model and its rival when both are fitted to the same data.

To separate causal from non-causal correlation, we need to assure ourselves that the relationships in our model are *identifiable* with the theory on which causation is based.

A very simple distinction we can make among the variables that we see moving together is that between endogenous and exogenous (or, more accurately, predetermined) variables. To go back to our model of the coffee market, we may observe the quantity of coffee bought, produced and in stocks, as well as the price of coffee and world income all moving together. But even in this mixture of effects, we can still separate out world income as being exogenous and hence we can be clear that its causal effect on the other variables is asymmetric. Also past values of these variables have an asymmetric effect on current values.

Identifiability of a relation essentially implies that, given the supposed causal foundation of the model, the data are capable of estimating the relation, as opposed to inadvertently estimating another relation *of the same form within the same causal structure.* Thus, if an equation in the structure is identifiable, we can proceed to estimation in the knowledge that we are estimating the causal relation we want, not another relation of the same form which either happens to be another behavioural equation in the structure or an artificial hybrid relation derived from it. That we must bother about such complexities arises because an observed outcome (of an endogenous variable)is the product of many inter-related agencies, and the separate effect of each on the relationship cannot be observed directly; indeed, it requires the explicit formulation of the inherent inter-relatedness to 'observe' each effect *in*directly. In actuality we cannot, except under very special circumstances, deal with one relationship at a time.

What all this implies is that if cause, *qua* cause, is to be separated in a model from effect, so that no variable can appear to be both a cause and effect at the same time, then we can only observe the reduced form of the model, not the structural form. Of course, we need the structure—at least the structural parameters—because these (parametrically) represent the theory on which the structure is based. However, the structural form has as many equations as there are endogenous variables, and so does the reduced form. Moreover, the *coefficients* of the predetermined variables in the reduced form are functions of the *parameters* of the structural form. Since we can estimate the reduced form coefficients directly from observed variables, the problem reduces to solving for the parameters of the structure from the coefficients of the reduced form. If we have just as many coefficients as there are parameters then the solution is unique and we can go ahead without any further difficulty. This is known as a *just* identifiable case. But if we have fewer coefficients in the reduced form than we have parameters in the structural form then the problem is not soluble at all; we have the *under-identifiable* case, and it is impossible to make meaningful causal statements. A much more usual case is of *many more* coefficients than parameters. In this—the *over-identifiable* case—we need to take into account, as additional information, that a unique set of structural parameters implies that the 'extra' reduced form coefficients must be more apparent than real: they must themselves be inter-related and hence their estimation must involve restrictions imposed upon them to produce a unique structure (for more details see Chapter 2).

Take as an example our model of the coffee market. In the most general notation of 1.8 we have five equations of the form

$$\phi_g [\chi, u; \alpha(g)] = 0 \qquad g = 1, \ldots, 5 \tag{1.8}$$

There are five endogenous variables DC_t, SC_t, PC_t, QC_t and STC_t and two predetermined variables Y_t and STC_{t-1}. Thus there are seven x variables for the five ϕ_g functions. We then assume that all the ϕ_g are linear in x, u and $\alpha(g)$. Then we can write the system 1.8 in linear form as

$$\sum_{j=1}^{7} \alpha_{gj} x_j = u_g \qquad g = 1, \ldots, 5 \tag{1.11}$$

α_{gj} is the coefficient of the jth variable in the gth equation. We have thus potentially thirty five (7 × 5) parameters α_{gj} to estimate. The first five x_j's are endogenous variables and we label them as y_j and the two predetermined variables z_k; the α_{gj} can be similarly relabelled by calling β_{gj} the coefficients attached to the endogenous variables y_j and γ_{gk} and the coefficients attached to the predetermined variables. The system 1.8 then becomes

$$\sum_{j=1}^{5} \beta_{gj} y_j + \sum_{k=1}^{2} \gamma_{gk} z_k = u_g \qquad g = 1, \ldots, 5 \tag{1.12}$$

If we wish to have a constant term in each equation, we add an exogenous variable z_0 and its coefficient γ_{g0} can then be the constant term. We then have to write the second summation above as

$$\sum_{k=0}^{2} \gamma_{gk} z_k$$

We shall do that in the subsequent discussion.

This addition brings the potential number of parameters to estimate up to forty : twenty-five β_{gj} and fifteen γ_{gk}. The system 1.12 is the structural form of our model. In each of the five equations, we can arbitrarily label one of the y_j as the dependent variable. This is equivalent to setting β_{gj}, attached to that variable, equal to 1, *a priori*, or dividing every parameter in an equation by one β_{gj}. This is a normalisation rule. Though arbitrary, it brings our model closer to models in applied work. We can set the $\beta_{gj} = 1$ when $g = j$. Thus, in the first equation, $\beta_{11} = 1$, in the second $\beta_{22} = 1$, and so on. We have now thirty-five distinct parameters (or ratios of parameters β_{gj}/β_{gg}, γ_{gk}/β_{gg}).

Now consider an alternative presentation of the system—its *reduced form*. Here each of the y_j is a function of only the predetermined variables z_k and since the *structural form* of the system, equation 1.11 or equation 1.12, is linear, the *reduced form* is linear as well. Let us write

$$y_g = \sum_{k=0}^{2} \pi_{gk} z_k + v_g \qquad (1.13)$$

There are five linear equations in 1.13, one for each of the five endogenous variables. There are three coefficients π_{gk} in each equation and hence fifteen π_{gk}—reduced form coefficients. What we would like to know is whether the π_{gk} bear a systematic relation to the β_{gj} and γ_{gk}. Is the equation system 1.13 derived from the system 1.12 or from any other system involving y_j and z_k positing a different causal structure between them? If we can relate β_{gj} and γ_{gk} uniquely to π_{gk}, i.e. if we can prove that the π_{gk} are derived from β_{gj} and γ_{gk} and them alone, then we have been able to identify the structural form parameters of our system. Then, indeed, the system 1.13 is not just any correlation between y_g and z_k but a systematic one implied by a causal structure.

It is not the intention in this book to prove the necessary and sufficient conditions required for uniqueness of the relation between the structural form parameter β_{gj}, γ_{gk} and the reduced form coefficients π_{gk}. That would require much more detail and in any case, this is much better done in other places (Fisher, 1966; Koopmans, 1950; Johnston, 1972). We can relate the sufficient conditions to the previous discussions of specifications and in a way which makes intuitive sense. In order to make this rather difficult but vital part of econometrics understandable, we shall try and look at the problem from different angles.

We must first be sure that in our structural system, we indeed do have five separate equations. None of them can be just a multiple proportion of the other or a combination of one or more other equations in the system. Thus there should be no superfluous equation in the system; the system must contain five or in general G *independent* equations. Then we say to ourselves, how can we relate the forty structural parameters to only fifteen reduced form coefficients? We cannot 'derive' from our fifteen π_{gk} the forty β_{gj} and γ_{gk}. We must restrict our system in some way. We do this in economic theory naturally by saying that some variables influence one variable but not another. Not every variable appears in every equation. Relating the model of the coffee economy in equations 1.3–1.7, to the system 1.10 and 1.12, we see that we have already assumed that D in 1.3 is linear. But more important, 1.3 has only two variables on the right-hand side: PC and Y. In all, the linearised version of 1.3 has three variables: two endogenous, DC and PC, and one predetermined, Y. Then of the five possible β_{gj} in this equation, three are zero and only two are non-zero. It is the first equation of our system ($g = 1$) hence we say that $\beta_{11} = 1$ and β_{12} (the coefficient of PC) is non-zero but β_{13}, β_{14} and β_{15}, the coefficients of QC, SC, and STC, are zero. The latter variables do not appear directly in the equation. Similarly, we may have a constant term and we have a non-zero coefficient for one predetermined variable Y_t but the other predetermined variable STC_{t-1} does not appear in the equation. Thus of the eight possible parameters in the first equation, four α_{gj}, three β_{ij} and one γ_{gk} are zero. We say then that there are *four zero restrictions* on the structural equation for DC. Similarly, equation 1.5 will only contain two variables–both endogenous with non-zero coefficients; there will be six zero restrictions on that equation. In a sense, we are saying that while the price of coffee (PC) influences both demand and output, income influences only demand but not output. Again in 1.6, demand and supply influence price but income does not directly enter that equation. Indirectly, of course, income influences price, demand, supply and output, and this indirect influence will be captured by the π_{gk}—the reduced form coefficients. But we must leave that for later. For the time being we are interested in knowing whether a variable directly enters an equation or not.

Of the forty possible parameters β_{gj} and γ_{gk}, we have already seen that four in the *DC* equation, six in the *QC* equation and five in the *PC* equation are zero. We are left with twenty-five non-zero parameters. Of these again, five are arbitrarily set equal to one. These are the β_{gg}. The remaining two relationships are identities—one for *SC* involving three variables and the other for *STC* involving four variables. There are in any case no unknown parameters to estimate in these identities since all the coefficients are set at one. We are therefore down to the parameters in the *DC* equation, one in the *QC* equation and two in the *PC* equation – five parameters plus three constant terms making in all eight parameters. Our fifteen reduced form coefficients can then be used to derive the eight parameter estimates.

In each equation where there are parameters to be estimated—those not set equal to zero, one or some other constant *a priori*—we use the following rule of thumb as a sufficient condition to ensure identifiability. *The number of zero restrictions in any equation should be greater than or equal to the number of equations excluding the one under consideration.* Thus in the *DC* equation, the number of zero restrictions—four—is just sufficient to identify the equation. In the *QC* equation on the other hand, we have more than enough restrictions (six) which exceed the number of equations (four) in the system excluding the one under consideration. The notion of zero restriction can be extended to include other homogenous restrictions. Often we say that two variables have the same parameter attached to them. Thus in the *PC* equation, we may wish to express *PC* as a function of *excess* supply, i.e. (*SC*–*DC*). In this case, the same parameter is attached to *SC* and *DC* but with opposite signs. This is a homogenous restriction since it enables us to cut down the number of parameters to be estimated to one instead of two. Zero restrictions are just a special case of homogenous restrictions.

The linear version of the model in equations 1.3 to 1.7 can

then be written in terms of the system of equations 1.12.

$$DC_t + \beta_{12} PC_t + 0QC_t + 0SC_t + 0STC_t + \gamma_{10} z_0 + \gamma_{11} Y_t + 0STC_{t-1} = u_{1t} \quad (1.14a)$$

$$-\beta_{21} DC_t + PC_t + 0QC_t + \beta_{21} SC_t + 0STC_{t-1} + \gamma_{20} z_0 + 0Y_t + 0STC_{t-1} = u_{2t} \quad (1.14b)$$

$$0DC_t + \beta_{32} PC_t + QC_t + 0SC_t + 0STC_t + \gamma_{30} z_0 + 0Y_t + 0STC_{t-1} = u_{3t} \quad (1.14c)$$

$$0DC_t + 0PC_t - QC_t + SC_t + 0STC_t + 0z_0 + 0Y_t - STC_{t-1} = 0 \quad (1.14d)$$

$$DC_t + 0PC_t - QC_t + 0SC_t + STC + 0z_0 + 0Y_t - STC_{t-1} = 0 \quad (1.14e)$$

Notice that we have written in the zero coefficients explicitly. This makes the task of counting the number of restrictions on each equation easy. In the second equation, two variables *DC* and *SC* have the same coefficient attached, β_{21}, though with opposite signs. This, as we said above, is a homogeneous restriction. Indeed, a homogeneous restriction of this kind can be translated into a zero restriction by adding an auxiliary variable which incorporates the information. We can in our case add excess supply *ESC* as an auxiliary variable and put it in the price equation in place of the two variables we have now. Correspondingly, we add an identity that $ESC_t = (SC_t - DC_t)$. Vice versa, all the identities we normally have in models can also be seen as devices for introducing auxiliary variables which incorporate homogeneous restrictions. This can be easily checked by substituting an identity, say for SC_t, in the price equation. The corresponding reduced form equation system of 1.13, then, is

$$DC_t = \pi_{10} z_0 + \pi_{11} Y_t + \pi_{12} STC_{t-1} + v_{1t} \quad (1.15a)$$

$$PC_t = \pi_{20} z_0 + \pi_{21} Y_t + \pi_{22} STC_{t-1} + v_{2t} \quad (1.15b)$$

$$QC_t = \pi_{30} z_0 + \pi_{31} Y_t + \pi_{32} STC_{t-1} + v_{3t} \quad (1.15c)$$

$$SC_t = \pi_{40} z_0 + \pi_{41} Y_t + \pi_{42} STC_{t-1} + v_{4t} \quad (1.15d)$$

$$STC_t = \pi_{50}z_0 + \pi_{51}Y_t + \pi_{52}STC_{t-1} + v_{5t} \quad (1.15e)$$

The relationship of the π_{gk}'s to the β_{gj}'s and the γ_{gk}'s has to be unique if the structural equations are identified. Another way therefore of thinking about identification is to derive a relationship between a structural equation and the corresponding reduced form equation. Let us take the *DC* equations 1.14a and 1.15a. Suppose instead of 1.14a, one was to take a weighted combination of all the reduced form equations and combine them with one equation for DC_t comparable to 1.14a. We can do this by using arbitrary weights δ_{11}, δ_{12}, δ_{13}, δ_{14}, δ_{15}. In terms of equation 1.12, our first equation would then be

$$\Sigma\delta_{ij}y_j + \Sigma\delta_{ij}\pi_{jk}z_k = \Sigma\delta_{ij}v_{jt}.$$

Alternatively, we can write in comparison to 1.14a

$$\delta_{11}DC_t + \delta_{12}PC_t + \delta_{13}QC_t + \delta_{14}ST_t + \delta_{15}STC_t$$
$$+ (\delta_{11}\pi_{10} + \delta_{12}\pi_{20} + \delta_{13}\pi_{30} + \delta_{14}\pi_{40} + \delta_{15}\pi_{50})z_0$$
$$+ (\delta_{11}\pi_{11} + \delta_{12}\pi_{21} + \delta_{13}\pi_{31} + \delta_{14}\pi_{41} + \delta_{15}\pi_{51})Y_t$$
$$+ (\delta_{11}\pi_{12} + \delta_{12}\pi_{22} + \delta_{13}\pi_{32} + \delta_{14}\pi_{42} + \delta_{15}\pi_{52})STC_{t-1}$$
$$= (\delta_{11}v_{1t} + \delta_{12}v_{2t} + \delta_{13}v_{3t} + \delta_{14}v_{4t} + \delta_{15}v_{5t}) \quad (1.16a)$$

Now 1.16a can be easily mistaken for a structural equation of system 1.13. It is a linear equation in y_g and z_k. How do we tell it apart from our 'true' structural equation 1.14a? The zero restrictions we have imposed *a priori* on 1.14a enable us to specify the conditions which 1.16a must satisfy to be a structural equation. Thus comparing the coefficients of 1.14a and 1.16a for each variable, we have

$$\delta_{11} = 1, \delta_{12} = \beta_{12}, \delta_{13} = \delta_{14} = \delta_{15} = 0$$

In addition, we also have restrictions on the predetermined variable coefficients. Incorporating δ_{ij} information from above, we have

$$\delta_{11}\pi_{10} + \delta_{12}\pi_{20} = \pi_{10} + \beta_{12}\pi_{20} = \gamma_{10} \quad (1.17a)$$
$$\delta_{11}\pi_{11} + \delta_{12}\pi_{21} = \pi_{10} + \beta_{12}\pi_{21} = \gamma_{11} \quad (1.17b)$$
$$\delta_{11}\pi_{12} + \delta_{12}\pi_{22} = \pi_{10} + \beta_{12}\pi_{22} = 0 \quad (1.17c)$$

Now while equation 1.16a looks like 1.14a since they are both linear equations, we have no problem in telling the two apart. Equation 1.16a can be mistaken for a structural equation such as 1.14a only if they are identical to each other. This is because in order to look exactly like 1.14a, equation 1.16a must satisfy the restrictions on δ_{ij} and the restriction on γ_{gk}. If it satisfies the restrictions on δ_{ij} and on the γ_{gk}, it will be identical to 1.14a.

The conditions 1.17a to 1.17c are derived by using the restrictions in β_{gj} and δ_{gj} as well as γ_{gk}. They can now be interpreted to solve the unknown parameters β_{12}, γ_{10} and γ_{11} in terms of the directly observable reduced form coefficients π_{gk}'s. Thus, solving 1.17c we have

$$\beta_{12} = -\pi_{10}/\pi_{22} \tag{1.18a}$$

In turn,

$$\gamma_{11} = (\pi_{10}\pi_{22} - \pi_{10}\pi_{21})/\pi_{22} \tag{1.18b}$$

$$\gamma_{10} = (\pi_{10}\pi_{22} - \pi_{10}\pi_{20})/\pi_{22} \tag{1.18c}$$

Knowing our reduced form coefficients and using the information incorporated in the zero restriction, we can derive a systematic relationship between the structural form parameters and the reduced form coefficients.

This exercise has been carried out for the *DC* equation. This equation is, however, a special case. Notice that the number of zero restrictions in the *DC* equation 1.14a exactly equals the number of equations in the system minus one. When this is the case, we have the sufficient condition for an equation to be *just identified*. Other equations in our model, e.g. QC_t, have more than the required number of restrictions— five instead of four. This then tells us that the equation is over-identified. What is involved in the discussion can be summarised by using a device similar to the one we used for the DC_t equation. By analogy, we have

$$\delta_{31} = 0, \quad \delta_{32} = \beta_{32}, \quad \delta_{33} = 1, \quad \delta_{34} = 0, \quad \delta_{35} = 0$$

and incorporating these δ_{ij} restrictions, we get

$$\beta_{32}\pi_{20} + \pi_{30} = \gamma_{30} \tag{1.19a}$$

$$\beta_{32}\pi_{21} + \pi_{31} = 0 \qquad (1.19b)$$

$$\beta_{32}\pi_{22} + \pi_{32} = 0 \qquad (1.19c)$$

Notice that in the three equations 1.19a to 1.19c we can solve for β_{32} and γ_{30} in terms of the π's, but we will have two solutions for β_{32}:

$$\beta_{32} = -\pi_{31}/\pi_{21} \qquad \text{or} \qquad \beta_{32} = -\pi_{32}/\pi_{22}$$

The equation is thus over-identified in the sense that we have multiple solutions for a parameter. This is not a serious handicap since we can choose either one of them. It is when the number of unknown parameters *exceeds* the number of equations that we can derive from the zero restrictions that we get the case of *under-identification*. This can be a case when we have an insufficient number of restrictions on an equation.

In the model above we have no under-identified equation. An example can, however, be provided from macroeconomics in terms of the IS–LM diagram. While the details are discussed in Chapter 8, we have in the IS–LM diagram two equations in income Y_t and rate of interest r_t but only one predetermined variable, money supply $\bar{M}$. We can write these two equations using the notation of 1.12 as

$$\beta_{11}Y_t + \beta_{12}r_t + \gamma_{10}z_0 + 0\bar{M}_t = u_{1t} \qquad (1.20a)$$

$$\beta_{21}Y_t + \beta_{22}r_t + \gamma_{20}z_0 + \gamma_{21}\bar{M}_t = u_{2t} \qquad (1.20b)$$

Equation 1.20a is the IS relationship and equation 1.20b is the LM relationship. We can normalise the two equations by setting $\beta_{11} = -1$ and $\beta_{22} = -1$. Notice however that equation 1.20a has one zero restriction, the coefficient of $\bar{M}_t$, but the equation 1.20b has none. Equation 1.20b is then under-identified by our sufficient condition that the number of zero restrictions should be at least equal to the number of equations less one, whereas 1.20a is just identified. We can quickly check this by writing a reduced form for the system on the lines of 1.13 and deriving as we did for the *DC* and *QC* equations, the following relationships

$$\pi_{10} + \beta_{12}\pi_{20} = \gamma_{10} \qquad (1.21a)$$

$$\pi_{11} + \beta_{12}\pi_{21} = 0 \qquad (1.21b)$$

$$\beta_{21}\pi_{20} + \pi_{21} = \gamma_{20} \qquad (1.22a)$$

$$\beta_{21}\pi_{21} + \pi_{22} = \gamma_{21} \qquad (1.22b)$$

Equations 1.21a and 1.21b which relate to the IS relationship can be easily solved for β_{12} and γ_{10}. It is clear from equations 1.22a and 1.22b that we have three structural form parameters—β_{21}, γ_{20} and γ_{21} but only two equations. Thus equation 1.20b, the LM relationship, is under-determined.

A geometric illustration may bring out these points clearly. In a famous article published nearly fifty years ago, E. J. Working (1927) analysed the identification problem in terms of the demand and supply diagram. In figure 1.1a, we have taken the IS–LM case. We see that the intersection of the two relationships (assumed linear as above in equations 1.20a–b) produced one point for a given level of money supply $\bar{M}_1$. If nothing changed the only observed point in the time series would be *a*, though perhaps random influences may produce the illusion of a scatter as in figure 1.1b.

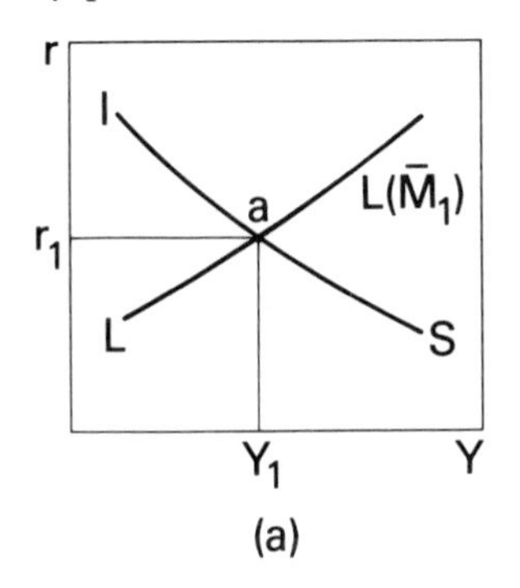

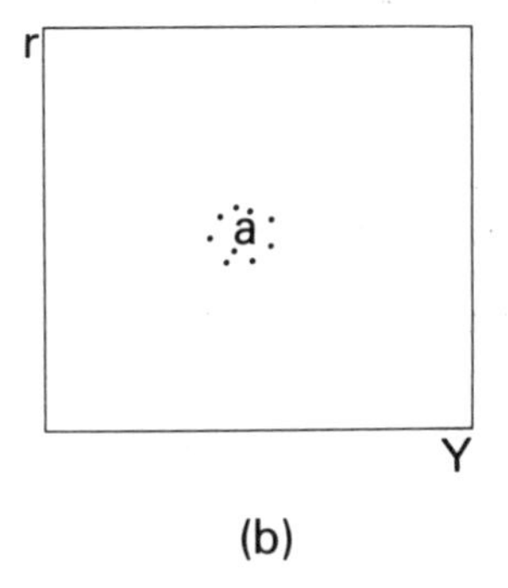

Fig. 1.1

Now it is clear that no relationship can be estimated from a point. Even the scatter round the point a in figure 1.1b will yield neither an IS nor an LM relationship. But the LM curve will shift when the money supply changes and this will trace a scatter of points lying along the IS curve. Figures 1.2a and 1.2b illustrate this, where figure 1.2b is the observed pattern arising from figure 1.2a. The scatter of points a to e generated by the shift of the LM relationship enables us to measure the IS relationship. Even some random variation round the intersection points will still enable us to observe an IS relationship. It is in this sense that the zero restriction on $\bar{M}$ in the IS equation identifies the IS equation.

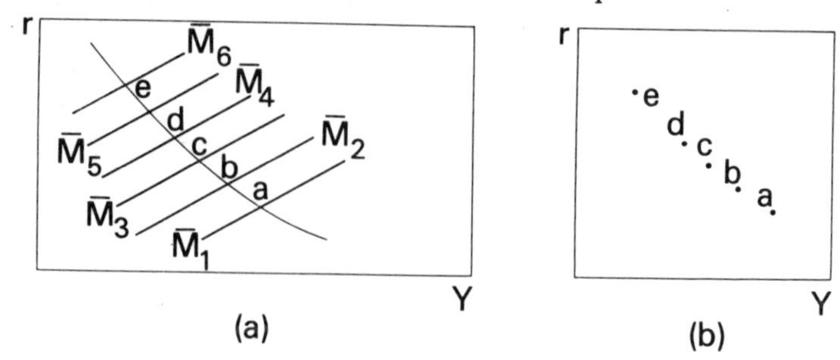

Fig. 1.2

Can we in some way measure the LM relationship when the zero restrictions are insufficient to identify it? This can be done if we have another type of restriction beside the zero and the homogeneous restrictions. Until now we have neglected any consideration of the error terms both in the structural form and in the reduced form. If we have some prior information on the relative error variances in the two equations, this will help identify one of the relationships. Let us say in context of figure 1.1a that even at a given level of money supply $\bar{M}$, the IS relationship fluctuates in a volatile manner due to the nature of businessmen's expectations. Thus the income/investment relationship derived from the IS relationship traces out a scatter of points as in figures 1.3a and b.

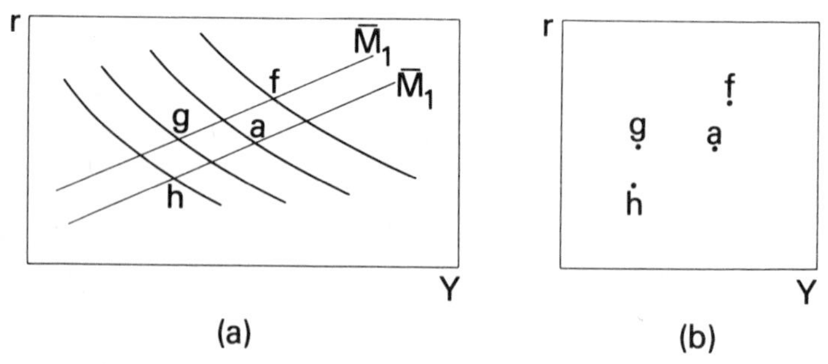

Fig. 1.3

The two $\overline{M}_1$ relationships are designed to illustrate that the LM relationship fluctuates due to random influences as well but by not as much as the IS relationship does. In this case the scatter of points a, f, g, h will be along the relatively less fluctuating LM relationship.

In order to formalise this argument, we can say that *a priori* we know the variance of u_{1t} to be a multiple of the variance of u_{2t}. This is a prior restriction.

$$\text{var}(u_{1t}) = K\,\text{var}(u_{2t}) \tag{1.23a}$$

To use this information, we can add an expression relating the reduced form errors v_{1t} and v_{2t} to the structural form errors u_{1t} and u_{2t}. Thus to equations 1.21a and 1.21b we add,

$$v_{1t} + \beta_{12}v_{2t} = u_{1t} \tag{1.21c}$$

and for (1.22c) we have

$$\beta_{21}v_{1t} + v_{2t} = u_{2t} \tag{1.22c}$$

By our assumption in 1.23a we have

$$\begin{aligned}\text{var}(u_{1t}) &= \text{var}(v_{1t}) + 2\beta_{12}\,\text{cov}(v_{1t}v_{2t}) + \beta_{12}^2\,\text{var}(v_{2t})\\ &= K\,\text{var}(u_{2t})\\ &= K[\beta_{21}^2\,\text{var}(v_{1t}) + 2\beta_{21}\,\text{cov}(v_{1t}v_{2t}) + \text{var}(v_{2t})]\end{aligned}$$

Therefore

$$\begin{aligned}&[(1-K\beta_{21}^2)\text{var}\,v_{1t} + 2(\beta_{12}-K\beta_{21})\text{cov}(v_{1t}v_{2t})\\ &+ (\beta_{12}^2 - K)\text{var}\,v_{2t}] = 0\end{aligned} \tag{1.23b}$$

Now in equation 1.23b, we see that the variances and convariances would be measurable from the reduced form equations for Y_t and r_t. We can derive an estimate of β_{12} since we have shown it is identified. Then if we can specify K from prior information, β_{21} is measurable from equation 1.23b. It only involves the solution of the quadratic equation in β_{21} and choosing the value which satisfies our prior knowledge about the sign of β_{21}. (This is by its nature a heuristic demonstration. For a rigorous proof see Fisher, 1965.) Once we have an estimate of β_{21} then equations 1.22a and 1.22b can be solved for γ_{20} and γ_{21}.

We use, therefore, all the prior information we possess—

zero and homogenous restrictions, ratios of error variances and perhaps other qualitative information such as the sign and size of parameters–in order to establish identifiability. (In some instances, we get nonlinear identifying restrictions as we shall see in Chapter 4. We have not dealt with the non-linearity problem here as it is fairly difficult to tackle on an informal basis.) This means, however, that we need to be sure that our restrictions are valid. As we shall see in Chapter 7, imposing invalid restrictions will mislead the econometrician to regard what is basically an under-identified model as an identified one. But such identification is spurious. It is necessary therefore that we have valid restrictions and that we should be able to test the validity of our restrictions. This takes us to the estimation problem.

Estimation

The technique of estimation most frequently used by econometricians (and used for estimating 1.1) is ordinary least squares (OLS) also called multiple regression. While we look at the details of the OLS method in the next chapter, we should say here that though computationally convenient, OLS is not entirely appropriate for an econometric situation. It is suitable much more for analysing the information from experiments where replication is possible and where we can rightly assume that our independent variables are non-stochastic or constant in repeated samples. In estimating, for example, the stimulus response relationship, the OLS technique provides a good method of estimating the mean response conditional upon a given set of stimuli and other controlled factors. Economists dealing with non-experimental situations do not have the opportunity for replication or for controlling their independent variables. These variables are in general not non-stochastic and the direction of causation is not irreversibly from the independent variables on the right-hand side to those on the left-hand side. Thus in equation 1.1 both price and income are stochastic variables and price is as much dependent on quantity demanded through equation 1.6 as is quantity a function of price. We are also interested in estimates of the price elasticity and income elasticity of demand, i.e. parameter estimation.

Another way of putting this is to go back to equation 1.1 and ask ourselves what the different numbers such as R^2 or t-ratios tell us. We say, for example, that since the t-ratio of β_1 is greater than two, income has a significant coefficient. We are testing here the null hypothesis of no relationship and finding a t-ratio of greater than two; we can safely reject the null hypothesis of no relationship between income and demand with 95% confidence. (We do not go into details of hypothesis testing; students can check it in books on econometric theory cited in the bibliography.) We can also test if the whole equation is statistically significant by an F-test which will again tell us that we can safely reject the null hypothesis of no relationship between Y and PC and DC. These, however, are not very dramatic conclusions. What is more, in the case of the price variable the t-ratio does not lead us to a correct inference because PC is not a truly independent variable. Our interest is more in estimating the joint relationship of all our endogenous variables among themselves and with the exogenous variables. The $\bar{R}^2$ for example for 1.1 is conditional upon DC being the dependent variable, but we could equally well make PC the dependent variable and obtain an equation with a different $\bar{R}^2$ and different coefficients and t-ratios. Equation 1.1 estimated by OLS artificially isolates one equation from a set of equations, leads to incorrect inference in the case of PC and only enables us to test rather simple and uninteresting null hypotheses.

We therefore need estimation techniques which concentrate on parameter estimates, make use of information in the complete model and yield test statistics which will enable us to test economically meaningful hypotheses, e.g. the particular set of restrictions we have chosen to impose on an equation. Not all techniques do these things adequately or to the same extent. As we shall see in Chapter 2, the method of instrumental variables ensures consistent (in a sense to be defined later) estimates of the parameters, and information from other equations in the model is implicitly taken into account when we choose the instruments. This technique also has the advantage that we treat all variables as stochastic. The instrumental variable technique has the disadvantage that it treats each equation separately. Another desirable property of parameter estimates is that they should have small variance. OLS satisfies this when its assumptions are valid. But when the OLS assumptions are not satisfied, we need other estimation techniques which can yield parameter estimates with relatively small variances.

Of much greater generality is the method of maximum likelihood. It is based on the assumption that the random errors (u_1, u_2, u_3 in the coffee market, say) have a known probability distribution, e.g. they are normally distributed either jointly or independently with zero mean and an unknown variance–covariance matrix. We proceed to form the probability density of the unobservable random errors which can be transformed in terms of the observed variables and parameters and then the likelihood function is maximised. The method does not yield straightforward linear normal equations when applied to a set of simultaneous equations and nonlinear techniques have to be used to solve the equations numerically. This makes the technique computationally demanding but with increasing size and speed of computers this has become a minor problem. The advantage of the method is in its flexibility. It can be adapted to situations of equations which are nonlinear in parameters. It treats all the endogenous variables jointly. Above all, for testing hypotheses about individual parameters or groups of them and for testing restrictions rigorously, the method of maximum likelihood is the most suitable.

As we go away from OLS, we encounter increasingly complex estimation methods. Some of them, such as the method of instrumental variables, are very similar to OLS and only slightly more demanding. Methods such as maximum likelihood are very computer-intensive. They also tend to be fairly sensitive to specification errors. If the equations or system of equations contains specification errors, e.g. variables excluded which should have been included, errors assumed to be temporally independent when they are not, variables assumed to be exogenous when they are not, etc., many of the properties of the parameter estimates yielded by these techniques are affected. We are back therefore at the problem of specification. This takes us into an area of *metatheory* where philosophical doubts can be raised about our practice.

Some Metatheory

A question we may pose at this stage is, can we ever ensure correct specification? If all our techniques assume correct specifications, what are the foundations on which such specification is to be based? As we have already mentioned before, often in practical studies, our method of specifying equations, of choosing among alternative specifications is the *post hoc* method of judging by OLS results. Even our belief that economic relationships are simultaneous is based only partly on economic theory; a much greater part is based on empirical results based on previous OLS estimates, rationalised *post hoc* by appeal to theory. Is it perhaps conceivable that our belief in simultaneity and the consequent search for better estimation techniques is in itself based on a gigantic specification error? This is a troublesome question. Such questions are often raised in informal discussion about the validity of econometric results. They have also been formally raised in methodological discussions by econometricians.

The main objection to the simultaneity approach has come from Professor Herman Wold. Wold has raised objection to the notion that a simultaneous equation system is a more truthful characterisation of the economic system. He prefers, on the grounds of both realism and methodology, a causal chain system whereby variables are linked to each other causally through time but where at any point in time, they show a unidirectional causation rather than simultaneous interdependence.

Methodologically, Wold finds that the notion of causality is not readily applicable to simultaneous systems. Causality in the laboratory sense of a stimulus–response relationship is *asymmetric*. A variable Y_1 is a function of Y_2, Y_2 being the 'cause' of Y_1, but then Y_2 cannot at the same time be an 'effect' of Y_1. A system of simultaneous equations where there is a set of variables which are jointly dependent upon each other and on a set of predetermined variables does not yield to an asymmetric causal interpretation. A *recursive system* where the causality is unidirectional can be so interpreted. (For a more rigorous definition of recursive systems, see the next chapter.)

Economists and econometricians have readily accepted the notion of simultaneous interaction. In general, we have two types of simultaneity occurring. One is where Y_1 is a function of Y_2 and Y_2 is a function of Y_1 (as well as other variables). This is a situation of circular causation. Thus, for example, consumption (Y_1) is a function of income (Y_2) but income is made up of consumption plus other items. Second is a situation where Y_1 is a function of Y_2 as well as another function of Y_2, or $Y_1 = f(Y_2)$ as well as $Y_1 = g(Y_2)$. This is *bicausality*. For example, quantity demanded (Y_1) is a function of price, but the quantity supplied (also equal to Y_1) is also a function of price. Wold believes that these situations arise because economic models are specified as equilibrium systems (e.g. Y_1 is both quantity demanded and quantity supplied only in equilibrium). Most often, these systems are equilibrium approximations of disequilibrium systems. A system in dynamic disequilibrium may be recursive in form but its static equilibrium analog will exhibit simultaneity. Let us take the example of a 'cobweb' system. Here demand is a function of current price and other variables, but supply is a function of the last period's price. Let us assume that the commodity is non-storable. Then we have

$$Q_t^d = \alpha_0 + \alpha_1 P_t + \alpha_2 X_t + u_t \qquad \text{demand equation} \tag{1.24}$$

$$Q_t^s = \beta_0 + \beta_1 P_{t-1} + \beta_2 Z_t + v_t \qquad \text{supply equation} \tag{1.25}$$

X_t and Z_t are some exogenous variables, P_t is price, Q^d and Q^s are quantities demanded and supplied, u and v are errors. Being a perishable commodity, Q_t^d and Q_t^s are equal to Q_t. The system then exhibits unidirectional causation–P_t is a function of Q_t and Q_t of P_{t-1}. Now the system will be in equilibrium if we add a third equation

$$P_t = P_{t-1} \tag{1.26}$$

Given this last equation, the system will then exhibit simultaneity if observed at equilibrium positions. P_{t-1} in the supply equation will be replaced by P_t and we will have a familiar system of two simultaneous equations. In the original system, the parameter β_1 has a causal interpretation in the asymmetric sense defined above. In the equilibrium system, this meaning is lost.

Equilibrium characterisation is only one reason why we 'observe' simultaneity rather than recursiveness. Another reason is that we may not have observations for a small enough time interval. Thus if we had daily or weekly observations we may be able to specify fine lags but these lags may have to be ignored if the data are quarterly or annual. Let us rewrite the equation above with a lag of θ.

$$Q_t^s = \beta_0 + \beta_1 P_{t-\theta} + \beta_2 Z_5 + v_t \tag{1.25a}$$

where $0 < \theta < 1$. If our observations are quarterly, θ may be a week, $\theta \simeq 1/13$. Lacking weekly data, we can specify the lag θ as zero and hence obtain a simultaneous system as a result of a specification error. The interdependent system then is an approximation to the 'true' recursive system. In the course of making the approximation, we make a specification error and change the stochastic specification of the model. For the supply equation above, by taking $\theta = 0$ we add to the error term v_t an element equal to $\beta_1 (P_{t-\theta} - P_t)$. The new error may be autocorrelated and also may be correlated with u_t when originally neither of the features may be present. The possibility of making a specification error is all the greater when our theoretical relationships are couched in terms of instantaneous time while our data are at discrete intervals. The problem of measurement of economic variables which we raised above thus reappears in the debate on simultaneity.

The possibility of making specification errors is regarded by Professor Liu as highly probable. He regards most if not all econometric relationships as being mis-specified. In each individual econometric equation, specification of variables to be included and excluded is usually done *post hoc* by looking at OLS results. Econometricians tend on the whole to restrict the number of variables to be included partly to gain degrees of freedom but also to preserve simplicity of the equation. Addition of variables also may not add significantly to R^2. In such a situation, many variables which should be included on theoretical or *a priori* grounds tend to be excluded. A specification error occurs thus by these variables being assigned zero coefficients when the true coefficients may be non-zero. There is also a tendency not to build 'grand' all-explaining models. Many variables are assumed exogenous when they are not 'truly' so. These variables should be properly classified as endogenous and equations should be included to explain them in the model. By labelling them as exogenous, a specification error of missing equations is added to the one of missing variables. There is in a sense not enough simultaneity in econometric models as specified; the world is much more simultaneous.

At this stage, the student in his bewilderment can be forgiven for crying 'plague on all your houses'. The problem of causality and simultaneity is philosophically difficult to solve. But in the more practical task of econometric research, where perfection is unattainable, there are solutions (admittedly partial) of the problem. We are faced with two divergent approaches both of which highlight the serious possibility of specification errors in econometric equations. We have to ask what the consequences are of making specification errors. In any particular equation, by making a specification error including an irrelevant variable, excluding a relevant one, suppressing a lag, etc., we alter the nature of the error term. We see an example of this in the case where the lag of supply behind price was so small that it had to be (mis)specified as zero. This added certain terms to the random error term equal to $\beta_1 (P_{t-\theta} - P_t)$. This addition may make the error term correlated with one of the included variables thus violating the OLS assumption. It may introduce autocorrelation in the error term. In any case, it would most likely raise the variance of the error term.

The consequences of a specification error are therefore *inconsistent* estimates of the parameters. This is due to the correlation of error terms with included variables. It also leads to *inefficient* estimates due to the higher error variance. Put in this way, the problem of specification error can be tackled by an appropriate estimation technique. If the nature of the specification error can be foreseen, e.g. if we can presume autocorrelation of errors, then the search for an appropriate estimation technique is made easier. In order to be able to foresee such errors, it is necessary to be rigorous in specifying the true relationship underlying the relationship to be estimated. The use of prior information from economic theory as well as other sources is helpful in this task. It also eases the task of choosing the appropriate estimation technique. In the next chapter, we look at the available estimation techniques and their limitations.

Bibliographical Notes

Estimation of demand equations was one of the earliest problems tackled by econometricians. Thus Benini pioneered estimation of the elasticity of demand for coffee in 1907 while even earlier Engel had estimated the elasticity of demand for wheat. For a survey of these, see Stigler (1954).

The aims of econometric research, especially the distinction between prediction and forecasting is drawn from Jacob Marschak 'Economic measurement for policy and prediction' in Hood and Koopmans (1953). Definitions of model and structure used in this chapter derive from Herbert Simon's 'Causal ordering and identifiability' in Hood and Koopmans (1953).

The measurement problem, especially of price indices, can lead to systematic biases. Thus Murray Kemp has shown that the use of unit value indices in international trade equations biases elasticities toward one, see M. Kemp (1962). The measurement of continuous time variables by discreet time points is a problem which has been taken up very recently, see articles by Bergstrom (1966), Wymer (1972) and Sargan (1974) and Phillips (1972).

The subject of identification is vast. There is an early treatment by Koopmans, Rubin and Leipnik in 'Measuring the equation system of dynamic economics' in Koopmans (1950), also there is Koopmans 'Identification problems in economic model construction' in Hood and Koopmans (1953) as well as H. Simon's article cited above. For an intuitive understanding see Chapter 2 in Klein: *An Introduction to Econometrics* (1962). For the most unified treatment see Franklin Fisher's *The Identification Problem in Econometrics* (1966) and many of his articles cited in the bibliography at the end of this book, especially Fisher (1965) for the case of error variance restrictions. Besides this, most textbooks on econometric theory also provide a good exposition of the problem. See, Christ *Econometric Models and Methods* (1966) Chapter VII, and Johnston *Econometric Methods* (2nd edn, 1972).

On the problem of metatheory see Franklin Fisher's IDA pamphlet cited in the bibliography. I have discussed the same issue in the context of the recent work in econometric history in Desai (1968). The articles by Strotz and Wold (1960) and by Liu (1960) are the important references, see also Ando, Fisher and Simon: *The Structure of Social Science Models* (1963). On the problem of mis-specification see Fisher (1961a).

A useful treatment of the interaction of various types of mis-specification, e.g. simultaneity, serial correlation, missing variables, is in Hendry (1975).

2
Estimation

We continue our discussion of estimation in this chapter. Our emphasis will be more on the technical details of estimation methods and their properties rather than on the metatheoretical issues which we examined above. It is still desirable, however, to begin at a fairly high level of generality before coming to specific issues. Recall from the previous chapter our description of a model as given in equation 1.8

$$\phi_g\,[\chi, u; \alpha(g)] \;=\; 0$$

We specify this model by:

(a) classifying our observable χ variables into endogenous (y) and predetermined (z) and further distinguish among the predetermined variables exogenous variables (x) and lagged endogenous variables (denoted as y_{-t} for some lag t) and the number of equations (G) in the model; and

(b) using economic theory and any other sources of prior information we possess to specify functional forms for ϕ_g (linear, loglinear, nonlinear) and *at the same time* the nature of the error process u (additive, multiplicative, autoregressive, etc). The functional form will, of course, specify the nature of variables as well as of parameters.

In the major part of this chapter we shall assume under (b)

that our model is linear in parameters and in variables and that the error terms are additive. Our discussion of nonlinear models towards the end of the chapter will be very brief though we shall come up with interesting examples of non-linearity (in parameters) in Chapters 4 and 5.

Whereas in the last chapter we avoided the use of matrix notation, in this chapter it is unavoidable. The discussion in this chapter has to be sketchy and hence should be invariably supplemented by some of the standard textbooks now available. Full references will, therefore, be given on all points at the end of the chapter. No proofs whatsoever are provided and only the bare essential definitions for our subsequent discussion are given.

These limitations may give the present chapter the appearance of a shopping list of estimation methods. Estimation methods are often loosely described in terms of power—e.g. high powered, a euphemism for complexity—and the temptation is to shop for high powered methods. A word of caution is therefore immediately in order. We choose estimation methods as tools in a much wider context and never for the sake of their complexity. The wider context defines the problem and then the choice of the appropriate method is made on the basis of well-defined criteria. Indeed, in every case where there is choice, we should choose the simplest of all the available techniques. This also implies that we shall seek to employ complex, 'high powered' techniques only when the problem at hand cannot be adequately tackled by a simpler technique. Invariably, simplicity will mean computational simplicity.

With these preliminaries let us specify a linear simultaneous equation model corresponding to equation 1.8 as

$$By_t' + \Gamma_1 x_t' + \Gamma_2 y_{t-1}' = u_t' \qquad t = 1, \ldots, N \tag{2.1}$$

B is a $G \times G$ matrix of coefficients of endogenous variables, Γ_1 is a $G \times K$ matrix of exogenous variable coefficients and Γ_2 is a $G \times G$ matrix of coefficients of lagged endogenous variables. y_t' is a $G \times 1$ vector of endogenous variables and y_{t-1}' denotes their value lagged one period, x_t' is a $K \times 1$ vector of exogenous variables and u_t' is a $G \times 1$ vector of unobservable random errors. (All our observations are assumed to be at regular discrete intervals. We ignore the problem of models with variables specified in continuous time. We also assume for the time being a one-period lag.) Readers will notice that equations 1.12 are the same as 2.1 but written out explicitly rather than in matrix form.

The econometric problem is that of obtaining estimates of all the unrestricted elements of B, Γ_1, Γ_2 and of the variance matrix Σ of u', i.e. all the elements not set *a priori* equal to zero, unity or some other homogeneous restriction. The true values of the parameters are unknown to us and will remain so. The best we can do is to obtain estimates of the parameters with desirable properties from the sample information we have in y_t' and x_t'. What then are the desirable properties?

These are stated primarily in terms of bias and variance of the *estimator*. If we call a parameter λ, then the *estimator* of λ, call it l, is a function of the observations y' and x'—a method of estimating λ. When l takes a specific value $\hat{l}$, we call it an *estimate*. Since the u_t' are random variables and our model is linear, the estimators will be random variables themselves. Consequently, the estimator will have distributions with moments of at least second order. (We shall not deal with the cases where this may not be so.) Then

the *bias* of an estimator is defined as the distance between its expected value and the true parameter: bias $= E(l) - \lambda$, where E is the expectations operator, and

the *variance* of the estimator is defined as the expected value of the square of the distance between the estimator and its expected value: variance of $l = E[l - E(l)]^2$.

It is also useful to define a related distance measure in terms of *expected* (*or mean*) *squared error*. This is the expected value of the square of the distance between the estimator and the true parameter : MSE of $l = E[l - \lambda]^2$. The MSE can be decomposed into the variance of the estimator and the square of the bias: MSE of $l =$ variance of $l +$ (bias)^2.

In general we desire estimators which are unbiased and which have minimum variance among comparable rival estimators. We may have to settle for less than this and in some cases we shall live with a small mean squared error. An unbiased estimator is important since it tells us that the mass of the probability density function of the estimator is concentrated around the true parameter value. An individual estimate should, however, always be distinguished from the estimator and its expected value. An individual estimate can fall anywhere in the full range of the possible values of the estimator. We can, however, use the unbiasedness property of the estimator to gauge the probability of an individual estimate falling a certain distance away from the true parameter value. Variance, similarly, is desired to be small so as to get as small a spread as possible of the estimator around its expected value. If an estimator has minimum variance among comparable estimators then it is called an *efficient* estimator.

Although unbiasedness and efficiency are desirable properties, often they are too strong requirements. As we shall see below, the non-experimental nature of economic data forces us to settle for weaker properties. Corresponding to unbiasedness is the *consistency* of an estimator. In as much as an estimator is a function of the observations, it may be influenced by the size of the sample N. One can imagine a sequence of estimators l_N obtained from samples of increasing size N, say $l_{10}, l_{20}, l_{30} \ldots$. The estimator is then called *consistent* if the probability of its being within a small distance of the true parameter gets larger as the sample size gets larger. Thus if $\epsilon > 0$ is any arbitrary small number, l is a consistent estimator of λ if

$$\lim_{N \to \infty} \Pr\{|l_N - \lambda| < \epsilon\} = 1 \tag{2.2}$$

The definition then says that as the sample size N approaches infinity (in the limit) the probability that the distance between l_N and λ is smaller than ϵ approaches unity. Consistency is a property of estimators based on large samples and in as much as it is a limiting phenomenon it is called an *asymptotic* property. Equation 2.2 is commonly expressed as

$$\text{plim } l_N = \lambda \tag{2.2a}$$

Correspondingly, we can also define *asymptotic efficiency* of an estimator, *asymptotic unbiasedness* and other properties relating not just to the moments but to the nature of the limiting distribution of the estimator, such as *asymptotic normality*. We shall not do so since it will take us into more detail than we wish to go into (see Christ, 1966; Dhrymes, 1970). It is important to note here that the property of unbiasedness is independent of sample size whereas consistency is not. In choosing a consistent estimator, therefore, we may also want to know how large the sample size needs to be for the estimator to converge to the true parameter value.

With these desirable properties of estimators in mind, let us look at the problem of estimation. As we look at different estimators and estimation methods in turn, it would be useful to structure the discussion as follows.

The classification is made in terms of equation 2.1 which is quite general for our purposes. We also indicate at the same time the chapters where applications of these models occur in the text.

1 *Static models*: $\Gamma_2 = \phi$ (null)—no lagged endogenous variables present.
(a) *Static single equation models*: $G = 1, z = x$ (Chapters 3 and 5).
(b) *Seemingly unrelated regression equations*: Here a multiple equation static model has no interaction among the endogenous variables in the deterministic part of the model. $G > 1$, B diagonal ($\beta_{ij} = 0$ for $i \neq j$ all i and all j) (Chapter 3).
(c) *Static simultaneous equation models*: $G > 1$, B non-diagonal (Chapter 4).

2 *Dynamic models*: Γ_2 non-null.
(a) *Dynamic single equation models*: $G = 1$ (Chapter 6).
(b) *Dynamic multiple equation models*: $G > 1$ (Chapters 7 and 8).

In the above we also have classified models according to information on B, G and Γ_2. It is understood that the remaining 'parameters' of equation 2.1, K, Γ_1, Σ, are unrestricted. Also, except where we have mentioned a restriction, e.g. B diagonal, the appropriate parameters B, G and Γ_2 are also unrestricted.

We shall then go on to discuss the method of maximum likelihood. This will help us frame our discussion of testing restrictions along appropriate lines. Our discussion of testing restrictions will be against the general background of testing hypotheses. We shall discuss three well-known methods of testing restrictions—the Wald test, the Lagrangean multiplier test and the likelihood ratio test. Our discussion of maximum likelihood estimators will also help in tackling problems of nonlinear models.

We will take single equations first, 1(a) and then 2(a), and follow up with a discussion of 1(c), 1(b) and then finally 2(b).

1(a) Static Single Equation Models

In terms of 2.1, $G = 1$ and $\Gamma_2 = \phi$. This is the multiple regression model. We shall discuss the properties of the ordinary least squares (OLS) estimator in this context. If x_t' are fixed nonstochastic variables in repeated samples OLS is a linear *unbiased* and *efficient* estimator. If x_t' are stochastic, OLS is *consistent* and *asymptotically efficient*. In order for these properties to hold we require that the model satisfy some requirement concerning the random error term. These are that the u's have zero expectation, constant variance and be unrelated among each other and with the independent variables. Setting $\beta_{11} = -1$, we have in terms of 2.1

$$y' = \Gamma_1 x' + u \tag{2.3}$$

$$y_t = \sum_{j=1}^{k} \gamma_{1j} x_{jt} + u_t \qquad t = 1, \ldots, N \tag{2.3a}$$

We have written 2.3 for all N observations by making y' and u' $1 \times N$ vectors and x' a $k \times N$ matrix. The requirements for 2.3 are: (a) $E(u') = 0$; (b) $E(uu') = \sigma^2 I_N$, where I_N denotes a $N \times N$ unit matrix; (c) $E(x'u) = x'E(u) = 0$; (d) x' is a matrix of rank k and therefore $(x'x)^{-1}$ exists. The first requirement is obvious. The second one says that error variances are equal for all errors. Errors are *homoscedastic*. The third requirement is for the case where x's are fixed regressors and it ensures the independence of x's and u's. The fourth requirement says that the independent variables should not be perfectly correlated among each other. If these requirements are met, then the OLS estimator of Γ_1 is a best linear unbiased estimator (BLUE). The estimator of σ^2 is also unbiased. If x' are stochastic regressors then we replace requirement (c) by (c′) plim $\left(\frac{x'u'}{N}\right) = 0$. The OLS estimator is then *consistent* and *asymptotically efficient*. If the u' are normally independently distributed then the OLS estimates of Γ_1 are also normally distributed. As is well known the OLS estimator is written as (ˆ denotes an estimate)

$$\hat{\Gamma}_1' = (x'x)^{-1} x'y \tag{2.4}$$

where under (a), (b), (c) requirements

$$E(\hat{\Gamma}_1') = \Gamma_1' \qquad \text{variance } (\hat{\Gamma}_1') = \sigma^2 (x'x)^{-1}$$

Heteroscedasticity

In the context of 2.3 if the requirement of homoscedastic errors–requirement (b)–is not satisfied, we have the case of heteroscedasticity. This is expressed as (b′) $E(uu') = \sigma^2 \Omega$, where Ω is a $N \times N$ matrix. This case can be further divided into two: a situation where Ω is a diagonal matrix, this is when the errors are independent of each other but have unequal variances; and another situation where the errors may be correlated with each other causing Ω to be non-diagonal though the error variance may be equal in this case.

Taking the situation of a diagonal Ω first, this may arise if we have, for example, y and x arranged to increasing size. Or again it may arise when our y and x observations are averages of groups of observations but these groups are of unequal size. Heteroscedasticity then has the effect of causing the OLS estimator to be *inefficient* though *unbiased*. We have to find ways of incorporating the information on the nature of random errors into the model. This may be done in the first of the two examples above by deflating all the variables by a size variable which will make them of comparable size. This is frequently the logic when, for example, in investment functions the dependent as well as independent variables are deflated by capital stock (see Chapter 6 for details). Sometimes the entire equation is transformed in a nonlinear fashion, e.g. by taking logarithms of all variables. These approximations have to be made because we do not know the true nature of the heteroscedasticity. If we knew Ω then we could use Aitken's generalised least squares (GLS) estimator which is *unbiased* and *efficient*. The estimator is given by ($\tilde{}$ indicates a GLS estimate)

$$\tilde{\Gamma}_1' = (x'\Omega^{-1}x)^{-1}(x'\Omega^{-1}y) \qquad (2.5)$$

Then

$$E(\tilde{\Gamma}_1') = \Gamma_1' \qquad \text{and} \qquad \mathrm{var}(\tilde{\Gamma}_1') = \sigma^2(x'\Omega^{-1}x)^{-1}$$

Equation 2.5 is comparable to 2.4 since in the OLS case $\Omega = I$.

In many cases Ω will be unknown. A two-stage procedure may then have to be adopted where in the first stage *consistent* estimates of u are obtained which in turn give an estimate of Ω. This estimate of Ω can then be used in 2.5 in place of the true Ω. In some cases it may happen that knowing the nature of the heteroscedasticity will also indicate that Ω is a singular matrix. This happens in the situation where errors are dependent on each other. This is the case of autocorrelation of errors.

Autocorrelation

There are many reasons why time series may be autocorrelated. The primary ones are the influence of inertia, the slowness of response to a given change, the durability of goods etc. All these bring out the influence of past values of the independent or dependent variables on the current value of the dependent variable. Omission of any such important influence would lead to specification error. Mis-specification is therefore one of the reasons for autocorrelation of errors. Another reason is that time series are often available only in moving average form, e.g. overlapping decennial averages. Such moving average processes, by introducing common terms in successive observations, introduce autocorrelation. In cross-section regressions, autocorrelation is harder to interpret but it has been taken as evidence of the possible presence of non-linearities in the true relationship which is approximated by a linear equation. This is also then an example of mis-specification.

We may have in equation 2.3a additional information about the error process, for example, errors may follow a first-order autoregressive pattern.

$$u' = \rho u'_{-1} + \epsilon' \tag{2.6}$$

$$u_t = \rho u_{t-1} + \epsilon_t \tag{2.6a}$$

where $|\rho| \leqslant 1$ and $E(\epsilon\epsilon') = \sigma_\epsilon^2 I$.

Other possibilities are that the errors may be autoregressive but of a higher order or that they may be of a moving average form. These two possibilities can be written as

$$u_t = \sum_{i=1}^{r} \rho_i u_{t-1} + \epsilon_t \quad r\text{th order autoregressive process} \tag{2.6b}$$

$$u_t = \sum_{i=0}^{m} \mu_i \epsilon_{t-i} \quad m\text{th order moving average process} \tag{2.6c}$$

In each of 2.6, 2.6a, 2.6b and 2.6c we assume that the ϵ's are truly random homoscedastic errors. For the present we shall confine ourselves to 2.6 together with 2.3. In this case, OLS estimates are still *unbiased* but *inefficient*. If we know the value of ρ *a priori* then a problem arises that Ω becomes singular (for proof, see Christ, 1966, or Johnston 1972). Thus a two-step procedure has to be adopted. There are a variety of methods available here.

In the simple case of equation 2.3 where all the independent variables are uncorrelated with the error and there is no lagged dependent variable present, we can use the Durbin–Watson (*DW* or *d*) statistic to test for the presence of autocorrelation. We know that the asymptotic value of the Durbin–Watson statistic approaches $2(1 - \rho)$ where ρ is the autoregressive coefficient. Tables for the upper and lower values of the *d*-statistic are available for testing for the presence of autocorrelation among errors. If the computed value of *d* is between the lower and upper values then we cannot reject the null hypothesis of zero autocorrelation. If it is below the lower value then the presence of positive autocorrelation is indicated.

(1) The first method is to estimate Γ_1 by OLS and compute the residuals $\hat{u}$. At this moment, we have the choice of computing the *d*-statistics as follows

$$d = \sum_{t=2}^{N} (\hat{u}_t - \hat{u}_{t-1})^2 / \sum_{t=2}^{N} \hat{u}_{t-1}^2 \quad (2.7)$$

and then compute $\hat{\rho}$ — the estimated value of ρ — by using the asymptotic formula $\rho = 1 - d/2$. Alternatively, we can use the $\hat{u}_t$ series to estimate ρ by a simple homogenous regression

$$\hat{u}_t = \rho \hat{u}_{t-1} + \epsilon_t$$

and by OLS:

$$\hat{\rho} = \sum_{t=2}^{N} \hat{u}_t \hat{u}_{t-1} / \sum_{t=2}^{N} (\hat{u}_{t-1})^2 \quad (2.8)$$

Notice that the summation in 2.7 and 2.8 is over $(N-1)$ observations. We may in some cases know u_0 and use the information. The second stage is to use the estimated $\hat{\rho}$ to combine equations 2.1 and 2.6 for transforming y and x's as follows:

$$(y' - \hat{\rho} y'_{-1}) = \Gamma_1 (x' - \hat{\rho} x'_{-1}) + (u' - \hat{\rho} u'_{-1}) \quad (2.9)$$

or for 2.3a

$$(y_t - \hat{\rho} y_{t-1}) = \sum_j \gamma_{1j} (x_{jt} - \hat{\rho} x_{jt-1}) + (u_t - \hat{\rho} u_{t-1}) \quad (2.9a)$$

The parameters γ_{1j} can now be estimated by OLS from equation 2.9a treating the transformed variable $(y_t' - \hat{\rho} y'_{t-1})$ as the new dependent variable and the corresponding transformed independent variables $(x_{jt} - \hat{\rho} x_{jt-1})$ as the new independent variables. The transformed error term now satisfies OLS assumptions.

(2) A second method is to substitute 2.6 into 2.3 directly and obtain

$$y' = \Gamma_1 x' - \rho \Gamma_1 x'_{-1} + \rho y'_{-1} + \epsilon' \quad (2.10)$$

$$y_t = \sum_j \gamma_{1j} x_{jt} - \rho \sum_j \gamma_{1j} x_{jt-1} + \rho y_{t-1} + \epsilon_t . \quad (2.10a)$$

Equation 2.10 can be estimated by OLS. We now have k coefficients Γ_1 of x_t and k coefficients $\rho\Gamma_1$ of x_{t-1} plus the coefficient ρ of y_{t-1} to estimate. We have therefore $2k + 1$ coefficients to estimate $k + 1$ parameters γ_{1j} and ρ. This leads to overdetermination. One solution is to take the estimate of

ρ from the coefficient of y_{t-1} and transform the variables again as in equation 2.9 above with the help of this $\hat{\rho}$.

(3) A maximum likelihood method devised by Hildreth and Lu (1960) avoids a direct estimate of ρ. This method is computer-intensive since it involves the running of many more regressions than either of the two methods above. The method takes different values of ρ between -1 and $+1$, say at intervals of 0.1 or 0.05. For each value of ρ, equation 2.3 is transformed as in 2.9 above and OLS estimates are obtained. The next stage is to plot for each value of ρ which minimises $\Sigma \hat{\epsilon}_t^2$. That value of ρ is then the optimal estimate of ρ and the corresponding estimates of Γ_1 are taken as the optimal estimates of Γ_1.

(4) An alternative approach is to recognise that 2.9 or 2.10 involve nonlinearities in the parameters Γ_1 and ρ. A maximum likelihood estimate designed by J. D. Sargan (1964) directly formulates the likelihood function of ϵ in equation 2.10 and proceeds to maximise the concentrated log-likelihood function with respect to Γ_1 and ρ. The resulting equations are nonlinear and can be estimated by an iterative Newton–Raphson method given some initial value of ρ. Standard errors can also be obtained for these parameter estimates. We shall discuss the maximum likelihood method further below (see also Chapter 7 for further discussion).

We have already noticed two cases where the OLS assumptions regarding the error term break down and either GLS or some maximum likelihood method has to be resorted to. The GLS methods retain strong resemblance with OLS. Thus, in the case of first-order autoregression, methods (1) and (2) described above apply OLS in two separate stages. In the second stage, we apply a transformation which makes the estimation method formally identical to GLS but similar sets of linear normal equations have to be solved as in OLS. A more serious problem occurs when we depart from the simple static formulation of equation 2.1 and introduce dynamic specifications.

2(a) Dynamic Single Equation

We still have in the context of 2.1 $G = 1$, but now Γ_2 is no longer null. We have a lagged dependent variable in our equation. Thus instead of 2.3

$$y' = \Gamma_1 x' + \Gamma_2 y'_{-1} + u' \tag{2.11}$$

So 2.11 can be written as

$$y_t = \sum_{j=1}^{k} \gamma_{1j} x_{jt} + \gamma_2 y_{t-1} + u_t \tag{2.11a}$$

This equation is dynamic because the past history of y is relevant to its current value. As we shall see later, such equations can arise from many different assumptions. Partial adjustment models and adaptive expectation models yield equations similar to 2.11 (see Chapter 6 for examples).

The transition from equation 2.3 to 2.11 has one obvious implication. We can no longer assume that our independent variables are nonstochastic since y'_{-1} is a stochastic variable. If y'_{-1} as well as x' satisfies the requirement (c′), i.e. if y'_{-1} is independent of the error term, then we obtain *consistent* and *asymptotically efficient* estimates of Γ_1 and Γ_2. The estimation problem becomes difficult if we have any grounds for believing that the error term may be serially correlated. Models incorporating adaptive expectations or the permanent income hypothesis in time series analysis lead to serial correlation of errors. Of the four methods we discussed above for dealing with autoregressive errors in a static single equation model not all are applicable for the case of a dynamic single equation with autoregressive errors. (Once again we deal with autoregressive rather than moving average errors.)

We can no longer test the null hypothesis of no autocorrelation by using the *DW* statistic. This is because if the errors are autoregressive, following a pattern such as 2.6 then requirement (c′) is no longer met. y_{t-1} and u_t are correlated through u_{t-1} even asymptotically. This violation of (c′) then means that the estimates of Γ_2 (or rather γ_2, since it is a scalar) are *inconsistent*. Inconsistent parameter estimates affect our residuals which are in turn our estimates of the random error term. These are also *inconsistent*. Indeed, it has been shown that OLS estimates of the parameter bias the computed *DW* statistic towards a value of 2—towards an acceptance of the null hypothesis of zero autocorrelation when the true model is one of positive autoregression in errors. We have therefore to reject OLS in favour of a consistent estimator and this is provided by the instrumental variable (IV) estimator (but see Durbin, 1971, for the correct test).

Instrumental Variable Estimator

The OLS estimator is a linear estimator in terms of x's and y's. Now we look for additional variables, M, which will serve as instruments and the instrumental variable estimator is then a linear function of M, x and y. The instrumental variables, M, have to satisfy two requirements: (c″) the instruments must be independent of the error term plim $\left[\frac{1}{N}(M'u)\right] = 0$. This is necessary but not sufficient. In a sense for each independent variable that fails to satisfy requirement (c′), we seek at least one instrumental variable which will satisfy requirement (c″). The second requirement is that these instruments which we want to replace our independent variable with must be (highly) correlated with that independent variable (d') i.e. that $M'x$ is nonsingular. Suppose in 2.3 we want to replace each of the k independent variables by an instrumental variable. Then the IV estimator of Γ_1 (denoted by $\hat{\hat{}}$) is

$$\hat{\hat{\Gamma}}_1' = (M'x)^{-1}(M'y) \tag{2.12}$$

Note that for OLS, $M = x$ since the x's satisfy (c′). The IV estimator is a consistent estimator, hence

$$\text{plim}\,(\hat{\hat{\Gamma}}_1') = \Gamma_1' \tag{2.13}$$

only the asymptotic variance-covariance matrix of $\hat{\hat{\Gamma}}_1$ can be worked out and this is

$$\text{asy var}(\hat{\hat{\Gamma}}_1) = \text{plim}\left[\sigma^2\left(\frac{M'x}{N}\right)^{-1}\right] \tag{2.14}$$

The higher the correlation between our instruments and the

original independent variables the lower will be the asymptotic variance. In the limiting case, a perfect correlation between M and x will take us back to the OLS case.

Returning to the case of a dynamic single equation with autoregressive errors, we see then that in equation 2.11 along with the possibility that errors may follow a pattern such as 2.6, we need an instrument for y_{t-1}. This will enable us to obtain a consistent estimate of γ_2. We have available two straightforward choices. Since the x's are exogenous, they clearly satisfy requirement (c′) and our equation says that y and the set of x's are related. Thus any lagged exogenous variables, any x_{jt-1} out of the k possible variables, will serve as an instrument. Alternatively, we may form a linear combination of all the x variables and the lagged value of such a linear combination can also serve as an instrument. Indeed, since the correlation between y and all the x's will exceed that between y and any one of the x's, the latter alternative—a linear combination of all the x's—will give us smaller asymptotic variances for the parameter estimates. In the limit, there will be perfect correlation between M and x which reduces the IV estimator to the OLS case, which by definition is minimum variance among the class of linear estimators.

One way to choose the linear combination of x's is to regress y on the set of x's. This is an auxiliary regression and does not really constitute a causal model. We write this as

$$y_t = \Sigma p_j x_{jt} + v_t \tag{2.15}$$

Having estimated p_j, we form

$$\hat{y}_t = \Sigma \hat{p}_j x_{jt} = y_t - \hat{v}_t \tag{2.15a}$$

and then $\hat{y}_{t-1}$ is an instrument for y_{t-1} in 2.11. The IV estimator can then be formed as

$$\begin{pmatrix} \Sigma\hat{\hat{\gamma}}_{1j} \\ \\ \hat{\hat{\gamma}}_2 \end{pmatrix} = \begin{bmatrix} x'x & x'y_{-1} \\ \\ \hat{y}'_{-1}x & \hat{y}'_{-1}y_{-1} \end{bmatrix}^{-1} \begin{pmatrix} x'y \\ \\ \hat{y}'_{-1}y \end{pmatrix} \tag{2.16}$$

We shall see later on that this method of selecting instruments is of general applicability when we come to discuss simultaneous equations under 1(c) and 1(b). The method is known as the method of two-stage least squares (2SLS) in that context.

Choosing $\hat{y}_{-1}$ as an instrument for y_{-1} ensures us *consistent* estimates for γ_2. Then we can use the residuals to test the null hypothesis of no serial correlation in the errors. If we wish to improve the efficiency of our estimates, then we have to use the information contained in the residuals to estimate the variance–covariance matrix of errors ($\hat{\Omega}$) and try a GLS estimator to improve the efficiency of the estimator. This may be further improved by an iterative procedure where the GLS estimates of the parameters could be compared with the IV and the Ω matrix re-estimated until successive estimates of the parameters converge to a stable value. Of course, if Ω is $\sigma^2 I$, i.e. there is no autocorrelation in errors, there will be no gain in efficiency.

1(c) Static Simultaneous Equations Model

We have now $G > 1$ and B non-diagonal but Γ_2 is null. So 2.1 can be rewritten as a structural form (SF) system

$$By' + \Gamma_1 x' = u' \tag{2.17}$$

This is the simultaneous equation model. Since the errors are correlated across equations, $E(u'u) = \Sigma$ is non-diagonal and there is causal interaction among the endogenous variables through the elements of B, OLS is no longer appropriate as assumption (c′) is violated. If OLS is used on any equation of 2.17, biased and inefficient estimates would result. We need, therefore, an IV estimator to ensure consistency. The appropriate IV estimator is what we described above as the two-stage least squares estimator though any other method of choosing instruments will ensure consistency of estimates.

Corresponding to 2.17 we can write down the restricted reduced form (RRF) system

$$y' = -B^{-1}\Gamma_1 x' + B^{-1}u' = \Pi_1 x' + \epsilon' \tag{2.18}$$

This reduced form embodies all the information in 2.17 but casts it in terms of exogenous variables alone on the r.h.s. But then using the analogy of the auxiliary equation 2.15, the auxiliary system of equations corresponding to 2.17, called the unrestricted reduced form (URF) or the least squares reduced form (LSRF), can be written as

$$y' = P_1 x' + v' \qquad (2.19)$$

In 2.19 we do not use the information that P_1 is a product of B^{-1} and Γ_1. Indeed, the only information we use is that the endogenous and exogenous variables specified in 2.17 reappear respectively on the left-hand side and right-hand side of 2.19. The instrumental variable estimator or 2SLS estimator of 2.17 is formed by using $\hat{y}'$ from 2.19, $\hat{P}_1 x' = [(x'x)^{-1}x'y]' x'$, as an instrument vector for the endogenous variables which appear as independent variables in any equation in 2.17. Thus, say in the third equation we have y_3 as the dependent variable ($\beta_{33} = -1$) and y_1, y_2 and y_6 as independent variables with non-zero coefficients, then we use $\hat{y}_1$, $\hat{y}_2$ and $\hat{y}_6$ as instruments for that equation. We can repeat this process for each of the G equations and obtain consistent estimates of B (and, of course, Γ_1). If 2.17 is a just-identified system then we can go directly from an estimate of 2.18 to obtain consistent estimates of B and Γ_1, but in general most of the systems in econometrics are typically over-identified.

Notice here that 2.18 is a restricted version of 2.19. Thus any of the restrictions on B and Γ_1 in 2.17 will carry over to 2.18 in a suitable form but not to 2.19. If, however, a certain exogenous or endogenous variable is missing altogether from 2.17 when it should belong to the model, i.e. if 2.17 is mis-specified by exclusion of a variable which should be included, then that omission could carry over to 2.19. Thus 2.19 is unrestricted only with respect to the restrictions on the coefficient matrices B and Γ_1. There is an additional question of the testing of the validity of the restrictions by comparing 2.18 and 2.19 but we should leave this until later when we discuss the problem of testing restrictions. (Those in a hurry at this stage can consult Christ, 1966, pp 531–543.)

We have already discussed in the context of a single dynamic equation above that using a linear combination of exogenous variables as instruments as we do in the 2SLS case implies that, as far as efficiency is concerned, 2SLS estimators are best among IV estimators. This efficiency is, however, only asymptotic efficiency just as the estimator yields only consistent estimates. But the drawback of the 2SLS method is that it takes each equation separately from others. It uses no information from the other $(G-1)$ equations in the model other than what endogenous variables and exogenous variables appear in the entire model. There is, however, additional information in the error variance matrix Σ. Simultaneity among the y variables comes not only through the B matrix of endogenous variable coefficients but also through the covariances among the random error terms. The information contained in Σ if used in estimation can help improve the efficiency of the estimates.

It would be helpful at this stage to write out the Σ matrix explicitly:

$$E(u'u) = \mathbf{\Sigma} = \begin{pmatrix} \Sigma_{11} & \Sigma_{12} & \cdots & \Sigma_{1G} \\ \Sigma_{21} & \Sigma_{22} & & \vdots \\ \vdots & & \ddots & \vdots \\ \Sigma_{G1} & \cdots & \cdots & \Sigma_{GG} \end{pmatrix} \tag{2.20}$$

$\mathbf{\Sigma}$ is a symmetric matrix of variances and covariances of errors among equations. Each of the diagonal elements of $\mathbf{\Sigma}$ will itself be of the form Ω or $\sigma^2 I_N$. Thus Σ_{11} is an $N \times N$ matrix.

Now if $\mathbf{\Sigma}$ were diagonal, then there is no further cross-equation information contained in $\mathbf{\Sigma}$ that can improve the efficiency of the 2SLS estimator. But if $\mathbf{\Sigma}$ is non-diagonal, then a further step can be taken to improve the asymptotic efficiency of the 2SLS estimators. This further step takes us to a three-stage least squares (3SLS) method. It is a GLS analogue in the many equations case. After having obtained consistent estimates of B and Γ_1 by the 2SLS method, the residuals of the G equations are used to compute $\hat{\Sigma}$, an estimate of $\mathbf{\Sigma}$. This will be a consistent estimate. This then is incorporated into the model. All the equations of 2.17 are rewritten so that the parameters in B and Γ_1 form a vector, i.e. the first row of B, Γ_1, is written first, then the second row, and so on. The endogenous and exogenous variable matrices are suitably rewritten and then $\hat{\Sigma}$ is incorporated into the estimator in the GLS fashion. (It would involve us in much detailed notation to write the 3SLS estimator here but the general idea is conveyed. For details see Johnston, 1972, pp 395–398, Christ, 1966.)

1(b) Seemingly Unrelated Regression Equations (SURE)

Given our discussion of 3SLS above, this case can be easily dealt with. The idea here is that the B matrix may be an identity matrix and hence the y variables may *seem* independent of each other. The Σ matrix may, however, be non-diagonal. We shall come across this case in Chapter 3 when we study demand equations. Here we do not need an IV or 2SLS estimator since our estimates of Γ_1 by OLS would be consistent but their efficiency can be improved by using the OLS residuals to estimate Σ and incorporate this in GLS fashion in a second estimate of the Γ_1 matrix. This is then again a GLS analogue for many equations except that in this case B is an identity matrix.

2(b) Dynamic Multiple Equations

This is the most general of all the models we need to consider. Here we have $G > 1$, B non-diagonal, Γ_2 non-null and Σ non-diagonal. In addition, we shall consider a generalisation of the autoregressive error case in the single equation situation (equation 2.6). We can say that we have

$$By' + \Gamma_1 x' + \Gamma_2 y'_{-1} = u' \qquad (2.21)$$

$$u' = Ru'_{-1} + e' \qquad (2.22)$$

R is a $G \times G$ matrix and equation 2.22 can be called the vector autoregressive equation of the random errors. While 2.22 only incorporates a first-order case (just as 2.21 only includes a one-period lag in y), a generalisation can be easily made to higher order cases. Notice that R is not a symmetric matrix. Taking $G = 2$, we have for 2.22 explicitly

$$\begin{pmatrix} u_{1t} \\ u_{2t} \end{pmatrix} = \begin{bmatrix} \rho_{11} & \rho_{12} \\ \rho_{21} & \rho_{22} \end{bmatrix} \begin{pmatrix} u_{1t-1} \\ u_{2t-1} \end{pmatrix} + \begin{pmatrix} e_{1t} \\ e_{2t} \end{pmatrix} \qquad (2.23)$$

ρ_{ii} is the same as ρ in equation 2.6 since it is the coefficient of the own lagged term. But ρ_{12} is the influence of the lagged value of the second equation's error term (u_{2t-1}) on the first equation's error term of this period (u_{1t}). There is no reason at all why it should be equal to ρ_{21} since that tells us about the influence of the u_{1t-1} on u_{2t}.

Now a system such as 2.21 raises the problem of choice of instruments in the same way the dynamic single equation did. The restricted and unrestricted reduced forms of 2.21 respectively are

$$y' = \Pi_1 x' + \Pi_2 y'_{-1} + \epsilon' \tag{2.24}$$

$$y' = P_1 x' + P_2 y'_{-1} + v' \tag{2.25}$$

Now we clearly need instruments $\hat{y}'$ for the contemporaneous endogenous variables appearing with unrestricted coefficients in any row of B. If, however, we form instruments by using URF in 2.25 and forming $\hat{y}'$ as before, we run into a problem. If the errors are autoregressive as in 2.22, then y'_{-1} will be correlated with u' through u'_{-1}. Now if y'_{-1} enter $\hat{y}'$ with coefficients $\hat{P}_2$ then $\hat{y}'$ will in turn be correlated with u'. Thus it will not satisfy the requirement (c′) that an admissible instrument should. Not only that but we cannot really treat y'_{-1} as predetermined and use them as their own instruments. We need instruments for y' and for y'_{-1}. This is especially so since we cannot *test* for the presence of an autoregressive scheme such as 2.22 by OLS residuals of 2.21.

It would be safest, therefore, to assume 2.22 along with 2.21. Then in forming instruments $\hat{y}'$ delete y'_{-1} from the URF 2.25 and use only the exogenous variables as instruments. Then $\hat{y}'_{-1}$ can in turn be used as instruments for y'_{-1} as long as we take care to see that

$$\hat{y}' = \hat{P}_1 x' = [(x'x)^{-1} x'y]' x' \tag{2.26}$$

We shall see in Chapter 7 that systems such as 2.21 and 2.22 are not at all unusual. Indeed, ignoring 2.22 in a dynamic context will seriously affect the economic logic of the parameter estimates obtained. Once we are in a simultaneous dynamic context, we have to go the full length of specifying a scheme such as 2.22. Taking care of the autoregression in each equation separately as is often done means that we only test for the presence of ρ_{ii} and neglect ρ_{ij}. It will also lead us to choosing inappropriate instruments.

The presence of vector autoregressive errors also modifies the rules of thumb that are often used to check whether an equation in a system of equations is identified. The usual practice is to count the zero restrictions on B, Γ_1 and Γ_2. But notice that combining 2.21 and 2.22 we have

$$By' + \Gamma_1 x_t' + (\Gamma_2 - RB)y'_{-1} - R\Gamma_1 x'_{-1} - R\Gamma_2 y'_{-2} = e' \tag{2.27}$$

Now a zero restriction on Γ_2 if used as an identifying restriction in 2.21 can easily be invalid as in the transformed equation (2.27) the appropriate coefficient in $(\Gamma_2 - RB)$ matrix may not be zero. Let us illustrate this with an example. Take $G = 2$ as before:

$$\begin{bmatrix} 1 & \beta_{12} \\ \beta_{21} & 1 \end{bmatrix} \begin{pmatrix} y'_{1t} \\ y'_{2t} \end{pmatrix} + \begin{bmatrix} \gamma_{1,11} & \gamma_{1,12} & 0 \\ 0 & \gamma_{1,22} & \gamma_{1,23} \end{bmatrix} \begin{pmatrix} x'_{1t} \\ x'_{2t} \end{pmatrix} + \begin{pmatrix} 0 & \gamma_{2,12} \\ 0 & 0 \end{pmatrix} \begin{pmatrix} y'_{1t-1} \\ y'_{2t-1} \end{pmatrix} = \begin{pmatrix} u_{1t} \\ u_{2t} \end{pmatrix} \tag{2.28}$$

Here y'_{1t-1} is redundant since it has zero coefficients in both equations but has been put in for generality. There is one zero restriction on the first equation ($\gamma_{1,13} = 0$) and two zero restrictions on the second equation ($\gamma_{1,21} = 0$, $\gamma_{2,22} = 0$). The first equation is just-identified and the second over-identified by the order condition. Now if we combine 2.28 with 2.23 we get the explicit version of 2.27:

$$\begin{bmatrix} 1 & \beta_{12} \\ \beta_{21} & 1 \end{bmatrix} \begin{pmatrix} y'_{1t} \\ y'_{2t} \end{pmatrix} + \begin{bmatrix} \gamma_{1,11} & \gamma_{1,12} & \\ & \gamma_{1,22} & \gamma_{1,23} \end{bmatrix} \begin{pmatrix} x'_{1t} \\ x'_{2t} \\ x'_{3t} \end{pmatrix}$$
$$- \begin{bmatrix} (\rho_{11} + \rho_{12}\beta_{21}) & [(\rho_{11}\beta_{12} + \rho_{12}) - \gamma_{2,12}] \\ (\rho_{21} + \rho_{22}\beta_{21}) & (\rho_{12}\beta_{12} + \rho_{22}) \end{bmatrix} \begin{pmatrix} y'_{1t-1} \\ y'_{2t-1} \end{pmatrix}$$

$$-\begin{bmatrix} \rho_{11}\gamma_{1,\,11} & (\rho_{11}\gamma_{1,\,12}+\rho_{12}\gamma_{1,\,22}) & \rho_{12}\gamma_{1,\,23} \\ \rho_{21}\gamma_{1,\,11} & (\rho_{21}\gamma_{1,\,12}+\rho_{22}\gamma_{1,\,22}) & \rho_{22}\gamma_{1,\,23} \end{bmatrix}\begin{pmatrix} x'_{1t-1} \\ x'_{2t-1} \\ x'_{3t-1} \end{pmatrix}$$

$$-\begin{pmatrix} \rho_{11}\gamma_{2,\,12} \\ \rho_{21}\gamma_{2,\,12} \end{pmatrix}\begin{pmatrix} y'_{1t-2} \\ y'_{2t-2} \end{pmatrix} = \begin{pmatrix} e'_{1t} \\ e'_{2t} \end{pmatrix} \tag{2.29}$$

The system 2.29 now involves only one zero restriction each on the two equations. Only the zero restrictions on Γ_1 carry through to the transformed system, restrictions on Γ_2 vanish. There are of course nonlinear restrictions on the coefficients of 2.29. In 2.28 there are seven separate unrestricted parameters and in 2.23 there are four such parameters. In 2.29 there are eighteen separate coefficients, hence there are seven extra nonlinear restrictions on the coefficients of the system 2.29. These restrictions are the simultaneous equation counterpart of the single equation case we discussed above in the context of Professor Sargan's work. We shall encounter them again in Chapter 7.

In obtaining consistent estimates of 2.29, we need four instruments for the two pairs of lagged y variables. We can use linear combinations of the x variables using the analogue of equation 2.26 and then proceed to improve the asymptotic efficiency by using a 3SLS procedure. An alternative is to use appropriate instruments for 2.21 or 2.28 and use the residuals to obtain estimates of ρ_{ij} and then again iterate till the parameter estimates of 2.21 and of 2.22 converge to stable values.

As we discussed in Chapter 1, we may regard the typical situation in econometric models as not one of simultaneous causality as in 2.20 but one of recursive or unidirectional causation. This was the case with the two equations model 1.11 and 1.12 in Chapter 1. The conditions of recursiveness are

(i) B matrix triangular—elements either above or below the diagonal must be all zero.

(ii) Σ, the variance-covariance matrix of errors, must be diagonal

(iii) the errors must be non-autocorrelated with their own past values and the past values of the errors in other equations:

$$E(u_t u'_{t-\theta}) = 0 \quad \text{for all} \quad \theta > 0.$$

This assumption is of special importance when lagged endogenous variables are included as in 2.21. For 2.21 we require that θ be at least equal to 1.

If these assumptions are satisfied then OLS estimates of 2.20 are consistent and asymptotically efficient. In a sense, conditions (i), (ii) and (iii) make the system such that the endogenous variables appearing as independent variables can be their own instruments. Thus, in (1.11) and (1.12) we can first estimate (1.12) using P_{t-1} as its own instrument. Then $Q_t^S (= Q_t^D)$ can be treated as a predetermined variable in (1.11) since Q_t^S can be broken up into $\hat{Q}_t^S + \hat{v}_t$ as in the 2SLS equations 2.23b above. Now, by assumption (b), v_t and u_t are uncorrelated and $\hat{Q}_t^S$ is also uncorrelated with u_t since it is a linear combination of predetermined variables. Thus Q_t^S is uncorrelated with u_t and OLS estimates of 1.11 will not involve any inconsistency. This reasoning can be generalised to a system of many equations.

Full recursiveness is a stringent condition especially in large models and often we get a situation where B is not triangular but *block triangular*. This means that blocks of equations are independent of equations in other blocks but simultaneously interdependent among themselves. Imagine our G equations in 2.1 split into two blocks of G_1 and G_2. Then one block recursive representation of the B matrix could be

$$\begin{bmatrix} \mathbf{B}_{11} & \mathbf{B}_{12} \\ 0 & \mathbf{B}_{22} \end{bmatrix} \begin{bmatrix} \mathbf{y}_{G1} \\ \mathbf{y}_{G2} \end{bmatrix} \tag{2.30}$$

Here the bottom G_2 variables are interdependent among themselves but independent of the G_1 variables which are in their turn dependent on the G_2 variables. We need for block recursiveness the block diagonality of the Σ matrix, the errors of the G_1 equations being independent of those in the G_2 equations. This condition along with the block triangularity qualifies the $\mathbf{y}_{G2}$ as instruments for themselves in estimating the elements of $\mathbf{B}_{12}$.

Testing Restrictions

We have mentioned at various stages in Chapter 1 and in this chapter the importance of using economic theory to derive prior restrictions on our parameters. Having specified them *a priori*, we need to check whether our data enable us to confirm our hypothesis. In other words, we have to ask ourselves if placing all these restrictions is of any help when explaining the observed data. If not then an unrestricted estimate may do just as well. Since the restrictions embody our causal scheme, it is important to test them rigorously. We have to devise methods of estimation which will help us incorporate our restrictions systematically (e.g. impose them as additional constraints in the estimation problem) and then test them. Our objective function in econometric estimation at the OLS stage was to fit 'the best line' minimising the sums of squared residuals. We revised this since we were interested in parameter estimation and moved on to methods such as IV, which provides consistent parameter estimates, and 3SLS, which improves their asymptotic efficiency. We now move a stage further and say that our aim is to estimate our parameters subject to restrictions and to test the validity of our restrictions.

It is not our intention here to review the theory of hypothesis testing. We shall assume that readers are familiar with (or have ways of finding out about) the logic of t-tests and F-tests. Implicitly we used this at the outset of Chapter 1 when we asked about equation 1.1 whether t-ratios were above two and then said that the coefficient was statistically significant. In that case, as in many econometric problems, our null hypothesis was a rather simple one—that the true value of the coefficient was zero. We did not use any other information such as the true value of the income coefficient should be not only not zero but positive. Our alternative hypothesis was thus left rather vague. If we had used this information we would see that our test should be a one-tailed test, which as a rule is the case in econometrics. A particular restriction may be that the sum of coefficients in an equation be unity (e.g. if we are testing for constant returns to scale in a production function). We can devise an appropriate t-statistic to see if the data reject this restriction. Alternatively, we can estimate the parameters subject to the restriction that the coefficients sum to one. This would clearly give us one degree of freedom since one of the coefficients can be derived from all the others. To test whether our restriction is valid, we could compare the restricted estimates with the unrestricted estimates. For example, we could compare the estimates of the RRF in 2.21 with the URF in 2.22 and choose that which is more in agreement with the data. But this is rather a vague way of putting it. In order to talk more systematically about it, we need to talk about the ML method and the likelihood ratio test.

We briefly mentioned the method of maximum likelihood in connection with Sargan's method of estimating equations with a first-order autoregressive error. The ML method is applicable in many more cases, indeed in every case mentioned in this chapter. To take the single equation case of 2.3 as an example, we make an assumption in addition to (a) to (d) made in OLS. This assumption is that the u's are independently normally distributed with mean zero and a constant variance σ^2. (We need not assume the distribution to be normal, but this is the most usual assumption.) We form the likelihood function of all u's given this information. Since the u's are normally distributed, $(y' - \Gamma_1 x')$ a linear function of u's is also normally distributed. We have then the likelihood function of all the N u's as follows

$$L(u; 0, \sigma^2) = \frac{1}{(\sigma^2)^N (2\pi)^{N/2}} \exp - \left[\frac{1}{2\sigma^2} u'u\right] \tag{2.31}$$

Substituting $u' = y' - \Gamma_1 x'$ we have

$$= \frac{1}{(\sigma^2)^N (2\pi)^{N/2}} \exp - \left[\frac{1}{2\sigma^2}(y' - \Gamma_1 x')(y' - \Gamma_1 x')'\right] \tag{2.32}$$

If $E(uu') = \Omega$ instead of $\sigma^2 I$, we can easily incorporate this by writing

$$= \frac{1}{|\det \mathbf{\Omega}|^N (2\pi)^{N/2}} \exp - \left[(y' - \Gamma_1 x') \mathbf{\Omega}^{-1} (y' - \Gamma_1 x')' \right] \quad (2.33)$$

Det $\mathbf{\Omega}$ is the determinant of $\mathbf{\Omega}$.

Our next step is to maximise the logarithm of the likelihood function with respect to the unknown parameters $\Gamma_1 \sigma^2$ (or $\mathbf{\Omega}$). It is easy to first solve out the ML estimator of σ^2 or $\mathbf{\Omega}$ and then substitute it in 2.33 to obtain the *concentrated* log-likelihood function and proceed to maximise that with respect to Γ_1. In the case of 2.1, the normal equations to be solved are identical for OLS and ML if all the assumptions are satisfied. Given the parameter estimates we can also compute the value of the likelihood function for the particular sample. Our estimates are consistent, asymptotically efficient and normally distributed.

The ML method can be readily adapted to the many-equation situation such as 2.17. Here we assume that the u's are jointly normally distributed with mean zero and a variance-covariance matrix $\mathbf{\Sigma}$. In this case we may begin with some set of consistent estimates and a consistent estimate of $\mathbf{\Sigma}$ before maximising the likelihood function which would be very similar to that of 2.33. Starting with consistent estimates, ML will help us derive asymptotically efficient estimates. In this sense for a system such as 2.17, the ML method is close to 3SLS. Similarly, the estimation problem in 2.21 and 2.22 can be tackled by forming the likelihood function of e_{1t} and e_{2t}, assuming them to be normally independently distributed and once again proceed to maximise the likelihood function. Here again, it may help to start with some set of consistent estimates.

The relevance of the ML method for incorporating and testing restrictions can now be brought out. Like OLS, the ML method sets up an objective function which has to be maximised. As we know from economic theory, we can incorporate restrictions (constraints) by the method of Lagrange multipliers and maximise the objective function subject to these constraints. Each binding constraint lowers the value of the objective function at the optimum compared to the unconstrained optimum. In a similar way, we can compare the value of the likelihood function for the restricted and the unrestricted estimates. Suppose $L(R)$ is the value of the likelihood function in the restricted case and $L(UR)$ for the unrestricted case. The ratio λ, where

$$\lambda = \frac{L(R)}{L(UR)} \tag{2.34}$$

is called the likelihood ratio. For large sample cases, we have a theorem which says that $-2 \ln \lambda$ is distributed as χ^2 with as many degrees of freedom as the number of restrictions. This is extremely helpful because we can compute χ^2 corresponding to the computed λ and compare it to some pre-assigned critical level of χ^2 (e.g. for the 0.05 region) as in the *t*-test, and if the computed χ^2 is less than the critical value then we say that our restrictions are not rejected by the data.

The logic of the likelihood ratio test can be intuitively explained as follows. Our restrictions come from an *a priori* theoretical model which we use to interpret the available data. Now if our restrictions are valid, then the data are in some sense in agreement with our theory. Then imposing the restrictions on the data and estimating only the remaining (unrestricted) parameters should compare favourably with imposing no restrictions at all. Now the unrestricted equation will have the lowest residual variance by the minimum variance properties of OLS proved earlier. (These carry over to the maximum likelihood in the simple linear case.) So the restricted equation will have a smaller likelihood (or higher residual variance). But if the restrictions are valid then the loss in likelihood value should not be very great. Thus $\lambda < 1$ and hence $-2 \ln \lambda$ will be positive. For valid restrictions $-2 \ln \lambda$ will be in turn the permissible χ^2 value, i.e. the ratio λ will be within the limits of that obtainable purely due to random variation. The likelihood value of the restricted equation will be therefore in the neighbourhood of the true maximum given by the unrestricted equation.

If there is a great fall in the likelihood value then this tells us that the restrictions are not valid. This will appear as a value of $-2 \ln \lambda$ in excess of the critical value of χ^2 chosen for the test. (The critical value also depends on the number of restrictions, of course.) In the terms of the Lagrangean multiplier analogy discussed above, what we can say then is that if the restrictions are binding (in the sense of the programming problem) the data can be said to have rejected them. Thus zero shadow prices for the restrictions indicate acceptance of the restrictions and positive shadow prices lead to their rejection. Two other approaches similar to the likelihood ratio test should be briefly mentioned here. They are a Lagrange multiplier test and the Wald test.

An alternative approach would be to carry out a constrained maximisation. Thus the constraints in 2.36 can be added with appropriate Lagrangean multipliers to the ML problem 2.31–2.33. Then computing the value of the Lagrange multipliers and their variance will tell us about the validity of the restrictions. Once again it would take us too far away from our current concern to develop this notion but the similarity of the notions of likelihood ratio rest and Lagrange multiplier test should be noted. (See Silvey, 1970, pp. 59–64 and 79–84 for details on restricted least squares and restricted maximum likelihood.)

Another general method of testing restrictions is the one which perhaps most readily comes to mind. This is to estimate the unrestricted equation and then test by a suitable t-test or F-test whether the restrictions are satisfied or not. Thus instead of imposing the restrictions *a priori*, they can be tested *ex post*. A rigorous test statistic in this case has been developed and is known after its inventor as the Wald test (or W-test). This once again comes out to be a χ^2 test but again the details are not developed here. (See again Silvey, 1970, pp. 115–121 for a discussion of the Wald test and the likelihood ratio test, and also pp. 180–188.)

Let us say that we are estimating the demand curve for coffee in its log–linear form of 1.8 with the restriction that $(b_1' - b_2') = 0$. Now putting this restriction means that we hypothesise that the income elasticity is the same absolute size as the price elasticity and together they sum to zero. This clearly saves us estimating one of the two parameters since it is one restriction on 1.8—giving us one degree of freedom. We can estimate then

$$\ln DC_t = b'_0 + b'_1(\ln Y_t - \ln PC_t) + u'_t \qquad (2.35)$$

We can estimate 1.8 and 2.35 and then form the likelihood ratio $L(u')/L(u)$. As we said above, in the single equation case, the ML estimator is identical to OLS if all the assumptions (a) to (d) are satisfied. In this case, comparing the likelihood is the same as comparing the residual sums of squares (RSS). We have for this case to compare RSS (2.35) to RSS (1.8), twice the logarithm of the ratio of RSS(u)/RSS(u') is distributed as χ^2 with one degree of freedom.

The likelihood ratio test can be adapted to test for a larger number of restrictions. We shall see examples of its use in Chapter 3 and Chapter 7. In general, it can be adapted to test the validity of identifying restrictions, of the restriction that errors are autoregressive or whether the specification of an equation should be linear or nonlinear. Since prior restrictions are of great importance if we are to use economic theory seriously in econometric estimation, the likelihood ratio test is a vital tool for econometricians.

We also mentioned above that restrictions can be incorporated with Lagrange multipliers. It is possible, though rather involved, to estimate the values of the Lagrange multipliers and their asymptotic standard errors. A method for incorporating restrictions using GLS has been proposed by Theil and Goldberger (1960) and called by them the method of mixed estimation. Instead of incorporating the restriction directly in the estimated equation as we have done in the simple case of 2.40, or estimating the Lagrange multipliers, this method uses any information available on the parameters, such as unrestricted estimates and variances or purely prior information, and incorporates these as additional equations. Thus in addition to 2.1 we may have the linear restrictions

$$r' = \Gamma_1 R' + v \qquad (2.36)$$

r for example may be a vector of zero's. In the case of 2.35 we have one restriction which says

$$0 = [b'_1 \ b'_2]\begin{bmatrix} 1 \\ \\ -1 \end{bmatrix} \qquad (2.37)$$

We could add random errors to our restrictions and specify the variance structure. We may have an estimated value of one of our parameters from previous data and also the estimated variance of the estimate. Say this is an estimate of γ_{11} in 2.3, then we write

$$\hat{\gamma}_{11} = 1\gamma_{11} + \hat{v}_1 \tag{2.38}$$

with $E(\hat{v}_1^2)$ = variance of $\hat{\gamma}_{11}$. In general, we assume $E(v_1) = 0$, $E(v_1 v_1') = \Omega$. We put together 2.3 and 2.36 since

$$\begin{pmatrix} y' \\ \\ r' \end{pmatrix} = \Gamma_1 \begin{bmatrix} x' \\ \\ R' \end{bmatrix} + \begin{bmatrix} u \\ \\ v_1 \end{bmatrix} \tag{2.39}$$

$$E\left[\begin{pmatrix} u \\ \\ v_1 \end{pmatrix} (u\, v_1)\right] = \begin{bmatrix} \sigma^2 & 0 \\ \\ 0 & \Omega \end{bmatrix} \tag{2.40}$$

Given 2.40, we can form the GLS estimator of 2.39. This will also be a ML estimator if the errors are normally distributed. Then a likelihood ratio can be formed by comparing 2.3 with 2.39 and using 2.34. It can be generalised to the case of simultaneous equations. In Chapter 3, we shall see an example of an outside estimate of a parameter such as in 2.38.

We have confined ourselves to linear equations until now, i.e. equations linear in parameters. In economic theory, however, situations frequently arise where the specification has to be nonlinear. The liquidity preference function has to be nonlinear since the rate of interest reaches a point where the liquidity preference function reaches an asymptote. The constant elasticity of substitution (CES) production function which we shall come across in Chapter 4 is also nonlinear in parameters. (An early example of the CES type function was seen in 1.9.) Whereas a linear specification is a first approximation, we have increasingly to face up to the fact that it can be a totally misleading approximation. Thus if the true equation is 1.9 both 1.8 or 1.2 are inadequate approximations. A way has to be found of estimating 1.9 directly.

The ML method is helpful in this case. We form the likelihood function of u'' in 1.9 assuming it to be normally independently distributed with a constant variance. We can take a Taylor series expansion of the likelihood function in terms of some initial values of A, α, β and ρ. Thus treating the likelihood function in terms of the parameters

$$L(A, \alpha, \beta, \rho) = L(A_0, \alpha_0, \beta_0, \rho_0) + (\alpha - \alpha_0)L'_\alpha + (\beta - \beta_0)L'_\beta + (\rho - \rho_0)L'_\rho + (A - A_0)L'_A + R(A, \alpha, \beta, \rho) \quad (2.46)$$

where $L'_\alpha = \partial L/\partial\alpha$, etc. R is the remainder which we assume is small. Starting with $A_0, \alpha_0, \beta_0, \rho_0$, we can see the addition to the likelihood function made by estimating the terms such as $(\alpha - \alpha_0)$, etc. Having obtained a set of estimates, say $A_1, \alpha_1, \beta_1, \rho_1$, we again expand the function round this value and so on until we converge to our optimal estimates. This method thus treats nonlinear estimation as a series of iterative linear estimates. The advantage of doing this is once again that we can compare the likelihood values for a linear and a nonlinear case and test the validity of the non-linear specification. We shall see in Chapter 4 a use of the Taylor series expansion. The logic of the iterative ML method is shown in a number of cases such as the estimations 2.30 and 2.31 where we said that we begin with some set of estimates and converge to asymptotically efficient estimates by using ML. The computational problems involved are by no means easy but they are not insoluble.

We have confined ourselves to a rapid survey of different methods available to the econometrician and the problems posed by the peculiar non-experimental nature of the subject. One can never know the true nature of the random process or the true specification. It is advisable, however, to assume a fairly restrictive process, e.g. a highly autoregressive one at the outset and tackle the problem with the appropriate technique rather than start with the OLS method to begin with. This is essential if our answers are to be any more than mere numbers. The estimation problem is by no means the only one though it is one that can be tackled formally. Those involved in applied econometric work are plagued by crude data often with highly serially correlated time series, inadequate prior information from economic theory, conflicting specifications or non-quantifiable hypotheses. They have to tackle the problem to the best of their ability in limited time. It is only by looking at some of the examples of econometric work that we can learn how complex the task is. Not all these examples are by any means perfect but they represent a part of the cumulative experience which is an invaluable, though not always an unfailing, guide.

Bibliographical Notes

There are many good textbooks in this area at various levels of sophistication. At the introductory level, there are Allard (1974), and Thomas (1974). Johnston's *Econometric Methods* (1963, 1972) is now an established textbook which is a very clear exposition of the estimation problem. Goldberger (1964) is also comprehensive and has the distinction of having numerical examples of econometric models adequately worked out. Asymptotic theory is best covered by Christ (1966) and Dhrymes (1970). Christ's book covers mathematical economics prerequisites of econometrics very well and in discussing distribution theory has many interesting examples. Dhrymes's treatment is more formal. Dhrymes covers spectral analysis, a topic which we have not touched in this book. Malinvaud (1966, 1972) is an advanced treatment especially good for those who like a geometric treatment. Theil (1973) is the most recent of these books and comprehensive as well as rigorous in its approach. A compact treatment of identification and estimation is also to be found in Wallis (1971).

The problem of hypothesis testing is dealt with in many statistical theory textbooks and there is no need to mention any except Mood and Graybill (1974) which has recently been issued in its third edition. This book also has suggestions on each topic for further reading. Mood and Graybill is a good introduction for maximum likelihood methods. On testing restrictions, the basic reference used here is Silvey (1970). This book is indispensible for an understanding of the topic of testing restrictions. I have only briefly dealt with the Wald method, the Lagrange multiplier method and the likelihood ratio test. Silvey's treatment of all three methods is the best place for further information.

The standard references in autoregressive errors are of course Cochrane and Orcutt (1949), Durbin and Watson (1951) and Hildreth and Lu (1960). The general theoretical problem is treated in Mann and Wald's classic 1944 *Econometrica* article. Sargan's work over many years (1958, 1961, 1964a, 1964b) has been the major source of inspiration for further work in this field. Hendry (1971, 1974, 1975) has followed up the work on estimation problems in dynamic equations with autoregressive errors. Nonlinear estimation is a somewhat recent arrival in the econometrician's toolkit. Goldfeld and Quandt (1972) is the major treatment here. Klein in his *Textbook of Econometrics* pioneered a discussion of this problem in the first edition (1952), which has now been revised and reissued (1974). Klein and Bodkin (1967) have also tackled the problem of nonlinear estimation in production functions.

3
Static single equations: demand analysis

Introduction

The earliest applications of econometric techniques were to the estimation of demand curves and the study of family budgets. Curiosity about the standard of living of the working class and of the poor receiving public assistance led to investigation of family budgets in the late eighteenth century. By the middle of the nineteenth century, Engel had already established systematic empirical tendencies in the relationship between expenditure on food and the level of income of poor families. The inverse relationship between the market price of a commodity and the quantity bought had been familiar to economists even before the days of Adam Smith. Engel also pioneered the study of time series demand curves in 1861 by examining the effect of fluctuations in the harvest on the price of rye in Prussia for 1846–1861. Studies by Henry Moore and Henry Schultz in the twentieth century secured the theoretical and empirical foundations of demand analysis.

The reasons for the popularity of demand analysis can be summarised as:

1. *Availability of data*: Budget data have long been collected to investigate standards of living and to construct cost of living indices. Data on output of agricultural commodities and their prices have also been easy to collect.

2. *Prior information*: The notion of an inverse relationship between the price and quantity demanded of a good has appealed to economists for many years. More recently, this notion has been rigorously formulated on the foundations of utility theory and provides many prior restrictions on the parameters of demand equations. Empirical demand analysis is a way of testing these prior restrictions.

3. *Empirical relevance*: Interest in demand studies acquired a practical relevance during the agricultural depression of the 1920's and 1930's, when farmers and policy makers began to search for a formula for stabilising agricultural incomes. An accurate measurement of the price elasticity of demand became crucial to any rational policy making. Similarly, after the rationing during the Second World War, many governments utilised demand studies to predict the impact of derationing on prices and quantities demanded. Budget studies which were undertaken initially to investigate the causes of social unrest are today relevant for the comparison of standards of living between different groups of people and over time.

Utility Theory

As already mentioned above, the foundations of demand analysis are provided by utility theory. Since this is now a familiar chapter in textbooks on economics, we shall only mention the main points. We postulate a consumer with a utility function where total utility (U) is expressed as a function of quantities of goods consumed ($x_1, \ldots, x_n$)

$$U = U(x_1, \ldots, x_n) \tag{3.1}$$

We assume that the consumer's tastes and other relevant socio-economic information are contained in the form of function U. The consumer maximises U subject to a budget constraint which says that total expenditure on all items has to equal a given amount—generally called income.

$$\sum_{i=1}^{n} p_i x_i = y \tag{3.2}$$

Maximising 3.1 subject to 3.2, we get from the first-order conditions for a maximum

$$\left.\begin{aligned} U_i &= \lambda p_i \\ \sum_{i=1}^{n} p_i x_i &= y \end{aligned}\right\} i = 1, \ldots, n \tag{3.3}$$

λ is the Lagrange multiplier and can be interpreted as the marginal utility of income. Each U_i is itself a function of all the x_i. We can therefore solve the $(n + 1)$ equations in 3.3 in terms of $(n + 1)$ unknowns x_i and λ (except in some degenerate cases) and get

$$\left.\begin{aligned} x_i &= x^i(p_i, y) \\ \lambda &= \lambda(p_i, y) \end{aligned}\right\} i = 1, \ldots, n \tag{3.4}$$

The first n equations x^i are the demand equations expressing demand for the ith good in terms of all prices and income. In the $(n + 1)$th equation we have an unobservable variable λ as the dependent variable.

We shall derive some information about the λ equation from the other n equations later on.

Each of our n demand equations involves $(n + 1)$ independent variables and hence at least that number of parameters. One advantage of a formal approach using a utility function is that we can reduce the number of parameters or gain qualitative information about them before setting out to estimate them. We take up first the question of a single demand equation. For this we derive the following qualitative results.

1. *Homogeneity*. A demand function derived from 3.1 and 3.2 is homogeneous of degree zero, i.e. if we increase all prices and income in the same proportion then the quantity

demanded does not change. In terms of elasticities, we say that for a given commodity x_i *the sum of price elasticities and income elasticity is zero.*

2. *Slutsky effect.* It is easy to show by comparative static analysis of the first-order conditions that price effect can be separated into income and substitution effect. This, combined with second-order conditions for a maximum, gives us the result that the substitution effect with respect to own price change is always negative

$$\frac{\partial x_i}{\partial p_i} = \left.\frac{\partial x_i}{\partial p_i}\right|_{U=U^\circ} - x_i \frac{\partial x_i}{\partial y} \tag{3.5}$$

The first expression on the r.h.s. measures the effect of price change along the original indifference curve, i.e. keeping the level of utility U unchanged at initial level U°. But this is the substitution effect

$$\frac{\partial x_i}{\partial p_i} = s_{ii} - x_i \frac{\partial x_i}{\partial y} \tag{3.5a}$$

This expression ignores any change in λ, the marginal utility of income due to a price change. s_{ii} the own substitution term is always negative.

3. *Income term.* Nothing can be said in general about the sign of the income term. It could be positive or negative but for *normal* goods we expect it to be positive. The only information we have about the *size* of the income effect comes from Engel's empirical work which says that for necessities the income elasticity is usually less than one and for luxuries greater than one. For *inferior* goods, income effect and hence income elasticity may be negative.

4. *Other prices.* If a good is a substitute, its price will have a positive coefficient and, if a complement, a negative one. This is not very helpful unless we know from specific examples which commodities are likely to be complements or substitutes. If prices of all other commodities move equiproportionately then we can combine them into a composite commodity (x_c) with a composite price (p_c). This helps to reduce the number of parameters to be estimated.

Before we go on to consider an example of demand analysis in econometrics, a few qualifications to the above discussion should be mentioned. The approach is static and does not take into account dynamic considerations such as habit formation, the appearance of new goods, changes in tastes, etc. It takes no account of the socioeconomic and cultural factors which lead to the formation of tastes. The working class person who buys the daily tabloid, and the educated middle class person who buys the 'serious' daily newspaper are but two examples of the influence of class on consumption. Class and ethnic background, residential location, educational attainment, age, sex and family background are all important determinants of consumption. (Since tastes are subsumed in the form of the utility function, this amounts to saying that utility functions differ across individuals.) They are taken care of, if at all, as 'nuisance variables' which must be accounted for before studying the effect of the purely economic variables of prices and income.

A much more serious objection is that purchase is treated as consumption, thus making no allowance for the durability of goods, or monetary accumulation. Either the budget identity has to be understood as applying to total expenditure after saving or dis-saving decisions have been made, or decisions on saving and acquisition of financial assets have to be integrated with consumption. Usually the former alternative is taken and y is defined as total expenditure.

Finally, aggregation problems have to be faced. The utility function in 3.1 is meant to apply to an individual but, even for a family budget study, the aggregation of all the individual family members' utility functions into a family utility function (or aggregation of their demand functions) has to be performed. Much more serious is the problem with time series market demand curves. Since price changes have differential income effects these have to be aggregated. Usually these effects may be taken to be small or nearly identical but the assumptions underlying any such solution need to be carefully stated. Needless,to say, in actual work, the nature of the available data dictates what sort of function is specified. This is unavoidable but the considerations listed above indicate the care we have to take before we assume that any empirical results have general validity.

When we begin empirical work on demand analysis, our first task is to specify a form for the demand function x^i (and by implication for the utility function). The requirements of maximisation impose certain restrictions on the utility function (e.g. convexity and invariance under monotonic transformation), which in turn limit our choice of demand functions. Demand equations are, however, often specified on grounds of convenience of estimation and do not always correspond to a 'proper' utility function. An example of this is the Cobb–Douglas form or log–linear form of the demand function often adopted in empirical work.

$$\ln x_{it} = \alpha_{0i} + \alpha_{1i} \ln (y/p)_t + \sum_{j=1}^{n} \alpha_{(j+1)i} \ln p_{jt} + u_{it} \qquad (3.6)$$

Equation 3.6 was used by Stone in his classic work on consumer's expenditure in the UK and also by Tobin whose work we shall study in some detail below. p is the overall price index defined as a weighted geometric sum of all n prices, the weights being the average budget shares of the commodities. y is taken here as total money expenditure on all n goods.

$$\ln p_t = \Sigma w_i \ln p_{it}$$

where $w_i = (p_i x_i / y) = p_i x_i / \Sigma p_i x_i$. In this form, the demand function is very convenient for testing our prior restrictions mentioned above.

The Slutsky equation is easy to derive if we rearrange our equation as follows

$$\ln x_{it} = \alpha_{0i} + \alpha_{1i} \ln y_t + \sum_{j=1}^{n} (\alpha_{(j+1)i} - w_j \alpha_{1i}) \ln p_{jt} + u_{it} \qquad (3.7)$$

Equation 3.7 is now a specific demand equation corresponding to x^i in 3.4. The price elasticity is made up of two terms—income effect equal to $w_j \alpha_{1i}$ and $\alpha_{(j+1)i}$ which is proportional to the substitution effect.

The homogeneity requirements can now be stated in terms of elasticities of money income and prices and we have

$$\sum_j (\alpha_{(j+1)i} - w_j \alpha_{1i}) = -\alpha_{1i}$$

Now $\Sigma\alpha_{(j+1)i} - \alpha_{1i}\Sigma w_j = \Sigma\alpha_{(j+1)i} - \alpha_{1i}$. Hence, for homogeneity, we need $\Sigma\alpha_{(j+1)i} = 0$. But this means that one of the n elasticities can be derived from the remaining $(n-1)$. Equation 3.6 can therefore be rewritten as

$$\ln x_{it} = \alpha_{0i} + \alpha_{1i} \ln (y/p)_t + \sum_{j \neq k} \alpha_{(j+1)i} \ln (p_j/p_k) + u_{it} \tag{3.6a}$$

In a time series specification x_i and y have a common element due to increasing population and therefore it is advisable to deflate both x_i and y by population.

A problem with 3.6 is that it does not come from any reasonable utility function except in the very special case of income elasticity and own price elasticity being unity with all cross price elasticities being zero.

Later we shall discuss a demand function that is theoretically more satisfactory. For the present we shall stay with equation (3.6).

Exercise. It is often convenient to use p_t as a surrogate for all other prices and write 3.6 as

$$\ln x_{it} = \alpha_{0i} + \alpha_{1i} \ln (y_t/p_t)_t + \alpha_{2i} \ln (p_{it}/p_t) + u_{it}$$

What assumptions are being made about cross elasticities? Derive the appropriate restrictions for zero homogeneity.

Tobin's Study

We can now look at the details of Tobin's classic study of demand for food in the USA for 1913–1941 (Tobin, 1950). Tobin attempts to integrate the micro level demand curve for food by a family and the demand for food in the economy. He also pools the information in a cross section family budget study with the time series macroeconomic study. Tobin begins with a family demand curve for food.

$$\ln C_{jt} = \alpha_0 + \alpha_1 \ln Y_{jt} + \alpha_2 \ln Y_{jt-1} + \alpha_3 \ln P_t + \alpha_4 \ln Q_t + \alpha_5 \ln N_{jt} + u_{jt} \tag{3.8}$$

C_{jt} = quantity of food consumed by jth family in year t, whether purchased, received in kind or home-produced.

Y_{jt} = disposable family income for jth family in year t: money income plus income in kind including gifts in money or kind from other families less direct taxes and gifts to other families.
P_t = index of food prices average for year t
Q_t = index of prices of other consumer goods average for year t
N_{jt} = number of persons in the jth family in year t

This demand function is similar to 3.6 above except that the previous year's income has been introduced and family size has been added to allow for economies of size. (On problems of measuring family size see Notes at the end of the chapter.) We expect α_1, α_2 and α_4 to be positive and α_3 to be negative. In general, we expect α_5 to be positive; if it is less than one then we take this as an indication of economy of size. This, however, is an example of a nuisance variable. We have no prior information from economic theory about the sign or size of α_5. (Further nuisance variables such as residential location, race, occupation, etc. can also be introduced if we think they are relevant.) The homogeneity postulate requires that $\alpha_1 + \alpha_2 + \alpha_3 + \alpha_4 = 0$.

It should be noted at this stage that, in demand studies, we often cannot obtain a measure of the quantity demanded. We have to obtain a measure of the expenditure and deflate it by some appropriate deflator to approximate to the quantity demanded. This is an additional reason why demand studies were first concerned with agricultural commodities. A measure of quantity at a fairly disaggregated level is easier to obtain for these commodities. When we move on to study demand for all commodities, we shall need an expenditure measure to ensure comparability.

In order to derive a market demand function from 3.8, we have to make some postulate about the income and family size distributions at a point of time and over time. The assumption necessary and sufficient for aggregating 3.8 into a macro demand function is that every family shares a change in aggregate income in proportion to its income and remains of the same size. Given this assumption we can aggregate 3.8 for the market as:

$$\ln S_t = \ln C_t = A_0 + \alpha_1 \ln Y_t + \alpha_2 \ln Y_{t-1} + \alpha_3 \ln P_t + \alpha_4 \ln Q_t + u_t \tag{3.9}$$

where S_t is per capita supply of food and equals per capita demand and Y_t is per capita income.

Tobin chooses to write 3.9 with $\ln P_t$ as the dependent variable (assuming therefore quantity supplied to be given at time t) when estimating. We can write this as

$$\ln P_t = b_0 + b_1 \ln S_t + b_2 \ln Y_t + b_3 \ln Y_{t-1} + b_4 \ln Q_t + e_t \tag{3.10}$$

For data from 1913–1941, Tobin estimated 3.10 by ordinary least squares and obtained the following (after dropping Y'_{t-1} since it was non significant).

$$\hat{b}_1 = \underset{(0.42)}{-3.56} \rightarrow \hat{\alpha}_3 = -0.28$$

$$\hat{b}_2 = \underset{(0.09)}{0.97} \rightarrow \hat{\alpha}_1 = 0.27$$

$$\hat{b}_4 = \underset{(0.09)}{0.22} \rightarrow \hat{\alpha}_4 = 0.06$$

$$R^2 = 0.93$$

Since the parameters α_i can be solved from the coefficients b_i, standard errors for the α_i can be obtained from the standard errors of b_i. Tobin obtained the following 95% confidence intervals for the α_i

$$0.22 < \alpha_1 < 0.35$$

$$-0.38 < \alpha_3 < -0.23$$

$$0.01 < \alpha_4 < 0.12$$

The elasticities are thus all significantly different from zero though low, as one would expect, because food is a necessity. The point estimates sum to 0.05 but Tobin does not test the homogeneity postulate at this stage. He proceeds to obtain another set of estimates for the parameters α_i by the method of pooling cross-section family budget information with time series data. The reasons for doing this are two. First, in any time series data there is likely to be *multicollinearity* due to a common trend in ln Y and ln S. While this does not bias the estimates, it makes them unreliable by raising the standard error. Very often, the sample estimate *may* have the wrong sign although in the true model the parameter has the right sign. The second reason is that, since the aggregate demand curve is based on family demand curves, it may improve the estimates to use some information from family budget data. The variance of aggregate income in time series data is likely to be much smaller than the variance of family income at a point of time. This greater variance in cross section data may provide an estimate of income elasticity with a much smaller standard error than the time series estimate. Tobin obtains an estimate of $(\alpha_1 + \alpha_2)$ from cross section data. It is useful to look at this from the point of view of Engel curves although this is a detour from the main argument.

Engel curves are relationships between the proportion of a family's budget spent on a certain item of expenditure say food, and its total income. Engel's law was stated with reference to expenditure on food and it said that the proportion spent on food declined with a raise in income. Another way to put this is that the elasticity of expenditure on food with respect to income was less than one. Engel's law has been seen to hold true with remarkable consistency over time and over different countries. It abstracts from the influence of relative prices since it is estimated at a point of time from cross section data. Also, since it is stated in terms of proportions and elasticities the linear–logarithmic relationship such as equation 3.7 or 3.8 above is the best form for it. In general we have

$$\ln v_{ij} = \ln (p_i x_i)_j = \beta_{0i} + \beta_{1i} \ln Y_j + \beta_{2i} \ln N_j + e_{ij} \quad (3.11)$$

where j indicates the family, N_j the family size for j, p_i the price of x_i, and Y_j the *money* income of the jth family. We presume that if v_i refers to food or any necessity $\beta_{1i} < 1$. Recent work by Houthakker (1957) indicates a remarkable consistency between countries regarding the estimated β_{1i} and β_{2i}. It is worthwhile summarising his results.

Houthakker's data consist of about 40 family budget surveys taken in 30 countries over different years. For each of these surveys, he had expenditure data on four groups of commodities–food, clothing, housing and miscellaneous. He also had data on family size. His formulation of the Engel curve was similar to equation 3.11 above except that *instead of money income he had total expenditure.* This substitution makes the estimation of Engel curves easier, since income data are hard to get and also likely to be misreported. As we shall see later, it also leads to some estimation problem.

As we can see from Table 3.1 Engel's law is amply confirmed by the results. Expenditure elasticity estimates for food in all the surveys are significantly greater than zero and less than one. They range from 0.344 to 0.731. Engel's law is framed in terms of income elasticity but the relationship between income and expenditure elasticity can be derived as

income elasticity of *i*th expenditure item	=	expenditure elasticity of *i*th expenditure item	×	elasticity of expenditure with respect to income	
$\eta_{i,\,Y}$	=	$\eta_{i,\,E}$	×	η_{EY}	(3.12)

η_{EY} is less than or equal to one usually so $\eta_{i,\,E}$ can be seen as an upper bound of $\eta_{i,\,y}$. Expenditure elasticities for clothing and miscellaneous are higher than one (though not always significantly so) in most cases.

The elasticity of food expenditure with respect to family size is always less than one. The evidence is therefore that large families enjoy economies of *size* in food expenditure. For the other three items, the elasticity of expenditure with respect to family size is negative. Note that the use of total expenditure rather than total income imposes some restrictions on the parameters of Engel curves commodity groups. The sum of expenditures on all the items is equal to total expenditure, which is used as an independent variable. It can be shown that the restrictions on the parameters given equation 3.11 are

$$\sum_i \beta_{1i}\left(\frac{p_i x_i}{y}\right) = 1 \quad \text{and} \quad \sum_i \beta_{2i}\left(\frac{p_i x_i}{y}\right) = 0$$

Exercise: Prove this.

Table 3.1 Partial elasticities for four expenditure groups with respect to total expenditure (b) and family size (c)

Country	Food		Clothing		Housing		Miscellaneous	
	b	c	b	c	b	c	b	c
Austria	.554	.351	1.767	—.350	.741	—.210	1.620	—.392
	(.019)	(.022)	(.055)	(.064)	(.038)	(.044)	(.022)	(.025)
Canada[a]	.647	.292	1.337	—.114	1.114	—.447	1.131	—.061
	(.008)	(.007)	(.092)	(.081)	(.043)	(.038)	(.036)	(.032)
Finland	.621	.272	1.622	—.310	.802	.008	1.445	—.367
	(.026)	(.019)	(.063)	(.047)	(.077)	(.056)	(.048)	(.036)
France[b]	.483	.466	1.158	.232	1.098	—.652	1.656	—.536
	(.020)	(.029)	(.024)	(.034)	(.048)	(.068)	(.029)	(.041)
Germany 1907	.537	.261	1.498	.061	.913	—.154	1.604	—.358
	(.018)	(.015)	(.045)	(.038)	(.026)	(.022)	(.046)	(.039)
Germany 1927–28	.598	.291	1.297	—.014	1.056	.476	1.474	—.481
manual workers	(.035)	(.019)	(.054)	(.029)	(.483)	(.262)	(.334)	(.181)
clerical workers	.501	.274	1.035	.226	.881	—.052	1.469	—.298
	(.030)	(.025)	(.059)	(.049)	(.070)	(.058)	(.089)	(.074)
government	.385	.319	.918	.149	.887	—.023	1.606	—.335
officials	(.027)	(.027)	(.079)	(.081)	(.054)	(.055)	(.069)	(.071)
all three groups[c]	.473	.295	1.049	.102	.906	.196	1.447	.034
	(.020)	(.015)	(.047)	(.036)	(.045)	(.035)	(.082)	(.063)
Ireland[g]	.597	.323	1.177	.009	.705	—.221	1.478	—.219
	(.019)	(.024)	(.307)	(.382)	(.021)	(.026)	(.025)	(.032)
Italy[d]	.602	.346	1.042	—.733	[e]		[e]	
	(.096)	(.312)	(.196)	(.733)				
Japan 1955	.556	.309	1.593	—.051	.861	—.383	1.416	—.178
	(.025)	(.027)	(.119)	(.128)	(.023)	(.024)	(.040)	(.043)
Lastiva[f]	.430	.482	1.094	—.065	1.024	.002	1.567	—.516
	(.030)	(.033)	(.077)	(.084)	(.059)	(.062)	(.037)	(.040)
Mexico[g]	.657	.248	[e]		[e]		[e]	
	(.017)	(.014)						

Netherlands	.714	.237	1.634	−.110	.514	.021	1.273	−.241
manual workers	(0.50)	(.014)	(.097)	(.027)	(.129)	(.036)	(.106)	(.029)
white collar	.490	.304	1.059	.034	.619	−.016	1.403	−.157
workers	(.025)	(.019)	(.043)	(.034)	(.044)	(.035)	(.045)	(.036)
both groups[c]	.502	.291	1.088	.001	.613	−.001	1.406	−.200
	(.022)	(.014)	(.045)	(.029)	(.036)	(.023)	(.041)	(.026)
Norway[h]	.515	.131	1.266	−.044	.800	.031	1.524	−.296
	(.048)	(.030)	(.237)	(.149)	(.144)	(.091)	(.050)	(.032)
Poland[i]	.731	.213	1.784	−.497	.662	−.068	1.774	−.534
	(.030)	(.027)	(.041)	(.036)	(.026)	(.022)	(.030)	(.026)
Sweden	.631	.311	1.119	.003	.803	−.008	1.446	−.269
	(.048)	(.048)	(.138)	(.138)	(.085)	(.084)	(.047)	(.046)
Switzerland	.460	.397	1.445	.044	.824	−.137	1.879	−.629
	(.036)	(.026)	(.075)	(.055)	(.242)	(.178)	(.118)	(.086)
United Kingdom,	.594	.294	1.042	.143	.553	−.072	1.793	−.390
working class	(.021)	(.019)	(.029)	(.026)	(.026)	(.023)	(.026)	(.023)
middle class	.344	.386	1.342	−.111	.346	.145	1.488	−.221
	(.019)	(.021)	(.154)	(.169)	(.031)	(.034)	(.016)	(.018)
both groups[c]	.519	.330	1.096	.139	.477	−.045	1.640	−.358
	(.027)	(.032)	(.057)	(.067)	(.023)	(.027)	(.027)	(.032)
United States 190[h]	.712	.158	1.435	.016	.839	−.111	1.561	−.241
	(.004)	(.002)	(.019)	(.012)	(.016)	(.010)	(.045)	(.028)
United States 1950,	.693	.224	1.399	.016	.764	−.155	1.367	−.111
large cities, north	(.017)	(.016)	(.059)	(.054)	(.011)	(.010)	(.011)	(.010)
suburbs, north	.664	.280	1.303	.135	.978	−.236	1.255	−.125
	(.029)	(.030)	(.090)	(.092)	(.115)	(.117)	(.108)	(.112)
small cities, north	.653	.258	1.367	.074	.810	−.237	1.370	−.068
	(.029)	(.028)	(.079)	(.076)	(.054)	(.052)	(.049)	(.047)
large cities, south	.685	.213	1.231	.134	.789	−.271	1.245	−.097
	(.015)	(.015)	(.055)	(.055)	(.040)	(.040)	(.021)	(.021)
suburbs, south	.698	.190	1.147	.175	.974	−.292	1.178	−.090
	(.037)	(.034)	(.062)	(.057)	(.085)	(.078)	(.036)	(.033)

Country	Food		Clothing		Housing		Miscellaneous	
	b	*c*	*b*	*c*	*b*	*c*	*b*	*c*
United States 1950,	.687	.235	1.068	.287	1.122	−.543	1.217	−.151
small cities, south	(.031)	(.032)	(.055)	(.057)	(.081)	(.083)	(.033)	(.034)
large cities, west	.682	.193	1.410	−.111	.654	−.182	1.243	−.044
	(.023)	(.021)	(.048)	(.045)	(.032)	(.029)	(.011)	(.010)
suburbs, west	.709	.225	1.285	.124	.933	−.401	1.081	−.111
	(.031)	(.028)	(.067)	(.061)	(.031)	(.028)	(.010)	(.010)
small cities, west	.645	.292	1.195	.145	.766	−.292	1.286	−.187
all classes of	.692	.221	1.280	.808	.895	−.287	1.248	−.082
cities	(.002)	(.002)	(.006)	(.006)	(.013)	(.012)	(.006)	(.006)

a Direct taxes (which are excluded from total and miscellaneous expenditure) estimated from other data in source.
b Based on breakdown by city (Paris, Rennes and 17 others combined) and total expenditure.
c Allowing for possible social-class differences in levels of Engel curves (see text).
d Based on breakdown by region (North vs. South), farm vs. non-farm, and total expenditure.
e Not computed because of insufficient data.
f Family size estimated from number of equivalent adults.
g Unweighted (see text).
h 'Normal' families only consisting of two adults and young children.
i Based on figures for individual households.

Note: Houthakkers' *b* corresponds to β_{1i} in equation 3.11 and *c* corresponds to β_{2i}.

Pooling of Cross Section and Time Series Data

We can now return to the main theme—the practice of pooling data from various sources. It is usual to interpret the cross section parameters in demand studies as representing long-run relationships, the time series variables then picking up the short-run relationships. This proposition has limited general validity. In consumption function studies, the long-run constancy of the average propensity to consume (APC) is said to be a long-run phenomenon while the single year cross section data show a declining APC. The reasons for interpreting the income elasticity of demand obtained from cross section data as a long-run parameter can be thought of as follows. In cross section data income usually represents a cluster of sociocultural circumstances as well as the purely economic variable. The large variability of observed income across families provides much more information on the nature of the relationship. Usually the large number of observations may also permit us to isolate the influence of the social and demographic 'nuisance variables' and so separate the pure income effect. In time series macro data, these factors change very little from one year to the next. In addition to these factors, if the cross section data pertain to a 'normal' year—one which has not witnessed a large rise or fall in income/employment from the previous years—one can treat the observed points as lying along the long-run equilibrium expenditure point for any family, given its sociocultural characteristics which change slowly over time and given its income which, by our assumption of a normal year, will be close to the long-run expected income of the family. If these assumptions cannot be reasonably made, then the cross section parameters lose their long-run character.

We can now go back to Tobin's study. As we have said above, Tobin estimates $(\alpha_1 + \alpha_2)$ from family budget data for 1941. He does this by assuming that in equation 3.8 for a given year P and Q are given constants (neglecting therefore regional variations in prices). Thus

$$\ln C_{jt} = \alpha_{00} + \alpha_1 \ln Y_{jt} + \alpha_2 \ln Y_{jt-1} + \alpha_5 \ln N_{jt} + u_{jt} \tag{3.8a}$$

$$\alpha_{00} = \alpha_0 + \alpha_3 \ln P_t + \alpha_4 \ln Q_t.$$

The only remaining difficulty about estimating the parameters of 3.8a is the non-availability of data on last year's income or multicollinearity between Y_{jt} and Y_{jt-1}. Tobin circumvented this by assuming that family incomes grow at the same rate on the average as aggregate income

$$Y_{jt}/Y_{jt-1} = Y_t/Y_{t-1}$$

Substituting this into 3.8a, the coefficient of $\ln Y_{jt}$ *can now* be written as $(\alpha_1 + \alpha_2)$ and the constant term α_{00} has an additional term $\alpha_2 \ln (Y_{t-1}/Y_t)$.

Exercise. Examine the consequence of omitting $\ln Y_{jt-1}$ altogether in 3.8a on the estimate of α_1.

A word of caution is appropriate here. Sometimes we do not have individual family data but average values for groups of families, grouped according to income range or location, etc. Aggregating 3.8 into group averages means that we should really have geometric rather than arithmetic averages of C_j and Y_j across families as our original equation is in logarithmic form. It may also be the case that even if geometric averages are available, the groups may be of unequal size. If the errors u_{jt} fulfil OLS assumptions of homoscedasticity then the errors of the group averages will be heteroscedastic and a weighted regression procedure will have to be adopted to ensure homoscedasticity.

Tobin obtains an estimate α $(\alpha_1 + \alpha_2)$ and α_5 from cross section data from the 1941 urban budget study by the Bureau of Labour Statistics. The result is

$$\underset{}{\bar{C}'} = 0.52 + \underset{(0.03)}{0.56}\ \bar{Y}' + \underset{(0.07)}{0.25}\ n' \qquad R^2 = 0.93 \tag{3.8b}$$

We can see that the results obtained are in conformity with Engel's law and with Houthakker's results given above. The economy of family size also shows up as it does in Houthakker's article cited above. Houthakker estimates the elasticity of food expenditure with respect to family size to be 0.28 on the average and also cites a result by Brady and Barber (1948) that in general the elasticity is 1/3 (and therefore called the cube-root law). Tobin's results are compatible with these earlier estimates.

Having estimated α and α_5 from cross section data, Tobin then goes back to the task of estimating the remaining parameters of equation 3.8b – namely, α_3, the own price elasticity and α_4 the cross elasticity. Since $\alpha = \alpha_1 + \alpha_2$ we can derive a residual estimate of either α_1 or α_2 given α. We arrange 3.10 to get

$$\ln P_t = b_0 + b_1 (\ln S_t - \hat{\alpha} \ln Y_t) + b_2 \Delta \ln Y_t + b_3 \ln Q_t + e_t \tag{3.10a}$$

Since α is known we label it $\hat{\alpha}$ and we can form the variable $(\ln S_t - \hat{\alpha} \ln Y_t)$. Equation 3.10a is a standard multiple regression problem in three independent variables. For 1913–1941 (29 observations) we have (standard errors in parentheses)

$$\begin{aligned} \hat{b}_1 &= -1.97(\pm 0.27) & \hat{\alpha}_1 &= 0.44 \\ \hat{b}_2 &= -0.24(\pm 0.10) & \hat{\alpha}_2 &= 0.12 \\ \hat{b}_3 &= -0.06(\pm 0.14) & \hat{\alpha}_3 &= -0.51 \\ & & \hat{\alpha}_4 &= -0.03 \\ R^2 &= 0.87 & \sum_{i=1}^{4} \alpha_i &= -0.02 \end{aligned}$$

Since b_3, the coefficient of $\ln Q_t$, is non-significant (its t-ratio < 1.90) we can drop it (equivalent to assuming $\alpha_4 = 0$). Doing this, Tobin obtained

$$\begin{aligned} \hat{b}_0 &= 2.95 & \hat{A}_0 &= 1.57 \\ \hat{b}_1 &= -1.88(0.14) & \hat{\alpha}_1 &= 0.45 \\ \hat{b}_2 &= -0.2\ (0.12) & \hat{\alpha}_2 &= 0.11 \\ (b_3 &= 0 \text{ by assumption}) & \hat{\alpha}_3 &= -0.53 \\ & & \hat{\alpha}_4 &= 0 \text{ by assumption} \\ R^2 &= 0.87 & & \end{aligned}$$

As before, the standard errors of the $\hat{\alpha}_i$ can be derived from the standard errors of $\hat{b}_i$. A test of the homogeneity postulate performed by Tobin showed that his results do not contradict the hypothesis.

We need at this stage some indication of the advantages of pooling time series and cross section data. In Tobin's case, he obtains a higher value for the income as well as price elasticity in the pooled estimate than in the unrestricted time series regression. The restricted estimates, however, assume that the time series parameter for income is the same as the cross section parameter. One question is whether this assumption is legitimate. We can also ask whether there are better ways of pooling information than the two-stage procedure adopted by Tobin. In recent years, there has been renewed discussion of the technique of pooling data and one of the test cases adopted for trying our new estimation procedures has been Tobin's study.

Let us take the second question first. When incorporating the cross section estimate of $\hat{\alpha}$ into the time series study, we are neglecting the information provided by the standard error of $\hat{\alpha}$. Clearly, if we could use this information, the efficiency of our estimates will improve. There are two ways of doing this. We could combine equation 3.9 with another equation indicating that the parameter is known to us up to an additive error and also that the estimated variance of the error is known. Thus,

$$0.56 = 1\,\alpha + \hat{\epsilon} \tag{3.13}$$

where var $\hat{\epsilon} = (0.03)^2$. Combining 3.9 and 3.13 we can use the mixed regressor approach of Theil and Goldberger (1961) and use the information of var $\hat{\epsilon}$ to improve our estimates of all the α_i. Recently Maddala (1973) has suggested a simultaneous estimation of 3.10 and 3.8a. He shows that this will result in efficient estimates of all the α_i. One then needs neither the approach of introducing $\hat{\alpha}$ with certainty nor the mixed regressor approach of introducing $\hat{\alpha}$ along with its standard error. Maddala obtains $\hat{\alpha} = 0.5355$ and $\hat{b} = -1.964$ compared to 0.56 and -1.88. He also obtains a covariance matrix for $\hat{\alpha}$ and $\hat{b}_1$ (as well as other parameters indicating a non-zero covariance for $\hat{\alpha}$ and $\hat{b}_1$). There is thus additional information and a gain in efficiency.

An interesting by-product of Maddala's work is a test of the restricted equation 3.10a against 3.10, the OLS unrestricted estimate. He does this by performing a likelihood ratio test for the two equations and obtains a χ^2 value of 17.12 for one degree of freedom thus rejecting the imposed restriction, indicating that the model is mis-specified. One reason for this could be that the cross section parameter α may not be the time series parameter and a specification error is made when we assume this. Even the Maddala simultaneous estimate is based on this assumption. One indication of the specification error is given by the presence of serial correlation among the disturbances. Tobin's study does not provide comparative information on serial correlation (his study predates the Durbin–Watson statistic). On recomputing with his data, it was found that the DW statistic for 3.10 was 1.37 and for 3.10a was 0.49. For 29 observations and five parameters, the test is inconclusive for 3.10 but leads to a rejection of the hypothesis of non-autocorrelated disturbances for 3.10a (Desai, 1974).

Tobin deals with the problem of serial correlation in 3.10a. While he did not provide the DW statistic, he plotted the difference between actual P_t and $\hat{P}_t$ computed from 3.10a, [i.e. antilog ($\ln \hat{P}_t$)]. He discovered a cyclical pattern of residuals and the von Neumann ratio was 0.68 indicating serial correlation. Tobin's solution was to first difference 3.10a and re-estimate as follows (dropping $\ln Q_t$ from 3.10a).

$$\Delta \ln P_t = b_1 \, \Delta(\ln S_t - \hat{\alpha} \ln Y_t) + (b_2 \Delta^2 \ln Y_t + e_t \quad (3.14)$$

He obtained

$$\hat{b}_1 = \underset{(0.18)}{-1.74} \qquad \hat{b}_2 = \underset{(0.08)}{-0.08}$$

The recomputed von Neumann ratio was 1.99 indicating to Tobin no significant serial correlation.

It should be remarked that Tobin should have plotted the difference between $\ln P_t$ and $\ln \hat{P}_t$ rather than their antilogs. One is really interested in the presence of serial correlation in e_t. One method available today would be to hypothesise that e_t follows a first-order autoregressive process (as indicated in Chapter 2)

$$e_t = \rho e_{t-1} + \xi_t \qquad (3.15)$$

and either estimate ρ from the asymptotic formula for DW $DW = 2(1 - \rho)$ or incorporate 3.15 into 3.10a by a Cochrane–Orcutt transformation. The procedures then available for estimating are outlined in Chapter 2 and need not be repeated here. Tobin's procedure in 3.14 is equivalent to assuming $\rho = 1$.

Exercise. Using $DW = 0.49$ for 3.10a and the asymptotic formula for ρ, compute the autoregressive coefficient for Δe_t.

The technique of pooling information is extremely useful when used in appropriate circumstances. When we have continuous cross section or 'panel' data available, i.e. a cross section of the same economic units over many years, we can put the technique to its best use. Not only does this help combat multicollinearity but it increases the efficiency of estimates. It is necessary, however, to test carefully the restrictions imposed. In the particular case of Tobin's demand study the restrictions are rejected but the technique is one of general applicability. We must also note Tobin's specification and test of the homogeneity condition of demand curves.

Tobin goes on to consider the problem of simultaneous equations bias in his model. As we saw above, the choice of $\ln P$ as the dependent variable implied that the causation was from a given quantity to price. If $\ln S$ is a function of lagged price, or if $\ln S$ is a function of price as well as other variables not included in the demand function, then identification is assumed by rank and order conditions. The variability of supply conditions in agricultural commodities is a useful identifying restriction as we have seen in Chapter 1 above. We do not discuss this aspect of Tobin's work here since we shall take up the identification problem in the next chapter.

Complete Sets of Demand Equations

In our discussion of the demand functions prefacing Tobin's study, we have only derived properties of a single demand equation. As we saw in the context of Engel curves, there may be restrictions imposed *across* equations due to the budget identity. We can now derive the properties of the complete set of n demand equations taken together which are relevant for estimation purposes. We shall then discuss some empirical studies.

1. *Engel aggregation.* The price weighted sum of income effects for all commodities is unity, $\sum_i p_i(\partial x_i/\partial y) = 1$.

2. *Cornot aggregation.* The price weighted sum of price effects for change in a given price is equal to the quantity of the commodity $\sum_i p_i(\partial x_i/\partial p_j) = -x_j$. This follows from the Slutsky equation and Engel aggregation.

3. *Symmetry.* From the Slutsky equation, we can derive that the matrix of specific substitution effects is symmetric and negative definite. In particular $s_{ii} < 0$ for all i and $s_{ij} = s_{ji}$ for $i \neq j$. This is an enormous advantage because for n commodities instead of having to estimate n^2 substitution terms, we only have to estimate $n(n+1)/2$ terms. Thus for $n = 10$ instead of 100, we only estimate 55 terms, a saving of 45 parameters to be estimated.

4. *Money flexibility.* An interesting parameter generated by estimation of a complete set is what Frisch called *money flexibility.* This has to do with the income elasticity of λ our Lagrangean multiplier. Since λ denotes marginal utility of income, the elasticity of λ with respect to y tells us about the diminishing marginal utility of income with respect to income. The reciprocal of the elasticity is easier to estimate. We expect marginal utility of income to decline with higher incomes and hence the elasticity is negative and so is the flexibility. If the elasticity were zero then there would be no utility gain by income redistribution. If negative, income distribution in favour of the poor raises the sum of total utilities. Thus money flexibility is a welfare measure and is most usually measured by the reciprocal of $\eta_{\lambda y}$:

$$\eta_{\lambda y} = \left(\frac{\partial \lambda}{\partial y}\frac{y}{\lambda}\right) \qquad \text{and} \qquad \phi = \eta_{\lambda y}^{-1}$$

If when price changes, income is changed to compensate for the changing marginal utility of income, we have what is called a matrix of specific substitution effects. This matrix is also symmetric and negative definite. Summing a row of this matrix and weighting by prices we can obtain a measure of $\eta_{\lambda y}$

$$\sum_i p_i(\partial x_i/\partial p_j)|_{d\lambda=0} = \frac{y(\partial x_j/\partial y)}{\eta_{\lambda y}} = \phi y(\partial x_j/\partial y)$$

This measure is obtained by summing the price weighted substitution terms for any particular price change. It is a cross equation measure and is available only for the complete set of demand equations. It is discussed in some detail because it is an example of additional information yielded from parameter estimates by a rigorous development of theory.

Homogeneity, Engel aggregation and the Slutsky conditions (from which Cournot aggregation follows) represent restrictions on the demand functions which follow from the theory of the consumer's utility maximising behaviour. If the theory is valid then the restrictions must be satisfied by a set of empirical demand estimates. An alternative is to estimate the set of demand equations with the restrictions imposed, e.g. in the substitution matrix estimate only $n(n+1)/2$ coefficients and compare the estimates with an unrestricted system. If the restrictions are valid then they must yield more efficient estimates of parameters than the unrestricted system. Once again, we can use the likelihood ratio test for comparing the restricted against the unrestricted system. The number of restrictions then gives us the number of degrees of freedom for the χ^2 statistic. In the demand system, we have the n homogeneity conditions (one for each of the n demand equations), one Engel aggregation condition and the $n(n-1)/2$ symmetric off-diagonal substitution terms, making $n+1+[n(n-1)/2] = (n^2+n+2)/2$ restrictions. For 10 commodities, this means fifty-six restrictions while the total number of parameters to be estimated is n^2 price terms and n income terms n^2+n or 110 in our example. We shall later examine in some detail an attempt to test these restrictions rigorously for a set of demand equations.

Form of the Utility Function—Additional Restrictions

It should be quite clear from the above discussion that while the notion of a downward sloping demand curve is intuitively appealing, empirically testable and practically useful, the full apparatus of utility theory yields many additional restrictions. In any case, to estimate all the $n(n+1)$ parameters of a complete set of demand equations is a formidable task to say the least, and one may not have enough observations. Econometricians have been exploring ways of imposing additional restrictions which would make life easier by reducing the number of parameters to be estimated. They have done this in two ways: by assuming an explicit form for the utility function or by imposing certain types of restrictions—such as additivity or separability—on the implicit utility function. The most famous example of the first in econometric research is Stone's work on the linear expenditure system which derives from the Bernoulli utility function (Stone, 1954). As for the second, there is a large body of literature on different variants of additivity and separability, each tried out on some body of data. Byron has tested a number of these on the Dutch data (1970) which have also been used by Barten (1969) for his studies. Deaton (1974) has recently comprehensively covered this area with UK data. We shall discuss these after taking up the Stone system.

Linear Expenditure System (LES)

The linear expenditure system is a set of n equations for the expenditure on each of the n items (rather than quantity) and can be written as

$$v_i = p_i x_i = x_i^* p_i + \alpha_i (y - \sum_{i=1}^{n} p_i x_i^*) + e_i \qquad (3.16)$$

As usual, e_i is a random error term, y is total expenditure or income, x_i is quantity and p_i is price, x_i^* are minimum or subsistence quantities and $\Sigma p_i x_i^*$ is a measure of *committed* expenditure. It can be shown that the utility function corresponding to 3.16 (except for the random error terms, e_i) is

$$U = \sum_{i=1}^{n} \alpha_i \log (x_i - x_i^*) \qquad (3.17)$$

Exercise. For $n = 2$, derive the linear expenditure function by maximising 3.17 subject to 3.2.

It can be seen that unless each of the nx_i are above their respective x_i^*, the consumer derives no positive utility from consumption. After having bought the minimum quantities, he can spend his remaining (or *supernumerary*) income on additional consumption. α_i is therefore the proportion of his supernumerary income a consumer spends on the ith commodity and α_i must therefore sum to one. Another way to see this is to sum 3.16 for all n items and set the sum by definition equal to y:

$$y = \sum_{i=1}^{n} p_i x_i = \Sigma p_i x_i^* + \Sigma \alpha_i (y - \Sigma p_i x_i^*) + \Sigma e_i$$

When $\Sigma \alpha_i = 1$, the two sides are equal to each other, assuming $\Sigma e_i = 0$.

For a set of n linear expenditure equations we have only $2n$ parameters to estimate—α_i and x_i^*—for each of the n commodities. This is instead of the $n(n + 1)$ parameters in an unrestricted demand system. The saving is clearly enormous: for ten commodities, we save ninety parameters. But this advantage can only be gained by estimating the n equations simultaneously. This is not straightforward as in each equation x_i^* appears nonlinearly along with α_i since we can write 3.16 as

$$v_i = (1 - \alpha_i) x_i^* p_i + \alpha_i y - \alpha_i \sum_{i \neq j} x_j^* p_j + e_i \qquad (3.16a)$$

The LES is therefore really a set of linear equations which are nonlinear in parameters. These equations can be estimated by linear methods if we proceed iteratively.

If we set $x_i^* = 0$ then 3.16 reduces to

$$v_i = \alpha_i y + e_i \qquad (3.18)$$

These are n linear Engel curves with the income elasticity for each item being unity. It is also easy to show that the demand equations corresponding to 3.18 each have an own price elasticity of unity. Thus for $x_i^* = 0$ we also have corresponding to 3.18 the only admissible set of Cobb–Douglas or nonlinear demand functions with unit price and income elasticities. (These propositions are simple enough for the reader to derive himself.)

Exercise. Show that the substitution matrix for 3.17 is diagonal. Derive also the matrix of price effects.

Exercise. Show that the demand equation corresponding to 3.16 is homegeneous of degree zero.

We can estimate from 3.18 all but one of the α_i. Since there is no constant term in 3.18, we have a case of homogeneous linear regression. We get our first estimates of α_i—call them $\hat{\alpha}_i^1$, we can use them in 3.16 as in the case of Tobin's study except that we have to estimate the x_i^* simultaneously. The n equations can be written in matrix form as

$$(\mathbf{v} - \hat{\boldsymbol{\alpha}}^1 y) = [(\hat{\boldsymbol{\alpha}}^1 i - \mathbf{I})\hat{\mathbf{p}}]\,\mathbf{x}^* + \mathbf{e} \qquad (3.19)$$

$\mathbf{v}, \mathbf{x}^*, \hat{\boldsymbol{\alpha}}^1$ and $\mathbf{e}$ are each $n \times 1$ vectors and i is an $n \times 1$ vector of 1's. $\mathbf{I}$ is an identity matrix and $\hat{\mathbf{p}}$ is a diagonal matrix with p_i as the ith diagonal element, y is a scalar. We can see that 3.19 is a linear regression problem where we have to estimate the vector x^* from the independent variable $(\hat{\boldsymbol{\alpha}}^1\,\mathbf{i} - \mathbf{I})\hat{\mathbf{p}}$ with the dependent variable being $(\mathbf{v} - \hat{\boldsymbol{\alpha}}^1 y)$. All we need is N observations where $N > n$. Having obtained our first estimates of x_i^* (label them $\hat{x}_i^{*1}$) we go back to 3.16 and estimate once again $(n-1)\alpha_i$ for the second time and then in turn estimate, with the help of these $\hat{\alpha}_i^2$, the second set of x_i^*. We iterate—repeat this procedure—until we get nearly identical estimates at two successive stages for the α_i and x_i^*.

Stone and his colleagues have applied this model to UK data. In a multi-country study, Goldberger and Gamalestos have applied the Stone model and the Cobb–Douglas demand function to a common set of data for US and Western European countries. In the first application of LES, Stone used UK data for 1920–1938 and confined himself to six commodity groups. The LES therefore required the estimation of 12 parameters rather than 42. As a comparison he took equation 3.18, for which $x_i^* = 0$. Table 3.2 summarises Stone's results for the naive and the LES case. Except for the case of drink and tobacco, the explanatory power of the LES is much better than the naive system. But what is more important is that the α_i are different for the two systems. We also see that the proportion of necessary ($p_i x_i^*$) to final expenditure (v_i) is much higher for the necessities (groups 1, 2 and 3) compared to the last three. This is a plausible result in the light of the Engel curve results we have seen. Once

Table. 3.2. Naive and iterative estimates of Stone's equations

	Naive		*Iterative*				
	α_i	$\sqrt{R^2}$	α_i	x_i^*	$\sqrt{R^2}$	$\bar{p}_i x_i^*$	v_i
1. Meat, fish, dairy products and fats	0.18	0.88	0.12	14	0.97	14	18
2. Fruit and vegetables	0.05	0.88	0.04	3	0.97	3	5
3. Drink and tobacco	0.11	0.95	0.06	10	0.57	10	12
4. Household running expenses	0.19	0.23	0.23	11	0.81	11	20
5. Durables	0.23	0.95	0.30	12	0.97	13	24
6. All other goods and services	0.24	0.98	0.25	15	0.97	15	25

basic needs have been satisfied, out of the additional money proportionately much more is spend on 'comforts and luxuries' rather than 'necessities'. It is also interesting to see that of the total expenditure of £104, £66 was for subsistence quantities. This is a measure of relative affluence. Stone's data are aggregative but given the fact that income as well as expenditure are unequally distributed, many people may be near or even below this level. Stone's system can be used to measure poverty income or minimum-need based income for inter-country or inter-regional (or if we have panel data, inter-family) comparative units. Watts (1967) has in fact used it in this way to generate inter-regional variations in poverty income for the US. Since x_i^* are estimated from the data rather than imposed on biological or nutritional grounds, we have here a social/cultural subsistence measure which is free to vary over time and space.

Additive/Separable Utility Functions

The utility function in 3.17 is explicity and is logarithmically additive in $(x_i - x_i^*)$. The notion of additivity is more general and can be put as

$$U = U[U^1(x_1) + U^2(x_2) + U^3(x_3) + \ldots + U^n(x_n)] \tag{3.20}$$

Here all the goods have separate utilities which are independent of the quantities of other goods consumed, total utility depending in some systematic way on the sum of individual utilities. One can also think of the n commodities being grouped into categories and the utility function satisfying group additivity

$$U = U[U^1(x^1) + U^2(x^2) + \ldots + U^m(x^m)] \tag{3.20a}$$

where for example, $x^1 = (x_1, x_2, x_3)$. Separability is a more general condition and for m groups we can write

$$U = U[U^1(x^1), U^2(x^2), \ldots, U^m(x^m)] \tag{3.20b}$$

The consequence of additivity, group additivity or separability is to put further restirctions on the parameters of the demand functions. Thus it can be shown that for group additivity, if we take a pair of commodities, one of which is in group I and the other in group J, then their income compensated price terms are symmetric and proportional to the product of their income effects, the factor of proportionality being related to the money flexibility measure. In terms of income and price elasticities we can write

$$(\eta_{ij}/w_j) + \eta_i = (\phi/y)\eta_i\eta_j = \theta\eta_i\eta_j = (\eta_{ji}/w_i) + \eta_j \tag{3.21}$$

where i is in group I and j in group J. η_{ij} is price elasticity of i with respect to j and η_i is the income elasticity of the ith commodity. (ϕ/y) is the money flexibility parameter and θ is an additivity parameter, w_i is the share of the ith commodity in total expenditure. For a separable utility function, we have a proportionality coefficient θ_{IJ} different for each pair of groups I and J. Similar restrictions can be derived for other grouping methods. Thus Pearce (1969) has a utility function which is separable between groups of commodities and additive within each group.

Estimation of Complete Sets of Demand Equations

The task of estimating a complete set of demand equations is thus a challenging one in econometrics. With increasing availability of data for a number of years and for many detailed items of consumer expenditure and the growth of computing facilities, many researchers have attempted this task. Pioneering work on Dutch data has been done by Theil (1965) and by Barten (1967, 1968, 1969). Byron (1970) has also worked on the same data rigorously testing the restrictions derived from theory. Both Barten and Byron came to negative conclusions about the validity of the restrictions. Deaton (1974) has again taken up the problem using UK data for 1900–1970. Not only is his work more recent but it is more comprehensive than previous work. We shall discuss his approach to illustrate the likelihood ratio method for testing restrictions in a multi-equation context.

Recall our equations 3.6, 3.6a and 3.7. An analogous systen of demand equations can be written for the set of n commodities. This is the *Rotterdam System.*

$$\hat{w}d(\ln \mathbf{x}) = bd(\ln \bar{y}) + Cd(\ln \mathbf{p}) \tag{3.22}$$

Our notation is somewhat different from Deaton's. $\hat{w}$ is a diagonal matrix with w_i, the share of ith commodity in total expenditure, along the diagonal; $\mathbf{x}$ is the vector of commodities, $\mathbf{p}$ that of prices; $\bar{y}$ is a scalar denoting real expenditure defined as

$$d(\ln \bar{y}) = w'd(\ln x) \simeq d(\ln y) - w'd(\ln p) \tag{3.23}$$

Equation 3.23 defines the proportionate change in real expenditure as a weighted sum of proportionate change in the quantities consumed, weights being w_i. This is approximated by the difference between proportionate change in money expenditure and a suitably weighted index of price change.

There are $n(n + 1)$ parameters. $n \times 1$ vector $\mathbf{b}$ gives us price weighted income effects $[b_i = p_i(\partial x_i/\partial y)]$. $\mathbf{C}$ is a $n \times n$ matrix of substitution effects or compensated price effects and is given as $y^{-1}\hat{p}S\hat{p}$. Thus an element $c_{ij} = p_i S_{ij} p_j / y$, where S_{ij} is defined as in equation 3.5.

The advantage of operating with the Rotterdam system is that it is log–linear and that restrictions defined earlier for the set of demand equations can be easily expressed in terms of b and C. It has the disadvantage that it cannot be derived from any well-behaved utility function as the LES system can. The LES on the other hand can be cast as a special case of 3.22.

Deaton summarises the restrictions on the system as follows:

(a) Engel aggregation $b'\iota = 1$
(b) Cournot aggregation $C'\iota = 1$
(c) Homogeneity $C\iota = 0$
(d) Symmetry $C = C'$
(e) Convexity $x'Cx \leqslant 0$ for all x
(f) Additivity $C = \phi(\hat{b} - bb')$

ι is a vector of 1's as before. ϕ is the inverse of the elasticity of the marginal utility of money and is the reciprocal of Frisch's money flexibility described above. The best way to understand conditions regarding additivity is to write the LES system as Deaton does:

$$\hat{p}x = \hat{p}x^* + b(y - p'x^*) \qquad (3.24)$$

This is just a matrix expression for 3.16. Now 3.24 satisfies $b'\iota = 1$. If we write $\mu_i = (p_i x_i^* / y)$ and w_i as $(p_i x_i / y)$ then $w = \mu + b(1 - \mu'\iota)$. Now ϕ can be defined following Frisch as $-(1 - \mu'\iota)$ for 3.24. Then we get by manipulation

$$\hat{w}d(\ln x) = b(\ln \bar{y}) + \phi(\hat{b} - bb')d(\ln p) \qquad (3.25)$$

Now comparing 3.22 with 3.25, we see that any additive system has $C = \phi(\hat{b} - bb')$. In the LES, strong assumptions are made about additivity and ϕ can be expressed as $-(1 - \mu'\iota)$ or as $-1 + y^{-1} p x^*$. This is therefore a stronger restriction on the utility function.

Deaton then sets up eight different models from the Rotterdam system imposing various restrictions. We shall discuss only a subset of these models here. The six models we shall discuss are summarised by Deaton as follows:

1. Rotterdam system unconstrained: b and C parametrised to give $b' = 1; \iota' \mathrm{C} = 0$
2. Rotterdam system with homogeneity: as in 1 and $C = 0$

3. Rotterdam system with symmetry: as in 1 and $C = C'$
4. Rotterdam system with additivity b and parametrised: $b'\iota = 1$, $C = \phi(\hat{b} - bb')$
5. LES: As in 4 but also $\phi = -1 + y^{-1}\hat{p}x^*$
6. No substitution: b parametrised $b'\iota = 1$, $C = 0$.

For these six models, estimating the complete set of equations by FIML, Deaton obtains values of the concentrated log-likelihood function. As we saw in Chapter 2, twice the log of the likelihood value ratio of the restricted and unrestricted system has a χ^2 distribution with the number of restrictions. Deaton tabulates twice the log-likelihood values for his six models in each of two versions—with intercepts and without intercepts. We give in Table 3.3 his result.

Table. 3.3. **Likelihood Values for Models of Consumer Behaviour**

Model	*Intercepts*	*No Intercepts*
1	4353.75(88)	4306.50(80)
2	4322.70(80)	4267.35(72)
3	4279.50(52)	4222.80(44)
4	4173.75(17)	4119.75(9)
5	4183.20(25)	4125.15(17)
6	4137.75(16)	4054.95(8)

The figures in parentheses are the number of unrestricted parameters to be estimated. Thus for nine commodity groups in a totally unrestricted system with no intercepts we would have 90 parameters, but imposing $b'\iota = 1$ and $\iota'C = 0$ means that we can derive one commodity group's parameters from the rest. This leaves us with 80 parameters. Adding eight intercepts gives us 88 parameters.

Now let us see how the likelihood ratio test will proceed. For model 1 compare the likelihood values with and without intercepts. There are eight extra restrictions imposed by the no intercept case. We look at the difference in the likelihood values 47.25 and compare it with χ^2 for eight degrees of freedom at the 95% level. There is no doubt that 47.25 exceeds the critical χ^2 value, hence we reject the restriction of zero intercepts.

Life is not always so simple, however. The likelihood ratio test is an asymptotic test and using it in a small sample situation may lead us to reject hypotheses otherwise valid. For restrictions within equations, there are certain correction factors which have to be used in a small sample situation as Deaton shows. Thus zero intercept, homogeneity or no-substitution effects are all within equation restrictions, but symmetry imposes cross equation restrictions and the number of restrictions is quite large compared to the number of observations (36/70).

We only indicate these complications but do not go into any further detail. Readers are warned to be wary of uncritical use of this test procedure. Deaton finds that he can safely reject the no-substitution case (model 6). Homogeneity is basic to any theory of rational consumer behaviour since it indicates no money illusion. Its rejection is, needless to say, problematical. But comparing model 2 with model 3, the additional restrictions imposed by symmetry are not rejected, though comparing model 1 and model 3, symmetry is rejected. This is not surprising: if homogeneity were accepted, symmetry seems to cause no further drastic drop in likelihood value, but homogeneity is rejected. Deaton finds, however, that since homogeneity is a weak restriction and symmetry is a strong one, this is quite favourable to consumer theory.

Additivity (model 4) is rejected when taken in the general Rotterdam model. Now the LES is not directly comparable to the unrestricted Rotterdam. The rejection of the one would not imply anything about the other. They are non-nested hypotheses. But the likelihood value appears to drop sharply when compared to Rotterdam unrestricted. Thus, though not as rigorous a test, we can reject LES.

It would seem, then, that these are substitution effects, these are symmetric as theory predicts and that additivity is not in general a valid restriction. The rejection of homogeneity is curious but since it is a weak restriction and a consequence of the budget constraint, Deaton is right in not taking it seriously. Deaton also obtained -2.8 as his estimate of the Frisch parameter.

Situations often arise in econometrics when restrictions derived from theory are rejected by data, and it is always a fine methodological point as to whether to discard the theory or to search for a new piece of data. As we stated in Chapter 1, the econometrician has to use whatever data are available. He does not generate them, he only accepts them as they come. We are testing, therefore, restrictions derived from a static utility theory of individual consumer behaviour on aggregative time series data. The theory does not allow for changing tastes, or for new goods or for any other kind of dynamic behaviour. The data after all span the inter-war years and post-war years and many changes took place in social practices (e.g. the growing habit of smoking among women) in the kinds of goods available (transistor radios, television and the motor car for example). The naive model skirts all these problems by allowing the data to generate estimates without imposing any structure on them. We do not know whether it does better due to the inadequate nature of consumer theory or due to peculiarities of the aggregative time series data. Such questions thus remain unresolved. The only clear indication is that the theory of consumer behaviour has many missing elements in it.

Conclusion

We know from all the available empirical work including Byron's results for the unrestricted model, that demand curves are downward sloping. Most goods seem to be normal. Byron found that only in the case of bread was there any trace of inferiority. The estimation of such simple demand curves is practically useful, for example for stabilising farm incomes or prices. It is when we want to go beyond this and say something about cross effects of prices on other quantities and make welfare predictions (about income-compensated price effects or about the size of the money flexibility parameter) that we find the evidence variable. The LES seems in this case quite powerful since it is derivable from an explicit utility function and generates many interesting parameters such as the estimate of minimum income. The presence of well specified economic theory yielding many restrictions and the availability of sample data is a combination that occurs only in demand theory. This provides us with opportunities to try out interesting estimation and testing techniques. As the theory of consumer behaviour is improved (e.g. in recent work by Lancaster, 1966) or as new data at a more detailed level become available, the challenge of testing prior restrictions of consumer theory on demand curves will remain one of the interesting unfinished tasks in econometric research.

Bibliographical Notes

Stigler's book on the history of ideas mentioned in the bibliographical notes to Chapter 1 is an indispensible source on the early work on demand analysis. The close link between the theoretical development in this field and their practical importance is illustrated by the correspondence between Henry Wallace who was in the early 1920's an editor of an Iowa agricultural newspaper [later Secretary of Agriculture in FDR's cabinet and Vice President 1940–44 and Presidential candidate 1948] and Henry Moore who was doing pioneering research in demand analysis. Some of this correspondence is quoted in Stigler. It shows how much accurate measurements of demand elasticities meant to the farmers' income expectations.

Development of the theory of consumer's behaviour is due to Slutsky (1915), Hicks and Allen (1934) and Hicks (1939). Henry Schuttz's monumental work *The Theory and Measurement of Demand* (1938) is a combination of economic theory and econometric practice of a very high standard. The postwar literature includes Wold and Jureen: *Demand Analysis* (1953), which once again combines theory and applications, and Houthakker and Prais: *The Analysis of Family Budgets* (1955). The latter book is interesting since it deals mainly with cross-section data. Recently (1973) it has been reissued in an abridged edition. Richard Stone's *Measurement of Consumer Expenditure in the UK* (1954) can be said to be the climax of the first cycle of investigations into demand analysis. A very readable account of the pioneer econometricians in this and other fields is in Christ (1952).

The theory of consumer behaviour and demand analysis in terms of the various restrictions is best stated in Goldberger (1967). Unfortunately this is not available in published form. Reference should also be made to Frisch (1959),

Pearce (1964). and the recent survey by Brown and Deaton (1972). For a discussion of notions of separability see Simmons (1974).

The linear expenditure system is also known as the Stone–Geary demand equation and was also independently developed by Klein and Rubin 1947–8. Recently there have been attempts to generalise the LES, see especially Deaton (1974), M. Brown and D. Heien (1972) and Pollak and Wales (1969).

On the problem of grouped data when the groups are of unequal size, see Aitchison and Prais (1954) and Malinvaud (1966, 1972).

A recent development has been to study demand in terms of characteristics rather than commodities and derive shadow prices of characteristics from prices of commodities. This was a linear algebraic formulation. See H. Makower (1957) for an early, if little known development. Gorman in two hitherto unpublished studies of demand for eggs (1956) and fish (1959) tried to estimate such demand structures. Recent work by Lancaster (1966) has generated much more interest in this area which is full of possibilities, see Boyle, Gorman and Pudney (1975).

A general class of utility functions has been recently introduced by Jorgenson, Christensen and Lau (1975); this is the transcendental logarithmic (translog) utility function. Their parallel or production function is discussed in Chapter 4. The translog is in second-order approximation to any general (utility) function such as equation 3.1.

4
Static multiple equations: production function

In the last chapter, we considered static demand equations. Even when looking at a set of n demand equations, we noticed that their interdependence arose from certain restrictions on parameters, e.g. Slutsky symmetry or Engel aggregation. There was, however, no *simultaneous* interaction between demands for different commodities as between prices and quantities in the sense that the variables on the right-hand side, prices and income, were considered given for the consumer. We now come to the problems of fitting production functions. Once again we are confined to static equations but now we have the problem of a set of *simultaneous static equations.* This raises questions of identification as well as of the appropriate estimation technique.

Corresponding to the notion of a demand curve is the notion of a supply curve. Elementary textbooks deal with the problem of consumer behaviour in relation to the former and the theory of the firm and of industry in relation to the latter. The equality of marginal cost and marginal revenue gives the profit maximising equilibrium of the firm and the comparative statics of short-run and long-run behaviour in response to changes in parameters such as input and output prices or technological change is then discussed. The equilibrium of a firm is, however, intertwined with the structure of the industry. It is difficult to make efficiency comparisons from the price–cost output relationships of a firm over time or of two firms unless we can establish similarity of market structures. The notion of a supply curve, useful as it is, breaks down as soon as we depart from competitive product markets. We need, therefore, a measurement of productive efficiency and a tool to analyse the firm's response to changing economic variables which is independent of market and industry conditions. Such a notion is the production function which as a *technological* relationship acting as a constraint for a profit maximising firm is invariant to economic and behavioural factors. Econometricians have therefore concentrated much more on the estimation of production functions than of cost functions or supply functions. The kind of questions which may be answered by production functions are the following.

1. *Returns to scale.* For some prescriptions of Pigovian welfare economics we may want to know whether a firm or an industry enjoys increasing or diminishing returns to scale.

2. *Allocation efficiency.* We may want to inquire whether firms purchase and utilise factor inputs in the most efficient way, i.e. matching the marginal products of factor inputs to their prices. Of particular interest here may be inter-firm comparisons in resource allocation.

3. *Returns to factors.* Related to the two questions above is the question of returns to a particular factor. It may be desirable to subsidise (or tax) the use of a particular input if returns to the factor are increasing (or diminishing) in a certain range. For example, we may wish to encourage the use of a high yielding variety of seeds or of fertilisers by subsidising them if there are increasing returns to them.

4. *Substitution.* A fundamental principle of economic behaviour is the tendency to substitute at the margin. Changes in the relative prices of inputs encourage corresponding substitution in the use of inputs by firms. We may want to know the extent to which substitution between inputs is possible. The degree of substitutability between inputs as

measured by the elasticity of substitution is crucial to the distribution of total output between different inputs. We can examine the effects of exogenous changes in inputs prices, for example, minimum wage legislation or depreciation allowances and changes in the quantities of inputs supplied, for example by immigration, on returns to factors and their shares in total output of an industry or a firm.

5. *Income shares.* The notion of the production function has also been applied at the macroeconomic level, although controversially, to explain the distribution of national income between income classes, i.e. wages and profits. The pioneering econometric estimation of a production function by Cobb and Douglas was undertaken precisely for this purpose. The starting point was the observed income shares of wages and profits in total income leading to a search for a production function in terms of output and inputs which would explain these observed shares. However, in recent years, there has been some doubt about the validity of an aggregate production function and the meaningfulness of empirical estimates using such a production function.

6. *Economic growth.* The notion of an aggregate production function has been used to provide empirical explanations of inter-country and inter-temporal differences in the economic growth of GNP. In these studies overall economic growth is apportioned as between different factors of production and often a residual remaining is labelled technical change. (For a discussion see Chapter 5.)

Whether we can answer these questions or not depends on whether we can *identify* the production function, i.e. isolate the purely technological relationships from the economic, behavioural and other historical relationships. Only if we can do this can we claim that our explanation of the relative efficiency of firms or the relative growth experiences of countries is invariant with respect to parameters such as prices, the structure of industry, size, previous experience, etc. Much controversy exists regarding the identifiability of a microeconomic production function from observable data relating to firms and the conditions under which such production functions retain their identifiability when aggregated over firms and industries.

The Neoclassical Production Function

What we have come to call the neoclassical production function was formalised first by Wicksell. Formally a production function expresses the output of a commodity as a function—sometimes a continuous and differentiable function of all its inputs. That is,

$$y = f(x_1, \ldots, x_n) \tag{4.1}$$

y being output and x_1 to x_n being inputs. As yet, however, this is an empty statement. We need to characterise the production function in greater detail. The first question relates to the level of aggregation to which the function refers. Is y the output of a plant, firm, industry or the economy? Microeconomic theory which uses the notion of production and cost functions relates to a firm producing a single homogeneous commodity. This concept of the firm is in many ways an abstraction in the age of assembly lines, product differentiation, giant multiproduct firms and conglomerates. As we saw above, the level of aggregation is often determined by statistical sources. The standard industrial classification (SIC) makes data available for industries' output at various levels of disaggregation—two digit, three digit, etc. Data at firm level in an industry come from censuses of manufacturing or sample surveys. While the whole notion of the neoclassical production function is currently in flux, we have greater confidence in it at the plant or firm level where we can hope to capture the technology of the production process. The production function is a *technological* relationship and the more closely we can approximate to the technological relationship between output and inputs by disaggregation, the more meaningful our results will be.

The second question concerns the dimensionality of our y and x_i variables. Are they stocks at a point of time or flows over a period of time? This is again a question of measurement which we referred to in Chapter 1 and of the difficulty of approximating a functional relationship defined in infinitesimal time to data which are available only in quarterly or annual intervals. We should take the greatest care that the output and input variables are defined in commensurate dimensions. Thus, if output is a flow variable, all inputs should be defined in flow terms. This is not as easy and trivial as it sounds. Ideally, a production function expresses a relation between a flow of output over a defined time interval and a flow of inputs over the same time interval or a relevant previous time interval. But variables are mostly available in stock terms—capital stock in terms of value of machinery and buildings and labour in terms of men employed or land in terms of acres. Care should be taken to measure the flow of input services from these stocks of inputs—value of capital services, manhours worked, the area sown. Inputs also are assumed to be homogeneous. We need manhours of labour of roughly equal skill and efficiency, acreage sown of similar quality and fertility of land, machines of similar vintage, and so on. Often, in the absence of these flow measures, there is a temptation to substitute the equivalent money valuation of these services as would prevail under competitive conditions given certain restrictive assumptions. We referred to this temptation in Chapter 1 where we mentioned that often the unit value of capital services is approximated by its competitive equilibrium expression, i.e. the price of capital stock multiplied by the sum of the rate of interest and the depreciation rate. This may lead to circularity in the argument for reasons we shall see later on.

We can now move on to the properties and parameters of the production function. The most important of these is the degree of substitutability between inputs. This is most easily discussed for a case of two inputs x_1 and x_2. The degree of substitutability is measured by the *elasticity of substitution* which is a parameter of the production function. The elasticity of substitution may be zero or infinity—what we call a fixed coefficient case and a linear isoquant case respectively. In the fixed proportion case, the inputs are combined in one proportion and this proportion cannot be varied. There may be other technologies available which combine the same two inputs in different proportions, but the important thing is that this proportion is fixed for the given technique and not continuously variable over different techniques. For the neoclassical production function proper, a continuous substitutability is crucial. This is familiar in the textbook diagrams of a smooth isoquant between two inputs. For a given level of output—along an isoquant—we define the *elasticity of substitution between two inputs as the proportional change in the input ratio corresponding to a unit proportional change in the ratio of the marginal products of the inputs*. Confining ourselves to $n = 2$ in equation 4.1, we have elasticity

$$\sigma = \frac{d(x_1/x_2)/(x_1/x_2)}{d\left(\frac{\partial f/\partial x_1}{\partial f/\partial x_2}\right)\Big/\left(\frac{\partial f/\partial x_1}{\partial f/\partial x_2}\right)} = \frac{d\ \ln(x_1/x_2)}{d\ \ln[(\partial f/\partial x_1)/(\partial f/\partial x_2)]} \tag{4.2}$$

The elasticity of substitution for a production function can be a constant or a variable. We shall deal with production functions which have constant elasticities of substitution. Elasticity can range from zero to infinity.

We have already referred to marginal products in the definition above. For a two-input production function, we can define the properties of the production function as follows

(a) $\partial f/\partial x_i > 0$ for all i, all marginal products are positive.
(b) $f(0, 0) = f(0, x_2) = f(x_1, 0) = 0$, all inputs are necessary for production.
(c) $\partial^2 f/\partial x_i^2 < 0$ for all i, diminishing marginal products.
(d) $\partial f/\partial x_i \to 0$ as $x_i \to \infty$ and $\partial f/\partial x_i \to \infty$ as $x_i \to 0$, the isoquants do not touch the axis.

The second parameter of the production function is the degree of homogeneity of the function which can be interpreted as a measure of returns to scale. We have already seen in the previous chapter that demand curves are homogeneous of degree zero. The degree of homogeneity is defined as the proportionate change in output resulting from an *equi-proportionate* change in all the inputs. If we increase both x_1 and x_2 by a proportion $\lambda > 0$, then output will go up by a proportion λ^r, where r is the degree of homogeneity of the function. For $r = 1$, we have constant returns to scale; for $r > 1$ increasing and $r < 1$ diminishing returns to scale.

Even given identical input quantities, there may be inter-firm variations in efficiency in terms of output produced. The same firm may also increase/diminish in efficiency over time. This may be due to non-measurable and unspecified inputs such as managerial ability or inter-regional differences in climate or accumulation of experience over time. Such variations are expressed by an efficiency parameter which determines the relative shift of the production function over firms or over time.

The substitution parameter, the efficiency parameter and the returns-to-scale parameter are then the three estimable parameters of interest to the econometrician. Before we go on to the problem of estimation of these parameters, let us look at some explicit forms of the production function. The most familiar is the Cobb–Douglas production function named after mathematician Charles Cobb and economist Paul Douglas. In this form it was first mentioned by Wicksell. The Cobb–Douglas production function is written as

$$y = A x_1^{\alpha_1} x_2^{\alpha_2} \tag{4.3}$$

In 4.3, α_1 and α_2 are respectively the elasticity of output with respect to x_1 and x_2, and the returns to scale parameter is $\alpha_1 + \alpha_2$ [since $A(\lambda x_1)^{\alpha_1} (\lambda x_2)^{\alpha_2} = \lambda^{(\alpha_1+\alpha_2)} A x_1^{\alpha_1} x_2^{\alpha_2}$ $= \lambda^{(\alpha_1+\alpha_2)} y$]. A is the efficiency parameter.

Exercise. Show that the elasticity of substitution is constant and equal to one for the Cobb–Douglas production function.

The popularity of the Cobb–Douglas production function stems from its simplicity and flexibility as well as the empirical support it has received from data for various industries and various countries. Taking logarithms of 4.3 we see that the Cobb–Douglas production function is linear in logarithms (log–linear or double-log for short). It is easy to generalise it for n inputs:

$$y = A \prod_{i=1}^{n} x_i^{\alpha_i}$$

The coefficients of inputs are easily interpretable in terms of elasticities and returns to scale. Lastly, it saves us the estimation of the elasticity of substitution by restricting it *a priori* to unity.

A recent rival to the Cobb–Douglas production function is the constant elasticity of substitution (CES) production function. This was first mentioned by H. D. Dickinson but it was estimated in 1961 by Arrow, Chenery, Minhas and Solow (ACMS or SMAC). What the CES production function lacks in simplicity it makes up for in its generality. It can be written as

$$y = A[\alpha_1 x_1^{-\rho} + \alpha_2 x_2^{-\rho}]^{-\mu/\rho} \tag{4.4}$$

Here A is once again the efficiency parameter, the returns to scale parameter is μ and the substitution parameter is ρ. The terms α_1 and α_2 are known as distribution parameters since we can relate the share of the two inputs in total output to α_1 and α_2.

Exercise. Show that the elasticity of substitution (σ) equals $1/(1+\rho)$ for the CES production function (take $\mu = 1$).

The CES function is more general than the Cobb–Douglas production function. This is because it can be shown that the Cobb–Douglas function is a special case of CES. It also looks more difficult since it is nonlinear in the parameter ρ. One cannot simply take logarithms of both sides and proceed because the term $-\mu/\rho \ln[\alpha_1 x_1^{-\rho} + \alpha_2 x_2^{-\rho}]$ cannot be evaluated without knowledge of $\alpha_1 + \alpha_2$ and ρ.

Exercise. Show that, as ρ approaches 0 or ∞, σ approaches 1 or 0 and the CES production function approaches the Cobb–Douglas or fixed coefficient production function. [Write 4.4 as $f(\rho)^{1/g(\rho)}$ and using L'Hospital's rule, let $\rho \to 0$.]

Estimation

From the discussion above, we can see that explicit production functions such as Cobb–Douglas and CES offer us in a convenient form of one or two parameters the main ingredients of interest, e.g. returns to scale or elasticity of substitution. More general forms can be formulated allowing for variable elasticity of substitution or with variable returns to scale. We turn, however, to the question of identifiability of the production function. We said above that our preference for the production function as against cost or supply functions was due to its invariance to certain economic factors such as prices or market conditions. We need to be sure, however, that in estimating the parameters of the production function from observed data, such invariance is preserved. We can interpret the estimated coefficients as parameters of a technological relationship rather than a mixture of technological and economic relationships only if we can ensure identifiability of the production function.

In discussing identifiability we shall confine ourselves to a production function at the microeconomic level in two inputs and we observe a sample of firms producing a homogeneous output (y) using two homogeneous inputs (x_1 and x_2) which are being bought and sold in competitive conditions and therefore their respective prices (p, p_1 and p_2) are exogenously given to the firms. These assumptions are made not because they make the problem easily soluble but precisely for the opposite reason that all the problems in estimating production functions can be illustrated in this example. For example, in a special case where we observe all the firms at a point of time, the production function becomes under-identified and cannot be meaningfully estimated by a straightforward OLS regression. This is known in the literature as the Marschak–Andrews problem and while it is a special case it is of great interest. Let us see why this problem arises.

The production function is a *technological* relationship between output and inputs. But the actual quantities of inputs *used* and output *produced* by a firm are a result of *economic* or behavioural decisions. A profit maximising firm operating under competitive conditions in factor and product markets faces an infinitely elastic demand curve at the market price for its output and infinitely elastic supply curves for its inputs at the going price for the inputs. Thus every firm faces an identical price for output and identical input prices.

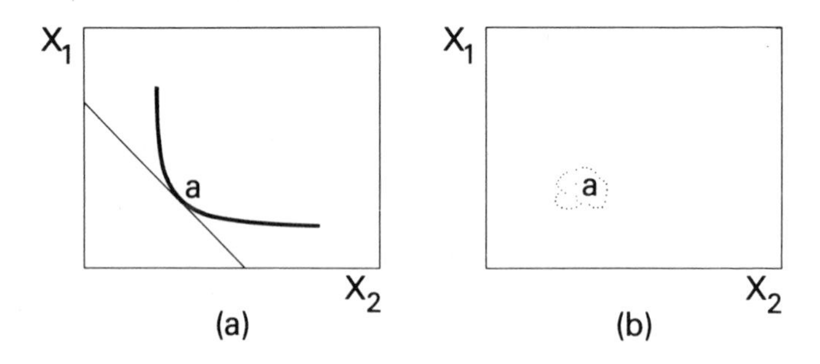

Fig. 4.1

The actual level of inputs used is decided by the profit maximising exercise equating the marginal revenue product to the exogenously given input price. Faced with identical production functions and a uniform input price ratio, the input ratio employed by all the firms at a point of time is identical. Thus every firm is on the same point of the isoquant except perhaps for scale differences and a random error at the given point in time for which we have data. What we wish to estimate is the isoquant, while what we observe is only one point on it. Hence the under-identification (see figure 4.1).

The problem arises because prices are not only exogenous to the firm but also because they do not vary. Any inter-firm or inter-temporal variation in prices will help us observe movements along the isoquants. In order to see this problem of under-identification in a more formal framework, let us set up the profit maximising behaviour of the entrepreneur facing given input and output prices and a production function. Thus, for the jth firm, total profits (R_j) are maximised subject to a constraint as follows

$$\left.\begin{aligned} \text{Max. } R_j &= py_j - p_1 x_{1j} - p_2 x_{2j} \\ \text{subject to } y_j &= f(x_{1j}, x_{2j}) \end{aligned}\right\} \quad (4.5)$$

We have the three familiar first order conditions

$$\left.\begin{aligned} pf_{1j} &= p(\partial f/\partial x_{1j}) = p_1 \\ pf_{2j} &= p(\partial f/\partial x_{2j}) = p_2 \\ y_j &= f(x_{1j}, x_{2j}) \end{aligned}\right\} \quad (4.6)$$

The three equations in 4.6 solve three endogenous variables y_j, x_{1j} and x_{2j} simultaneously, given the three prices p, p_1 and p_2 which appear as two price ratios p_1/p and p_2/p. The prices have no j subscripts since they are common to all the firms including the jth firm, but they are also constant at the given point of time. There are no exogenous *variables* in the system. In a more general framework, we may have five variables in all and we can solve any three of them holding two as exogenous. We are also interested in estimating the parameters of the production function—f_{1j} and f_{2j}. To estimate these two parameters, we need two restrictions in the system. These can be zero restrictions on the variables in the system. The third equation of the system includes all the *variables* in the system; the only excluded elements are the prices but they are *constant*. To put this another way, we cannot estimate the production function by OLS since the independent variables x_{1j} and x_{2j} are jointly dependent with y_j; we can estimate the parameters by instrumental variables (IV) but the system does not contain any exogenous variables which can be used as instruments. Let us illustrate this problem with a Cobb–Douglas production function as in equation 4.3. We have explicitly, instead of 4.6, the following system

$$\left.\begin{aligned} \alpha_1 (y_j/x_{1j}) &= (p_1/p) \\ \alpha_2 (y_j/x_{2j}) &= (p_2/p) \\ y_j &= A x_{1j}^{\alpha_1} x_{2j}^{\alpha_2} \end{aligned}\right\} \quad (4.7)$$

Imagine an econometric investigator estimating the parameters α_1 and α_2 of the production function, without taking into account the input demand equations. He has a log–linear equation in two independent variables $\ln x_1$ and $\ln x_2$ and he can proceed by OLS to estimate α_1 and α_2. The presence of the two input demand equations means, however, that $\ln x_1$ and $\ln x_2$ no longer satisfy OLS assumptions since by manipulating the first two equations in set 4.7 we have

$$\left.\begin{aligned} x_{1j} &= \left[\alpha_1\left(\frac{p}{p_1}\right)\right] y_j \\ x_{2j} &= \left[\alpha_2\left(\frac{p}{p_2}\right)\right] y_j \end{aligned}\right\} \qquad (4.7a)$$

Taking logarithms of the two equations in 4.7a we see that the 'independent' variables $\ln x_1$ and $\ln x_2$ are in fact dependent on the dependent variable $\ln y$ in their turn plus a constant $\ln\,[\alpha_i(p/p_i)]$. Thus, we have a situation in which OLS techniques lead to bias in the estimates if we ignore the other two equations in the system. If we do take account of the other equations, we have the identification problem. How do we solve this problem?

We have until now ignored a rather important stricture of Chapter 1. We have talked about estimation by OLS but we have not specified the nature of the random error term. Equations 4.6 or 4.7 are all deterministic and there is as yet no reason for random errors. Let us now assume that each of the equations in 4.6 or 4.7 are subject to random error. In the production function, we can rationalise the presence of random errors as being due to managerial efficiency in utilising the available inputs or as due to technical factors such as machine breakdown. For the two behavioural equations the ability of the entrepreneur to equate his marginal product to price can also be subject to a random error. This error is behavioural rather than technological. We rewrite 4.7 then

$$\left.\begin{aligned} \ln x_{1j} &= \ln[\alpha_1(p/p_1)] + \ln y_j + v_{1j} \\ \ln x_{2j} &= \ln[\alpha_2(p/p_2)] + \ln y_j + v_{2j} \\ \ln y_j &= \ln A + \alpha_1 \ln x_{1j} + \alpha_2 \ln x_{2j} + u_j \end{aligned}\right\} \qquad (4.8)$$

v_{1j}, v_{2j} and u_j are random errors satisfying the usual conditions about zero means and homoscedastic variances. The subscript

j denotes the jth firm in the sample. We have observations on x_{1j}, x_{2j} and y_j for the sample; we wish to estimate α_1, α_2 (and A) as well as the variances and covariances of the error terms v_{1j}, v_{2j} and u_j. As already explained above, the order conditions for identifiability are not satisfied by the above system. Thus, no direct estimate of α_1 and α_2 by OLS is possible.

A method of estimating α_1 and α_2 without a direct resort to OLS was suggested by Klein (1953). The method involves using the input demand equations in 4.7a to obtain an estimate of α_i as follows:

$$\alpha_i = \frac{p_i x_i}{py} \tag{4.9}$$

for all the j firms. α_i is the share of ith input in total output. Given our sample observations, we can derive an estimate of α_i from the geometric mean of the share of ith input over all firms.

$$\alpha_i = \prod_{j=1}^{j} \frac{p_i x_{ij}}{py_j} \tag{4.9a}$$

or

$$\ln \hat{\alpha}_i = \frac{1}{J} \sum_{j=1}^{J} [\ln(p_i x_{ij}) - \ln (py_j)] \tag{4.9b}$$

If the production function is assumed to obey constant returns to scale then of the two α_1's only one need be estimated since $\sum_{i=1}^{2} \alpha_i \approx 1$. The Klein estimator has been shown by Dhrymes (1962) to be *asymptotically unbiased and of such estimators it has the minimum variance.* (It is not, however, BLUE.) We may ask ourselves how Klein overcomes the Marschak–Andrews problem. We said above that we needed two restrictions to identify the two parameters. Klein has implicitly used two *nonlinear* restrictions which can be seen if we rearrange the three equations in 4.8 as

$$\left.\begin{aligned} \ln (p_1 x_{1j}) &= \ln \alpha_1 + \ln(py_i) + v_{1j} \\ \ln (p_2 x_{2j}) &= \ln \alpha_2 + \ln(py_j) + v_{2j} \\ \ln y_j &= \ln A + \alpha_1 \ln x_{1j} + \alpha_2 \ln x_{2j} + u_j \end{aligned}\right\} \tag{4.8a}$$

The two *nonlinear* restrictions are that the *constant terms in the first two equations are logarithms of the two parameters* α_1 *and* α_2 *in the third equation.* Thus while the Klein procedure does not estimate the production function directly, it uses the information that the input demand equations are jointly derived along with the production function in the course of a profit maximising exercise. Klein also assumes that the input and output prices are not only exogenous constants but that they are also *observable*. Thus we derive our estimates of *physical* productivity from data on *value* shares. In fact for the Klein estimates we need no data on physical outputs and inputs only total revenue and input payments. Data availability is a frequent constraint on estimates of econometric equations, and the Klein procedure uses the most easily available information.

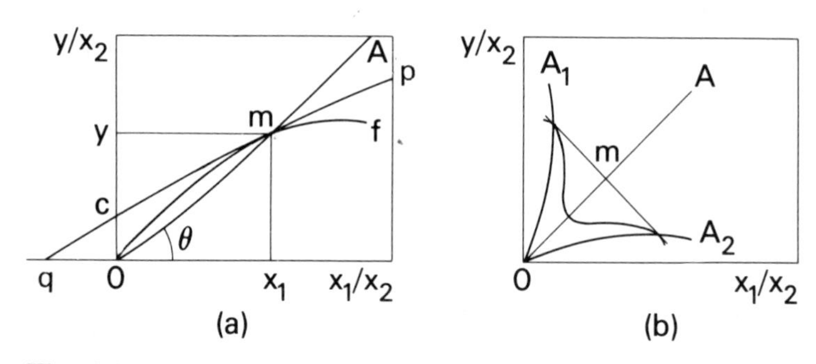

Fig. 4.2

(In their original investigation, Cobb and Douglas observed value shares first and noticed the remarkable constancy of labour income as a proportion of the total value of output. In order to explain this share, they proceeded to construct indexes of physical output and physical inputs of labour and capital. Then they estimated the parameters of the production function and found that these were indeed the value shares observed previously. The Klein procedure now comes back full circle and obviates the necessity for constructing the physical measures and directly takes the value share as an estimate of the Cobb–Douglas parameter. The interpretation of the value share as the ratio of marginal to average product depends crucially upon the existence of a Cobb–Douglas production function; of competitive factor and product markets and of profit maximisation.)

A geometric interpretation of the Klein procedure can now be put forward. We are no longer concerned with the isoquant map and the x_1, x_2 coordinates but with the derived demand curves and y, x_1 coordinates or the y, x_2 coordinates. For constant returns to scale we can take one of the two, say y, x_1. In figure 4.2a, *Of* is the production function given a certain level of x_2. The tangency of the production function with the price line *qcp* at point *m* gives us the level of input used (Ox_1) and output produced (Oy). *Om* is the size of the average product (given as tan θ) and for a Cobb–Douglas production function, marginal product is proportional to the average product, the factor of proportionality being the Cobb–Douglas parameter, α_1 in this case. If we take $p = 1$, then cy/oy is a measure of the share of x_1, in total output. A simple manipulation can show that this is equal to α_1 since at the tangency point *m*

$$\frac{\partial f}{\partial x_1} = \frac{p_1}{p} = \frac{cy}{ym} = \alpha_1 \frac{y}{x_1} = \alpha_1 \frac{mx_1}{ox_1}$$

Multiplying by ym/oy, we have

$$\frac{cy}{oy} = \frac{cy}{ym}\frac{ym}{oy} = \frac{p_1}{p}\frac{ym}{oy} = \frac{p_1}{p}\frac{ox_1}{oy} = \frac{ox_1}{oy}(\partial f/\partial x_1)$$

$$= \alpha_1 \left(\frac{mx_1}{ox_1}\frac{ym}{oy}\right) = \alpha_1$$

The statistical nature of the solution is then shown in figure 4.2b. At *m*, the marginal and average products are in a proportion α_1 to each other. The average products of all the firms are then distributed around the point m—OA_1 and OA_2 illustrate the deviations of observed average product round the mean value *OA*. The price ratio is a measure of the marginal product and, being an observable exogenous constant it can be measured without error. By evaluating the (geometric) mean of the observed average product (*OA*) we measure then the parameter α_1 given by the ratio of *om* to *qm*.

Klein's solution thus relies on value data to measure Cobb–Douglas parameters. It has the shortcoming that since value shares always have to add up to one, it is biased towards constant returns to scale. We also need to know something about the nature of the error terms and their variances and covariances if we need to estimate the standard error of $\hat{\alpha}_1$.

An alternative solution of the Marschak–Andrews problem has been proposed by Hoch (1958). This solution proceeds by putting restrictions on the error variance matrix rather than on the deterministic part of the model. We can see this by setting out 4.8 in a simplified fashion

$$\begin{aligned} \ln y_j &= \ln K_0 + \Sigma\, \alpha_i \ln x_{ij} + u_j \\ \ln x_{ij} &= \ln K_i + \ln y_j + v_{ij} \qquad i = 1, 2 \end{aligned} \tag{4.8b}$$

Writing the system as 4.8b rather than 4.8 is not just a change of notation but a change also in the theoretical premise. K_0 and K_i are now constants but the facts that $\ln K_i$ equals $\ln (\alpha_i p/p_1)$ and that the prices are observable are not used in solving the identifiability of the production function. All the information needed to solve the Marschak–Andrews problem is contained in the structure of 4.8b, especially the linear dependence of $\ln x_i$ on $\ln y$ and the variance–covariance matrix of the errors u_j and v_{ij}.

Hoch solves the Marschak–Andrews problem for two cases. The first case is where there is no transmission of errors from the production function to the behavioural equation or vice versa. This occurs when input demand depends not on actual output but anticipated output y^*. For the case of agricultural production, this is specially appropriate since inputs are committed first and actual output appears at the end of the process (flow input/point output case). If we have $\ln y_j^*$ for $\ln y_j$ in the equations for $\ln x_{ij}$, the OLS estimation of the production function is appropriate since $\ln x_{ij}$ are uncorrelated with u_j.

The second case is where we have y_j rather than y_j^* in the x_{ij} equation but the error covariances are still zero. Thus $E(uv_1) = E(uv_2) = E(v_1 v_2) = 0$. The equations in 4.8b can now be used to write down the variances and covariances of $\ln y$, $\ln x_1$ and $\ln x_2$. We obtain six variances and covariances: var $\ln y$, var $\ln x_1$, var $\ln x_2$, cov $\ln y \ln x_1$, cov $\ln y \ln x_2$ and cov $\ln x_1 \ln x_2$. These will be in terms of α_1, α_2 and the variances of the error terms. We can derive sample estimates of the variances and covariances of our observed variables $\ln y$, $\ln x_1$ and $\ln x_2$ from available data. Given these six sample moments we have to estimate five parameters: α_1, α_2, var u, var v_1 and var v_2. We have here a case of over-identification. Hoch proceeds by deriving consistent estimates of var v_1 and var v_2 from sample moments. He then derives the expressions for *plim* $\hat{\alpha}_1$, *plim* $\hat{\alpha}_2$ and *plim* $\widehat{\text{var}}\, u$, where ˆ denotes OLS estimates. Thus from 4.8b we have by simple manipulation,

$$\left.\begin{aligned} \ln y &= C_0 + \frac{1}{(1-\Sigma\alpha_i)}(\Sigma\alpha_i v_i + u) \\ \ln x_i &= C_i + \frac{1}{(1-\Sigma\alpha_i)}(\Sigma\alpha_i v_i + u) + v_i \qquad i = 1, 2 \end{aligned}\right\} \quad (4.8c)$$

Now we write $D = 1/(1 - \Sigma\alpha_i)$. [Notice that Hoch's expression requires strictly diminishing returns to be non-explosive. An alternative is to estimate only $(n - 1)\alpha_i$'s.] We have then

$$\left.\begin{aligned} \text{var} \ln y &= D^2(\sum_i \alpha_i^2 \text{ var } v_i + \text{var } u) \\ \text{var} \ln x_i &= \text{var} \ln y + 2D\alpha_i \text{ var } v_i + \text{var } v_i \qquad i = 1, 2 \\ \text{cov} \ln y \ln x_i &= \text{var} \ln y + D\alpha_i \text{ var } v_i \qquad i = 1, 2 \\ \text{cov} \ln x_1 \ln x_2 &= \text{var} \ln y + D\sum_{i=1}^{2} \alpha_i \text{ var } v_i \end{aligned}\right\} \quad (4.10)$$

(Hoch's expression can be generalised for many inputs. We have confined ourselves to $n = 2$.) Notice that var $\ln x_i$ as well as all the covariances are greater than var $\ln y$. These, however, are population rather than sample moments. It is worthwhile checking our sample moments to see whether they satisfy this inequality though a rigorous test of significance has not yet been developed. If our sampling moments do not satisfy this inequality, we may doubt the validity of our specification. Now from the equations in 4.10 we get the expressions for population moments of v_i

$$\text{var } v_i = \text{var } \ln y + \text{var } \ln x_i - 2 \text{ cov } \ln y \ln x_i \tag{4.11a}$$

which carries over to sample moments and we write

$$\widetilde{\text{var}}\ v_i = \widetilde{\text{var}} \ln y + \widetilde{\text{var}} \ln x_i - 2\ \widetilde{\text{cov}} \ln y \ln x_i$$

For α_i and var u we have

$$\left.\begin{aligned} \text{plim } (\hat{\alpha}_i) &= \frac{\alpha_i + \dfrac{\text{var } u}{\text{var } v_i}}{1 + \text{var } u \displaystyle\sum_{i=1}^{2} \frac{1}{\text{var } v_i}} \\ \text{plim } \widehat{\text{var}}\ (u) &= \frac{\text{var } u}{1 + \text{var } u \displaystyle\sum_{i} \frac{1}{\text{var } v_i}} \end{aligned}\right\} \tag{4.11b}$$

Notice that all the terms on the r.h.s. are population moments. We have consistent estimates for var v_i. We get $\hat{\alpha}_i$ and $\widehat{\text{var}}\ u$ from OLS estimates and therefore we can derive expressions for α_i and var u from 4.11b. Only for the special and clearly impossible case of var $u = 0$ will plim $(\hat{\alpha}_i) = \alpha_i$. By specifying the model explicitly and imposing plausible prior restrictions on the errors, Hoch has devised a method for consistent estimation of the production function parameters.

In the third case he goes further and lets $E(v_1 v_2) \neq 0$. The remaining restrictions now imply that the error in the technological relation is independent of those in the behavioural relations. If we are concerned with agricultural production functions, this seems reasonable since the error in the production function may be due to the weather. Given this additional parameter $E(v_1 v_2)$ to estimate we have six parameters and six equations. As before we can write out the expressions for the population moments of $\ln y$, $\ln x_1$ and $\ln x_2$.

$$\left.\begin{aligned} \text{var } \ln y &= D^2 (\alpha_1^2 \text{ var } v_1 + \alpha_2^2 \text{ var } v_2 \\ &\quad + 2\alpha_1 \alpha_2 \text{ cov } v_1 v_2) + \text{var } u \\ \text{cov } \ln y \ln x_i &= \text{var } \ln y + D(\alpha_i \text{ var } v_i + \alpha_j \text{ cov } v_i v_j) \\ \text{var } \ln x_i &= 2 \text{ cov } \ln y \ln x_i - \text{var } \ln y + \text{var } v_i \\ \text{cov } \ln x_1 \ln x_2 &= \text{cov } \ln y \ln x_1 + \text{cov } \ln y \ln x_2 \\ &\quad - \text{var } \ln y + \text{cov } v_1 v_2 \end{aligned}\right\} \tag{4.12}$$

var v_1, var v_2 and cov $v_1 v_2$ can be estimated as in 4.11a above from sample moments. The two equations for cov ln y ln x_i can be used to yield estimates of α_i and the var ln y, e.g. to give estimates of var u. This is a just-identified case and therefore we have an equal number of equations and unknowns. If, however, we wish to further relax the assumptions of about $E(uv_i)$ then we will have two more parameters than equations and the Marschak–Andrews problem will occur.

Hoch's solutions of the Marschak–Andrews problem seem more complicated than Klein's solution. They differ in making use of different bits of information contained in system 4.8. Hoch neglects the information on prices as well as the nonlinear restrictions on the constant terms in the input demand equations. Klein on the other hand uses no information about the error terms.

Let us now look at a more general situation where prices vary as well as outputs and inputs. This variation in prices can be inter-temporal or inter-firm. The inter-firm variation may be due to non-competitive conditions or to regional variations and constraints on factor mobility. The variability of prices may then afford the needed restrictions on the production function. We can then proceed to estimate the parameters by instrumental variables using the prices as instruments or by indirect least squares. We need to be sure, however, that prices are exogenous and for this we must look carefully at the economic and institutional conditions in the particular industry we are studying. An example of a careful use of institutional information for identification is provided by Marc Nerlove's study of returns to scale in the electricity generating industry. This is again a cross section of electricity generating firms in the USA, but prices can be seen to vary for reasons such as regional variation, individual firm bargaining with labour unions and variability in the riskiness of the individual firms. The features of the industry imply that output price is fixed by regulating agencies and output is also exogenous to the firm. This means that profit maximisation is equivalent to cost minimisation for a given level of output. Nerlove derives the minimum total cost function in terms of output level (y_j) and input prices. Let us illustrate the problem by recasting the profit maximisation problem in 4.5 as a cost minimisation problem. We have then total cost (TC) for the two-input case (ignoring once again the random error terms for the time being):

$$\begin{aligned} \text{Min } TC_j &= p_{1j}x_{1j} + p_{2j}x_{2j} \\ \text{subject to } y_j &= f(x_{1j}, x_{2j}) \end{aligned} \qquad (4.13)$$

We get for a Cobb–Douglas production function, the first-order conditions

$$\left.\begin{aligned} p_{1j} &= \lambda\alpha_1 (y_j/x_{1j}) \\ p_{2j} &= \lambda\alpha_2 (y_j/x_{2j}) \\ y_j &= A x_{1j}{}^{\alpha_1} x_{2j}{}^{\alpha_2} \end{aligned}\right\} \qquad (4.14)$$

λ is the Lagrangean multiplier and can be interpreted as the marginal cost for the given level of output. We can solve out one of the x_{ij} in terms of the other by taking the ratio of the two first-order conditons. Thus,

$$\frac{p_{1j}}{p_{2j}} = \frac{\alpha_1}{\alpha_2}\frac{x_{2j}}{x_{1j}}$$

Replacing x_{1j} in the production function, we have

$$y_j = A\left[\frac{\alpha_1}{\alpha_2}\left(\frac{p_{2j}x_{2j}}{p_{1j}}\right)^{\alpha_1}\right] x_{2j}{}^{\alpha_2}$$

$$\left[y_j A^{-1}\left(\frac{\alpha_1 p_{2j}}{\alpha_2 p_{1j}}\right)^{-\alpha_1}\right]^{1/(\alpha_1+\alpha_2)} = x_{2j}p_{2j}$$

We can get a similar expression for $p_{1j}x_{1j}$ and we have

$$TC_j = y_j{}^{1/(\alpha_1+\alpha_2)} p_{2j}{}^{\alpha_2/(\alpha_1+\alpha_2)} p_{1j}{}^{\alpha_1/(\alpha_1+\alpha_2)} \left[A^{-1}\left(\frac{\alpha_1}{\alpha_2 p_{1j}}\right)^{-\alpha_1} + A^{-1}\left(\frac{\alpha_2}{\alpha_1 p_{2j}}\right)^{-\alpha_2}\right]^{1/(\alpha_1+\alpha_2)} \qquad (4.15)$$

Now we have an equation for total cost in terms of output level and the price of inputs. Prices are exogenous variables and output level is also exogenous. It is appropriate to fit a total cost function here because the institutional conditions give the identifying restrictions by providing for variable prices and exogeneity of total revenue. Any error term attached to the cost equation will be a compound of u_j, v_{1j} and v_{2j} but since output is exogenous we have no simultaneous equation bias. Taking logarithms of both sides, we can use OLS. We have one degree of freedom since we have only two parameters and three coefficients. They can be suitably normalised by one of the input prices expressing the independent variables as $\ln TC_j - \ln p_{2j}$ and independent variables $\ln y_j$ and $(\ln p_{1j} - \ln p_{2j})$.

Nerlove's method, like Klein's, has the advantage that it uses more readily available data. Thus there is no need to gather data on physical inputs. This is, however, not advisable unless one is quite sure that economic considerations justify such a procedure. Very often one may be ignoring important variables because they are difficult to measure. This may lead to biased results. This can be illustrated by looking at the problems in estimating the parameters of the CES production function.

The Marschak–Andrews problem carries over to the fitting of CES production functions. However, in the estimation of CES production functions, nonlinearity has initially posed a bigger problem than the simultaneous equations aspect. Most attempts at estimation have been single equation approaches either using OLS on one of the input demand equations to derive estimates of ρ; or some iterative nonlinear technique to obtain direct estimates of the CES parameters. The problem of estimating the parameters of a set of simultaneous equations where one of them is nonlinear in parameters and the others are (log) linear is rather difficult to tackle. Some sort of linear approximation of the CES function seems to be required.

The initial attempt at fitting the CES function was made by Arrow, Chenery, Minhas and Solow. In the course of their estimation, they pointed out a variety of ways in which the CES parameters can be estimated. They also illustrated the use of the CES in making international comparisons of productive efficiency and for testing the predictions of the factor price equalisation theorem. We shall follow their approach here. ACMS fit CES production function on the assumption of constant returns to scale or $\mu = 1$. Thus we have instead of 4.4 (simplifying $\alpha_2 = 1 - \alpha_1$).

$$y = A[\alpha_1 x_1^{-\rho} + (1-\alpha_1)x_2^{-\rho}]^{-1/\rho} \tag{4.4a}$$

Instead of estimating 4.4a directly, ACMS evaluated the marginal product of one of the inputs–in their case of labour –let us say x_1.

$$\frac{\partial y}{\partial x_1} = A^{-\rho}\alpha_1 \left(\frac{y}{x_1}\right)^{1+\rho} \tag{4.16}$$

Setting $\partial y/\partial x_1 = p_1/p$ as before, we have

$$\frac{p_1}{p} = A^{-\rho}\alpha_1 (y/x_1)^{1+\rho} \tag{4.16a}$$

At this stage, they assumed that (p_1/p) was the exogenously given variable. By taking logarithms and rearranging we get (after adding the customary error term)

$$\ln(y/x_1)_t = \ln(A^{\rho}/\alpha_1) + \sigma \ln[p_1/p]_t + u_t \tag{4.16b}$$

ACMS' data were inter-country cross section data on twenty-four industries. They had the average product of labour (y/x_1) and the real wage rate (p_1/p) for each industry in each country. A crucial hypothesis to be tested here is whether

$\sigma = 1$, i.e. if the industry obeys a Cobb–Douglas production function. They did this by computing the t-statistic $(\hat{\sigma} - 1)/s\hat{\sigma}$, the term $s\hat{\sigma}$ being the standard error of $\hat{\sigma}$. They found that in fourteen out of twenty-four industries $\hat{\sigma}$ was significantly different from one at 90% or higher confidence level, thus confirming their expectation that the Cobb–Douglas production was a special case. While they do not dwell on the estimation of A and α_1, these can also be easily obtained. One way is to assume, as they did, that $A = 1$ which is valid for a cross section, and derive $\hat{\alpha}_1$ from 4.16b; or with $\hat{\sigma}$ obtained from 4.16b go back to 4.4a and derive estimates of A and α_1 from the resulting linear equation. The ACMS method has the advantage that it does not need data on the second input capital. Capital data are usually either unobtainable or non-comparable over time or across countries. The method also has simplicity since a log–linear equation is derived from the nonlinear production function.

Its biggest drawback is the failure to specify other relationships in the model such as the demand for capital.

Since ACMS had data pertaining to an inter-country cross section, they could treat the real wage w or (p_1/p) as a variable, which cannot be done in the pure case of a cross section of firms in an industry which we discussed above. It is not clear, however, whether to choose (p_1/p) or (y/x_1) as exogenous, or neither of them. One way to check the validity of the ACMS method is to obtain data on the other input, capital, and estimate σ again by a regression of (y/x_2) on (p_2/p). Dhrymes [1965] has done this in the context of a larger study testing for market imperfections. He computed the value of capital stock for industries in the US (inter-state cross section) by a formula

$$x_2 = \frac{py - p_1 x_1}{p_2} \tag{4.17}$$

Dhrymes discovered that for his sample of seventeen industries with inter-state cross section data in most cases the ACMS method yielded the result that $\hat{\sigma}$ was significantly different from one, while with the same data using ln (y/x_2) as dependent variable resulted in $\hat{\sigma}$ not being different from one. The ACMS estimator therefore appeared to be biased downward. One reason for the downward bias in the ACMS estimate could be their assumption of perfection in factor markets. If the labour market is imperfectly competitive, equation 4.16a is no longer valid. Instead of equating the marginal product to the real factor price, we have

$$\frac{\partial y}{\partial x_1} = \frac{1+\epsilon}{1+\eta}(p_1/p) = \phi(t)(p_1/p) \tag{4.16c}$$

where ϵ and η are respectively the inverses of the elasticity of supply of labour and the elasticity of demand for the product. The comparable estimation equation then is, instead of 4.16b,

$$\ln(y/x_1) = \ln(A^{\rho}/\alpha_1) + \sigma \ln \phi_t + \sigma \ln (p_1/p) + u_t \tag{4.16d}$$

The omission of the ϕ_t term therefore leads to a specification bias in $\hat{\sigma}$ and the bias is equal to $b\phi$, where b is the slope of the regression line between ln ϕ_t and ln (p_1/p). Thus if, for example, in markets with a low real wage, the elasticity of supply is high then b would be negative, showing a downward bias in $\hat{\sigma}$ estimated by ACMS method.

An alternative exploration of the ACMS method has been made by Maddala and Kadane [1966]. Their approach is to reverse the relationship of dependent and independent variables in 4.16b and regress ln (p_1/p) on ln (y/x_1) to obtain an estimate of $(1 + \rho)$ or $1/\sigma$. They first show the ACMS estimate of $\sigma[S_1]$ will always be lower than their (MK) estimate (S_2).

Exercise: Prove that the ACMS estimate of σ will always be lower than the MK estimate.

Estimating σ by their method and comparing it with ACMS method, MK get almost exactly opposite results. Whereas ACMS have 14 out of 24 industries with $\hat{\sigma}$ different from unity at the 90% level, MK get only 3 out of 24 industries with $\hat{\sigma}$ different from unity. They also show in a Monte-Carlo study that S_2 has uniformly less bias and in most cases lower mean square error than S_1.

While the ACMS method has been shown to have a downward bias, neither the Dhrymes method nor the MK method is necessarily any better. All three estimators have some bias and we need to work out this bias in the same way as we showed above in our discussion of Hoch's formula. This emphasises once again the need to treat the production function as one of a set of simultaneous equations and the importance of explicitly specifying the relations between the random error terms of these equations. We now turn to this task.

In order to treat the CES production function and the consequent input demand functions as a system, we have to obtain a linear approximation of the CES function. This is done by taking a Taylor series expansion round $\rho = 0$. At $\rho = 0$, we already know the CES is equivalent to Cobb–Douglas. We add the first-order term and neglect higher order terms. This yields a log–linear production function. It also has the advantage that in contrast to the ACMS approach, we do not need to assume constant returns to scale, i.e. $\mu = 1$. Then we get the following three equations (once again defining $\alpha_2 = 1 - \alpha_1$).

$$\left.\begin{aligned}
\ln y &= A + \mu\alpha_1 \ln x_1 + \mu(1-\alpha_1)\ln x_2 \\
&\quad - \tfrac{1}{2}\mu\rho\alpha_1(1-\alpha_1)[\ln x_1 - \ln x_2]^2 + u \\
\left(\frac{\rho}{\mu}+1\right)\ln y - (\rho+1)\ln x_1 &= \ln[p_1 A^{\rho/\mu}(p\mu\alpha_1)^{-1}] \\
&\quad + v_1 \\
\left(\frac{\rho}{\mu}+1\right)\ln y - (\rho+1)\ln x_2 & \\
&= \ln[p_2 A^{\rho/\mu}(p\mu)^{-1}(1-\alpha_1)^{-1}] + v_2
\end{aligned}\right\} \quad (4.18)$$

In the system above we clearly see that the production function reduces to Cobb–Douglas for $\rho = 0$ and the input demand equations reduce to the type we studied in Hoch's problem. The important thing is that even if $\rho \neq 0$ and $\mu \neq 1$, we have three equations which are log–linear in the parameters. Compared to the Cobb–Douglas case, we have a larger number of parameters to estimate and therefore we should carefully examine the possibilities of identification by prior restrictions on the errors. Kmenta (1967) has worked out consistent estimators under different alternative assumptions about the variance/covariance matrix of error terms. In order to simplify the discussion of Kmenta's method, we rewrite 4.18:

$$\left.\begin{aligned}
\ln y_t - \mu\alpha_1 \ln x_{1t} - \mu(1-\alpha_1)\ln x_{2t} & \\
+ \tfrac{1}{2}\mu\rho\alpha_1(1-\alpha_1)(\ln x_{1t} - \ln x_{2t})^2 &= \ln k_0 + u_t \\
(\rho/\mu + 1)\ln y_t - (\rho+1)\ln x_{1t} &= \ln k_1 + v_{1t} \\
(\rho/\mu + 1)\ln y_t - (\rho+1)\ln x_{2t} &= \ln k_2 + v_{2t}
\end{aligned}\right\} \quad (4.18a)$$

Case 1. $E(u_t v_{it}) = E(v_{1t} v_{2t}) = 0$. Given the independence of v_{1t} and v_{2t} the two input demand equations can be used to estimate $(\rho/\mu + 1)/(\rho + 1)$ consistently. In fact, each of them is just identified and we could use either of them. But the estimates derived from either have to be in agreement with each other since they involve the same parameters. Kmenta therefore multiplies them together to get, in terms of sample moments, a quadratic equation.

$$\hat{F}^2 \ \hat{\text{var}} \ln y + \hat{F}(\hat{\text{cov}} \ln y \ln x_1 + \hat{\text{cov}} \ln y \ln x_2) + \hat{\text{cov}} \ln x_1 \ln x_2 = 0 \tag{4.19}$$

$\hat{F}$ is then the estimate of $F = [\rho/(\mu + 1)]/(1 + \rho)$ derived by solving the quadratic equations. Of the two roots (which will be real) we choose that which minimises the residual sum of squares in the production function which can now be rewritten

$$\ln y = a_0 + a_1 \ln z_{1t} + a_2 \ln z_{2t} + a_3 \ln z_{3t} + e_t \tag{4.20}$$

where

$$a_0 = \ln A/(1 - Fa_1 - Fa_2)$$

$$\mu\alpha_1 = a_1/(1 - Fa_1 - Fa_2)$$

$$\mu(1 - \alpha_1) = a_2/(1 - Fa_1 - Fa_2)$$

$$-\tfrac{1}{2}\rho\mu\alpha_1(1 - \alpha_1) = a_3/(1 - Fa_1 - Fa_2)$$

$$\ln z_{1t} = F \ln y_t - \ln x_{1t}$$

$$\ln z_{2t} = F \ln y_t - \ln x_{2t}$$

$$\ln z_{3t} = (\ln x_{1t} - \ln x_{2t})^2$$

and e_t is proportional to u_t. Once we have estimated F, then we form z_{1t}, z_{2t} and z_{3t} and proceed to estimate the coefficients a_0, a_1, a_2 and a_3 which will give us the parameter estimates. These estimates are consistent if the error variance matrix is diagonal as assumed. This corresponds to Hoch's case where profit maximisation proceeds according to expected rather than actual output. Since use is made of the just-identified input demand equations, the method is called modified indirect least squares.

Case 2. We have assumed above that the factor and product prices are identical for each t-observation. Let us now look at the ACMS case where, given an inter-country cross section, we can take prices to be variable but we assume them to be exogenous. Without much rewriting, we can subtract one of the input demand equations from the other and have

$$\ln x_{2t} - \ln x_{1t} = \frac{1}{1+\rho}\frac{(1-\alpha_1)}{\alpha_1} - \frac{1}{(1+\rho)}(\ln p_1 - \ln p_2)_t$$

$$+ \frac{1}{(1+\rho)}(v_{2t} - v_{1t}) \qquad (4.21)$$

Again we assume $E(v_{1t}v_{2t}) = 0$ and obtain a consistent estimate of 1 $(1 + \rho)$ by OLS. The next step is to obtain from the above regression computed values of $(\ln x_{2t} - \ln x_{1t})$ and of $(v_{2t} - v_{1t})/(1 + \rho)$, the error term. We need then computed values of $\ln x_{1t}$ or $\ln x_{2t}$ which can be worked out as

$$\ln x_{2t} = b_0 + b_1 \ln\left(\frac{p_2}{p}\right)_t + b_2 \ln\left(\frac{p_2}{p_1}\right)_t + b_3\left(\frac{p_2}{p_1}\right)$$

$$+ b_4 \epsilon_{1t}^2 + b_5 \epsilon_{2t} \qquad (4.22)$$

b_0 to b_4 are reduced form coefficients, ϵ_{1t} is the error term of the regression above of which we now have computed values, ϵ_{2t} is the reduced form error term combining u_t, v_{1t} and v_{2t}. From equation 4.21 we have $(\widehat{\ln x_{2t} - \ln x_{1t}})$ and from 4.22 we have $\widehat{\ln x_{2t}}$. We also have ϵ_{1t} and ϵ_{2t}, all the error covariances except the var u_t. We now have a modified 2SLS procedure using $\widehat{\ln x_{2t}}$ and $(\widehat{\ln x_{2t} - \ln x_{1t}})$ in the $\ln y_t$ equation.

Once again, we have had to emphasise the details of the estimation procedure to a considerable degree. This is to bring out the overwhelming importance of treating the production function as a system of equations. This simultaneity arises from the behavioural or economic-theoretic background of the problem. It entails, however, a search for a sophisticated estimation procedure. The specification of the economic relationship and the econometric estimation problem are intimately tied up together in the case of the production function. Neglecting the estimation problem in favour of a simple technique such as OLS only means that the results will not bear an economic interpretation.

Up to now, we have confined our discussion to the estimation of a production function with two inputs. We also assumed competitive conditions in product and factor markets. We can now look at the extensions of the production function to (i) the n-input case and (ii) the aggregate production function. We can only look at each of these aspects in brief but we shall indicate the broad lines of development.

(i) *n-input Production Function*. At the beginning of this chapter, we emphasised that inputs and outputs should be as homogeneous as possible. The homogeneity of inputs is difficult to achieve unless we disaggregate inputs into a number of categories. Thus a catch-all variable called 'labour' hides more than it reveals. Cross-classification by degree of skill and perhaps length of service may more closely approximate a labour input of equal skill and efficiency. There may be other relevant inputs. In agricultural production functions, water, fertilisers and pesticides may be included. Machines of different vintage, even if the same production process, should be specified if they improve over time. The crucial factor here is that the inputs specified be homogeneous and distinguishable according to a relationship of substitutability or complementarity with respect to one another.

The introduction of many inputs calls for a redefinition of the concept of elasticity of substitution. While comparing the degree of substitutability between pairs of inputs as their marginal product ratio changes, the *ceteris paribus* conditions regarding other inputs have to be carefully specified. Here, as in the case of the demand curve, the number of parameters to be estimated also increases rapidly.

In the two-input cases, our definition of the elasticity of substitution related to change in input ratio as the relative marginal product ratio changed. In the n-input case, one way of defining elasticity is to examine the relative change in the demand for the ith input by the firm as the price of jth input changes, *all other input quantities and/or prices remaining fixed.* For the Cobb–Douglas production function the generalisation to n inputs is easy. The elasticity of the ith input demand with respect to the jth price change is unity for all i and j when the other $n - 1$ prices and quantities are kept fixed. If one wants to specify that the elasticity of the substitution between pairs of inputs (as defined above) is different for different i combinations, we have to use the

CES production function. In its n-input version, the most general case is the following:

$$y = A[\Sigma\alpha_i x_i^{-\rho_i}]^{-1/\rho} \tag{4.23}$$

If $\rho_i = \rho$ for all i, we have the simplest extension of the two-inputs CES production function. For $\rho_i = \rho$, the elasticity of substitution is $1/(1+\rho)$ for all i, j pairs. In equation 4.23, the elasticity will be different according to the choice of i, j. The above version can also be extended to group inputs into subclasses so that the 'within-subclass' elasticity is different from the 'between-subclass' elasticity. For such a situation we have

$$y = A[\sum_{i=1}^{k}\sum_{j=1}^{n_i}(\alpha_j x_{ij})^{-\rho_i}]^{-1/\rho} \tag{4.24}$$

Here we have k subclasses with n_i inputs in each ith subclass. It must be emphasised that while such generalisations are interesting, the problems of estimating these parameters are formidable. The Cobb–Douglas production function while most restrictive about the elasticity of substitution is the easiest to estimate. Hoch's estimator in the two-input case carries over to the n-input case. In the CES case, the Kmenta approximation can be generalised to n inputs to yield what is called the transcendental logarithmic production function.

(ii) *Aggregate Production Functions.* At the beginning of this chapter, we listed various questions we could answer with the help of production functions and we briefly indicated that inter-country and inter-temporal comparisons of growth rates as well as the study of macroeconomic income distribution were among the questions often answered by using an aggregate production function. In our discussion up to now we have indicated that the desired specification of the production function should be at a micro level–an individual firm or a particular plant. As far as possible inputs should be specified in terms of flows of homogeneous input services. Much applied econometric work, however, looks at an industry or country when fitting production functions. Thus in their pioneering study Cobb and Douglas fitted a production function for the US economy over a number of years. The work by Arrow and others cited above consisted of inter-country cross section data for two-digit level industries. How legitimate is the notion of an aggregate production function with aggregate inputs labour and capital?

The predictive performance of the aggregate Cobb–Douglas production function has been consistently high. Douglas (1948) in his Presidential Address to the American Economic Association summarised a large body of cross section and time series results for different countries and industries for which the Cobb–Douglas production function estimates (by OLS) fitted remarkably well. It was also striking that the exponent of the labour variable was close to the observed share of wages in total income. Since this result can be established through a combination of the Cobb–Douglas production function and the marginal productivity theory of distribution, it was widely accepted that the Cobb–Douglas production function was a valid representation of aggregate technology and that its predictions confirmed the marginal productivity theory of distribution. In a catch phrase, one could assert that the world was Cobb–Douglas. Even the introduction of the CES production function did not disturb this view since, in many cases, the elasticity of substitution turned out to be not significantly different from one (as the MK reversal of ACMS results showed).

The objections to such a simplified view of the world were first raised and sustained over a long period by Joan Robinson. The marginal productivity theory was originally stated at the microeconomic level and the meaningfulness of marginal product at aggregate level was questioned. It is now known that these objections relate to measurability of capital but also that they go deeper. The question is what are the conditions under which microeconomic production functions can be aggregated to yield a two-input Cobb–Douglas (or for that matter CES) production function. In particular, such an aggregate needs to be *invariant to market prices and the economic behaviour of entrepreneurs* for its pretension to being a technological relationship to be taken seriously. The measurability of capital is important here not only because capital goods may be more heterogeneous in terms of age and productivity than labour but also because capitalists' investment behaviour may lead to fluctuations in the value of capital independent of any technological factors. The only way to aggregate two disparate units of capital would be to take their market values but this already implies that market values are adequate measures of productivity, i.e. that micro-units value capital according to the dictates of the marginal productivity theory. Thus we may compute the flow price of capital as

$$c = P(r + \delta - \dot{P}/P)$$

where c is flow price, P stock price, r the discount rate, δ depreciation rate and $\dot{P}/P$ capital gain. This however derives from a world of complete certainty and equilibrium where everyone already values the capital goods in accordance with marginal productivity theory. One cannot measure separate capital goods this way, aggregate them into a macroeconomic capital measure and then proceed to 'test' the marginal productivity theory. Measures of aggregate inputs are thus dependent on market prices and economic behaviour and therefore cannot be invariant to them.

But there is still the evidence that Cobb–Douglas production functions fit well and predict the observed wage share. How do we explain this even if we do not attach economic meaning to the equation as a technological production function? This is a very complex and as yet controversial matter. In a recent simulation study, Franklin Fisher (1971) has provided one explanation. He has established that if the wage share happens to be roughly constant for whatever set of reasons, even though the true microeconomic production functions *do not* aggregate to a Cobb–Douglas production function, a Cobb–Douglas production function will still give a good fit and the exponent of labour will be a good explanation of the wage share. It is also necessary that the aggregate variables should roughly move together. The constancy of wage share, however, appears as the cause of the success of the Cobb–Douglas production function rather than its consequence. If wage shares are not constant then the Cobb–Douglas function will not perform well.

An aggregate production function thus appears to be a useful summary descriptive statistic. It need have no relation to the technology at the micro or macro level, but for predicting the course of output in the short run it may perform reasonably well. It is necessary to be clear therefore that the use of an aggregate production function should be confined to such purposes. One use to which it has been put is to provide an explanation of the factors contributing to economic growth. We turn in the next chapter to the measurement problems encountered if we use the production function to provide this explanation.

Bibliographical Notes

Literature on the theory and estimation of production functions is quite large. The early article by Cobb and Douglas (1928) is still worth reading and, in Murray Brown (1967), Douglas also explains the background to his research. For Klein's method of estimation the sources are Klein (1953) and Dhrymes (1962). Hoch's work is in his 1958 *Econometrica* article which was further extended in another article in *Econometrica* in 1962 and is generalised in Hoch and Mundlak (1965). The CES production function was first put forward by H. D. Dickinson and is also in Solow's *QJE* 1956 article on growth theory. Its estimation was first undertaken in Arrow, Chenery, Minhas and Solow, *RE Statistics* (1961). Some of the subsequent work is summarised in Nerlove's survey article in M. Brown (1967). There have been efforts to specify a variable elasticity of substitution production function but the general form for production functions has now been put forward by Jorgensen and his associates and covers all such cases, see Jorgensen *et al.* (1975).

On the debate concerning the validity of the aggregate production function, there are again many references but Fisher (1971) is a good point at which to start.

5
Measurement problems in econometric analysis: technical change

In the previous chapter, we concentrated on the problems of identification and estimation of the production function. We took for granted that the production function as well as the behavioural equations were correctly specified. We noted that the variables should all be measured in flow terms but we did not examine what this entailed. We now concentrate on the problem of measurement and the inter-related problem of specification.

The several attempts made in the last twenty years at measuring technical change at the aggregate and the industrial level illustrate the measurement problem. Technical change is the Great Unknown—the residual in economic theory. Attempts have been mainly confined to measuring the effects of technical change rather than explaining why it occurs. Unlike demand theory, there is no firm basis of economic theory from which we can obtain testable predictions. The problem in fact arises from the inadequacy of received production theory to explain certain observed economic phenomena. Empirical work using production functions has stumbled upon this residual and theory is only beginning to grapple with it.

One way to introduce technical change is to think of it as a shift of the production function over time. This is done by introducing a time variable among the arguments in the production function, e.g. equation 4.1 of Chapter 4. We have

$$y = f(x_1, \ldots x_n, t) \qquad (5.1)$$

Since the production function shift is a phenomenon taking place over time, we can make the role of time more explicit by dating all the inputs and outputs as follows:

$$y(t) = f[x_1(t), \ldots, x_n(t), t] \qquad (5.1a)$$

The extra time variable implies that an identical quantity of inputs at two different points of time—t and t'—will yield different quantities of output; in general if $t' > t$ then $y(t') > y(t)$ even when $x_i(t) = x_i(t')$ for all i. Technical change is then an upward shift of the production function. The problem of measuring technical change is that of measuring the shift while at the same time being reasonably sure that the measured inputs at the two points of time are indeed identical. If output as well as input quantities have changed at the two points of time, the problem of separating the shift of the production function from the effect of a sheer increase in inputs becomes an identification problem.

An alternative characterisation of technical change is through the efficiency parameter. If we can regard the efficiency parameter as a time dependent variable, then we can modify the explicitly production functions of Chapter 4 (equations 4.3 and 4.4) as follows:

$$y(t) = A(t)x_1(t)^{\alpha_1} x_2(t)^{\alpha_2} \qquad (5.2)$$

$$y(t) = A(t)[\alpha_1 x_1(t)^{-\rho} + (1-\alpha_1) x_2(t)^{-\rho}]^{-1/\rho} \qquad (5.3)$$

$A(t)$ is now the effect of technical change. Given identical input quantities, we have $y(t')/y(t) = A(t')/A(t)$ in both cases.

The problem of technical change arose in the context of an examination of the sources of US economic growth. We observe that over the last hundred years or more, per capita output/income in USA has grown and so has the stock of productive assets and the population. An obvious question to ask is how much of the growth of income is due to the growth of productive assets and how much due to the larger population. If output is a function of inputs alone as in equation 4.1, then we should be able to relate the growth of output to the growth of inputs. At this stage, our concern is with economic growth in the aggregate rather than with

changing productivity of inputs from growth of inputs themselves? Assuming w_i to be constant over time will lead to approximation errors, which will become more serious as our time span gets larger. Like many other insoluble problems, this is an index number problem. It is serious in this case because the measures we derive of $\dot{f}/f$ crucially depend upon the assumptions we make in this regard.

The problems above are of course only artificially separated. They are inextricably interwoven in one great AGGREGATION-MEASUREMENT-INDEX NUMBER problem. In what follows, we shall proceed historically and see how different authors tackled these problems.

The pioneering investigation was by Abramowitz (1950). He was concerned to analyse the reasons for the growth of the American economy over nearly a hundred years. Taking as his measure of output, net national product (NNP) per capita, Abramowitz observed that between the decade 1869–78 and the decade 1944–53, NNP per capita in 1929 constant prices had approximately quadrupled while population had more than tripled, giving an average annual growth rate of 3.5% per annum in NNP and 1.9% in NNP per capita. To explain this, he looked at the growth of two catch-all inputs—labour and capital. He measured labour by manhours, thus implicitly neglecting skill differences and age-sex-educational achievement composition and thereby assuming a mass of undifferentiated homogeneous labour input. He found that over the period, there was a slight decline in labour input per capita since, while population had grown, the working week had shortened and participation rates had also changed. Total capital, in which he included land, structures, producers' durable equipment, inventories and net foreign claims, had increased ten times and tripled in per capita terms.

Armed with an implicitly two-input production function, Abramowitz proceeded to measure the contribution of input growth to output growth by taking as his weights the share of each input in total output in the base period. He thus assumed that the $w_i(t)$ are constant and that they are measured by the income shares. The equation of earnings share with productivity weights can be easily rationalised by assuming that marginal products will be equal or proportionate to the real price of the input. Given these constant weights, Abramowitz obtained a combined index of resource input. He found that this index had grown by only 14% over the entire period. The remaining growth in output is then explained by the pure shift of what he calls the productivity of the combined unit of input. This grew by 250%. An overwhelming proportion of output growth was thus explained not by the growth of inputs but by a residual.

Abramowitz was clearly aware of many of the restrictive assumptions he had made. He checked against the selection of 1929 as base year by choosing an earlier year (our problem (b) above) but found that the results did not change much. His preference for a ten-year average as a basis for observation was designed to eliminate cyclical influences. In his more formal econometric measurement of technical change, Solow [1957] corrected for this probable source of error by taking annual observations. While Solow's time period (1909–1949) was different, his results were similar to those of Abramowitz.

Solow starts with a neoclassical production function with two inputs—capital and labour—and a shift variable represented by time. We have therefore as a special case of equation 5.1 above,

$$y = f(K, L, t) \ldots \qquad (5.5)$$

y, K and L are observed values of output, capital and labour at time t and t is a shift variable. All the variables are macroeconomic aggregates. The unit of observation is one year. Having specified equation 5.5, Solow further assumes that the effect of t—technical change—is to shift the production function in such a manner as to leave the marginal rate of substitution between K and L unchanged, if the capital–labour ratio is unchanged. He calls this neutral technical change. The ratio of marginal products of capital and labour remains constant before and after the shift. Any observed changes in the ratio or the ratio of inputs is then solely due to change in the relative price of these inputs. This can be written

$$y = A(t)g(K, L) \qquad (5.5a)$$

As we shall show subsequently, not every production function which can be written as 5.5 can be translated as 5.5a. We are implicitly assuming also that the inputs K and L themselves remain unchanged in any other way. Their marginal products are allowed to increase over time but they must do so at an equal growth rate. Since technical change occurs not in the inputs but 'outside' them as it were, such a technical change is also characterised as *disembodied.* Given 5.5a we can write, as in 5.4a above,

$$\dot{y}/y = \dot{A}/A + \frac{g_K K}{y}\frac{\dot{K}}{K} + \frac{g_L L}{y}\frac{\dot{L}}{L} \qquad (5.5b)$$

Now if we further define $(g_K K/y)$ as λ_K, the share of capital in total income, and $(g_L L/y)$ as λ_L, the share of labour in total income, we have

$$\dot{y}/y = \dot{A}/A + \lambda_K \dot{K}/K + \lambda_L \dot{L}/L \qquad (5.5c)$$

If we further assume that our classification of inputs into K and L is exhaustive, all income must go either to K or L and therefore $\lambda_K + \lambda_L = 1$. This is identical to assuming constant returns to scale and every input being paid its marginal product.

Then we have

$$(\dot{y}/y - \dot{L}/L) = \dot{A}/A + \lambda_K(\dot{K}/K - \dot{L}/L) \qquad (5.5d)$$

On the left-hand side we have the rate of growth of output per unit of labour and on the right-hand side growth of the capital labour ratio plus the shift factor $\dot{A}/A$. In fact, if we start by assuming that our production function in 5.5 is homogeneous of degree one, then we can directly move to an expression such as 5.5d except that now $\dot{A}/A$ is equal to $\dot{f}/f$

Equation 5.5d enables Solow to calculate $\dot{A}/A$ for each year given growth rates of output per unit of labour and of the capital–labour ratio as well as a measure of capital's share in total output. Unlike Abramowitz whose weights were constant, Solow takes λ_K to be variable and equal to λ_{Kt} for year t. He thus obtains a better approximation to a changing weight. His measure of labour is similar to that of Abramowitz–manhours worked. His measure of capital is not of available capital but of capital utilised to allow for under-utilisation of capital stock in times of depression. To get this, he multiplies his time series $K(t)$ by the ratio of employed persons to the total labour force. Thus while his approach is similar to Abramowitz' in assuming two inputs and approximating productivity by income share, Solow takes changing weights and specifies his capital input to approximate the *flow* of capital services rather than the stock of available capital.

His annual time series enables Solow to calculate technical change from 5.5d as

$$\left(\frac{\Delta y}{y} - \frac{\Delta L}{L}\right)_t - \lambda_{Kt}\left(\frac{\Delta K}{K} - \frac{\Delta L}{L}\right)_t = \left(\frac{\Delta A}{A}\right)_t \tag{5.5e}$$

Taking A_0 as 1, Solow adds on for each year $(\Delta A/A)_t$ to obtain a time series of $A(t)$. Deflating $(y/L)_t$ by $A(t)$ he can find out the contribution of growth in capital intensity $(K/L)_t$ on growth of output. It turns out that between 1909–1949, seven eighths of the total change in per capita output is accounted for by the shift and only one-eight by the growth of capital intensity. Solow's results are thus very similar to those of Abramowitz when taken over a long time span. The unit of time measurement problem and the problem of approximating changing weights both of which Solow has tackled better than Abramowitz do not seem to make much difference to the final result. A large portion of observed growth of output remains to be explained rather than labelled as technical change.

The task of explaining technical change is bound up with what is called the classification of technical change. Technical change is defined as a shift of the production function and it can be visualised as an inward shift of the isoquant in the case of two inputs. A shift of the production function can, however, affect the two inputs differently. After the shift, we may have a capital-using bias or a labour-using bias. The isoquant can change its shape as a result of the shift. This causes identification problems for the economist since, before and after the shift, we may observe two different input-ratios but it is hard to separate the influence of a change in the shape of the isoquant as against a change due to movements in relative prices. The concept of *neutral* technical change was devised to separate out (1) movements of the isoquant, (2) movements along the isoquant and (3) changes in the shape of the isoquant as a result of shift.

Two definitions of neutral technical change have been the mainstay of the discussion in this area. They are known after their authors as Hicks neutral and Harrod neutral. As we shall see, they are both of the disembodied type although they relate to changing efficiency (marginal products) of the inputs.

Hicks neutral. The marginal rate of substitution (ratio of marginal physical products) remains unchanged before and after the shift as long as the ratio of inputs remains constant (figure 5.1); or

$$\left.\frac{\partial(f_i/f_j)}{\partial t}\right|_{x_i/x_j} = 0$$

A general way of characterising the Hicks neutral technical change is to write our production function (equation 5.5) in terms of two inputs as

$$y = f[a_1(t)K, a_2(t)L] \tag{5.6}$$

$a_1(t)$ and $a_2(t)$ are efficiency factors. We measure inputs not just by their physical measures K and L but by their efficiency as inputs.

If they remain unchanged in efficiency over time then $a_1(t)$ and $a_2(t)$ are constants. Any improvement in these inputs is otherwise caught by these factors. The Hicks neutral technical change is then defined as a situation where $a_1(t)/a_2(t)$ is a constant.

Harrod neutral. The Harrod neutral technical change is defined as the rate of increase in efficiency of labour occurring when the marginal product of capital remains constant if the average product of capital (inverse of the capital output ratio) remains unchanged. For Harrod, $a_1(t)$ in equation 5.6 is constant and $a_2(t)$ is the rate of technical change. Since this has the effect of increasing the efficiency of labour (equivalent to an expansion in the physical quantity of labour), it is called the rate of labour augmentation. In our general notation, the rate of technical progress (R) can be defined as

$$R = \frac{\partial \ln f}{\partial t} \tag{5.7}$$

$$= \eta_K \frac{\dot{a}_1(t)}{a_1(t)} + \eta_L \frac{\dot{a}_2(t)}{a_2(t)} \tag{5.7a}$$

where η_K is the output elasticity of capital (equal to capital's share under neoclassical assumptions) and η_L is similarly

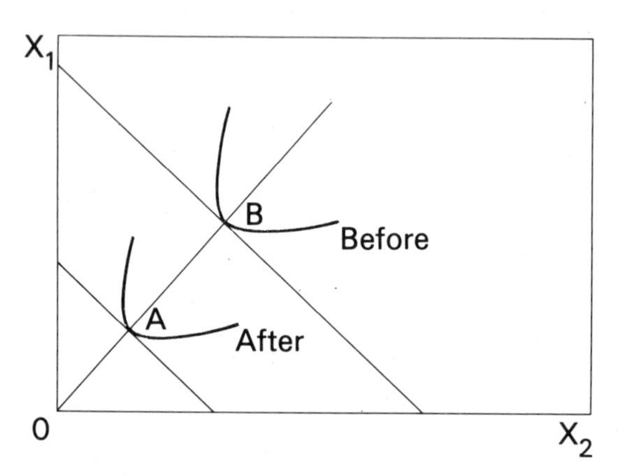

Fig. 5.1

defined. In Solow's case, by his assumption of Hicks neutrality, we have the two rates of change equal and

$$R = (\eta_K + \eta_L) \frac{\dot{a}(t)}{a(t)} \tag{5.7b}$$

$$= \dot{a}(t)/a(t) \qquad \text{(since income shares sum to one)} \tag{5.7c}$$

Exercise. If we assume the production function to be Cobb–Douglas, then it is impossible to distinguish between Hicks and Harrod neutrality since the parameters of the Cobb–Douglas production function give constant output elasticities of inputs. For Harrod neutrality, the ratio of marginal product to the average product of capital is constant but this is also the output elasticity of capital which is a parametric constant. Since the share of labour is also a constant, the Hicks neutrality condition is also satisfied simultaneously. Show this.

In the Hicks and Harrod neutral technical change, the improvement factor, $a_1(t)$ for example, applies equally to all capital stock whether new machines or hundred year old buildings. One can think of technical change as coming about due to new inventions and innovations which lead to greater productivity. The rate of adoption of these new inventions in reality depends on the rate of gross investment. If no investment is taking place then new inventions remain as blue prints. In this way of thinking, technical change in the form of higher productivity becomes *embodied* in new machines or new buildings. The date of birth–original construction–of the investment good indicates its productivity. This is known as the *vintage model* since the vintage of capital stock indicates its productivity.

Solow (1959) adopted a vintage model of capital to explain the rate of technical change in a study following his study cited above. The first assumption was that machines made this year were a constant percentage rate more productive than machines made last year and which are still in use this year. Let v indicate the date of construction of the machine, t the time at which the comparison is being made–thus Kv, t is a machine constructed at time v in use at time t. Corresponding to a machine of each vintage is a production function:

$$y_{vt} = F(K_{vt}, L_{vt}) \tag{5.8}$$

where y_{vt} is the output of a machine of vintage v in year t produced with inputs K_{vt} and the labour input associated with K_{vt}. Labour working on different machines is assumed to be homogeneous. Thus given equal quantities of labour working on machines of today's vintage and yesterday's vintage, the output of today's machine is λ percent higher than output from yesterday's machines. In particular, given equal inputs,

$$y_{v't}/y_{vt} = e^{\lambda(v-v')} \tag{5.9}$$

A second assumption of the Solow vintage model is behavioural. Since production is carried out on machines of different vintage, we need a behavioural rule which will determine the amount of labour used on each vintage machine. This is done by assuming that each unit of homogeneous labour input is paid a wage equal to its marginal product regardless of the vintage of machine it works with. This means that with a smooth neoclassical production function (isoquant asymptotic to the axes) no vintage ever goes out of production. (For an alternative characterisation see Johansen, 1959.) A third assumption is that machines of every vintage depreciate at a constant rate δ. Given these three assumptions the Solow model can be explicitly formulated for a Cobb–Douglas production function. As a special case of equation 5.8 we now have

$$y_{vt} = Be^{\lambda v} L_{vt}^{\alpha} K_{vt}^{(1-\alpha)} \tag{5.8a}$$

Total supply of labour over all vintages and total input over all vintages

$$L_t = \int_{-\infty}^{t} L_{vt} dv \tag{5.10a}$$

$$y_t = \int_{-\infty}^{t} y_{vt} dv \tag{5.10b}$$

Machines have productivity depending on vintage v and depreciate at rate δ. The number of machines produced in any one year is equal to the gross investment in that year, by definition. Therefore

$$K_{vt} = K_{vv} \exp[-\delta(t-v)] = I_v \exp[-\delta(t-v)] \tag{5.10c}$$

The first subscript referring to vintage year and the second to year of observation. A machine produced in 1960 still in use in 1970 is written

$$\begin{aligned} K_{1960,\,1970} &= \delta K_{1960,\,1970} \exp[-\delta(10)] \\ &= I_{1960} \exp[-\delta(10)] \end{aligned} \tag{5.10c'}$$

Let the wage rate be w_t and equating the marginal product of labour with the wage rate we have for each vintage v

$$w_t = \frac{\partial y_{vt}}{\partial L_{vt}} = B \exp(\lambda v) L_{vt}^{\alpha-1} \{I_v \exp[-\delta(t-v)]\}^{1-\alpha}$$

$$= \alpha B \exp[\lambda + \delta(1-\alpha)]v.\ L_{vt}^{\alpha-1} I_v^{1-\alpha}. \exp[-\delta(1-\alpha)t] \quad (5.11a)$$

Solving for L_{vt} we have

$$L_{vt} = (\alpha B)^{1/(1-\alpha)} \exp\{[\lambda/(1-\alpha)] + \delta\}v.\ \exp(-\delta t) I_v w_t^{1/(\alpha-1)} \quad (5.11b)$$

$$= h(t) \exp(\theta v).\ Iv$$

where $h(t) = B^{1/(1-\alpha)} \exp(-\delta t) w_t^{1/(\alpha-1)}$ and $\theta = \{[\lambda/(1-\alpha)] + \delta\}v$.

Given our behavioural assumptions, the amount of labour employed on any machine is a function of the wage rate, and the number of machines of that vintage originally produced. Due to exponential depreciation, however, this employment declines over time at a constant rate δ. The superior productivity of machines of younger vintage ensures that more labour will be employed for machines of more recent vintage than for older machines, *ceteris paribus*, since $\theta > 0$.

Aggregating labour over all vintages and output over all vintages we encounter the aggregate production function which incorporates the crucial vintage assumption

$$\left.\begin{aligned} y_t &= B\bar{e}^{[\delta/(1-\alpha)]t} L_t^{\alpha} J_t^{(1-\alpha)} \\ J_t &= \textstyle\int_{-\infty}^{t} e^{\theta v} I_v dv \end{aligned}\right\} \quad (5.12)$$

Instead of our usual measure of capital stock which adds up all previous investments equally, J_t is the *weighted* sum of past investments, the weights being determined by the rate of technical change embodied in the new machines. But we cannot have a measure J_t until we know λ and δ so no straightforward estimation of 5.12 is possible. Solow therefore takes *a priori* values of α and δ to obtain estimates of λ. A little manipulation of 5.12 can be made giving the following answer

$$\frac{(\dot{R} + \delta R)}{I_t} = B^{1/(1-\alpha)} e^{\lambda t/(1-\alpha)} \tag{5.13}$$

where $R_t = y_t^{1/(1-\alpha)}/L_t^{\alpha/(1-\alpha)}$ and $\dot{R} = dR/dt$. The left-hand side of 5.13 can be expressed as a dependent variable after taking logarithms of both sides, and the regression coefficient of t can be made to yield λ, given our assumed value of α. Solow assumed two alternative values for α of $\frac{2}{3}$ and $\frac{3}{4}$ and for δ of 0.04 (assuming a 25-year life of machines). One restriction is that the left-hand side of 5.13 must be positive. Solow found that for 1919–1953 there were five observations, 1920, 1930, 1933, 1936 and 1946 when $\Delta R_t + 0.04R_{t-1}$ was negative. The Solow model thus works only when GNP does not decline substantially—for years of depression it fails. Solow found that $\alpha = \frac{3}{4}$ gave a better fit and implied a λ estimate of 0.025 or $2\frac{1}{2}$% per annum.

Solow's problem can be posed in a much more general framework. He has to assume values of α and δ in order to be able to obtain a linear estimator for λ because his basic equation 5.12 has a nonlinearity in the form of the variable J_t. J_t is itself a function of λ, α and δ and therefore cannot be computed to estimate the parameters of 5.12. One approach would be to assume various alternative combinations for λ and δ and for each combination compute J_t and then the predicted value of output. We can then choose the combination that minimises the residual sum of squares. (This is similar to the Hildreth–Lu method for estimating the autoregressive parameter ρ discussed in Chapter 2 above, it is a general method for tackling nonlinearity in parameters.) This is cumbersome, however. Wickens (1970) has suggested a maximum likelihood approach to the joint estimation of α, δ and λ by using a Taylor series expansion of J_t round an initial value of θ. (This is another general method for tackling nonlinearities and we recall from Chapter 4 that Kmenta used it in order to obtain estimates of the CES production function.) This method avoids the problem Solow had about the negative values of the dependent variable in equation 5.13 for selected years. By adding disembodied technical change as well as embodied technical change, a more rigorous test of the hypothesis about the presence of embodied technical change can be carried out. As we have already indicated in Chapter 2, the advantage of using a maximum likelihood estimator is clear in such a case since we have in equation 5.12, coefficients which are nonlinear functions of the parameters. The FIML method generates the estimates of the coefficients as well as of the parameters and (more important) the asymptotic standard errors of the parameters can be derived from the variance–covariance matrix of the coefficient estimates.

Wickens starts with an equation similar to 5.12 but adds disembodied technical change going on at the rate μ. Then assuming CRTS and putting $(1-\alpha) = \beta$ the Wickens version of equation 5.12 is

$$\begin{aligned} y_t &= Ae^{(\mu - \delta\beta)t} L_t^{\alpha} J_t^{\beta} \\ J_t &= \int_v e^{(\lambda + \delta)v} I_v \, dv \end{aligned} \tag{5.12a}$$

Notice that for Solow the weighting factor was $\theta = [(\lambda/\beta) + \delta]$. Thus Wickens' parameter λ relates to Solow's λ with a proportionate factor β. This implies a modification in the process by which labour is allocated over different vintages. Comparing 5.12 to 5.12a we also notice that 5.12 assumes $\mu = 0$. Wickens proceeds to expand J_t round initial values of $(\lambda + \delta) = \theta_1$. [We also label $(\mu - \delta\beta) = \theta_2$.] J_t is clearly $f(\theta_1)$ and therefore

$$\begin{aligned} J_t &= f(\bar{\theta}_1) + (\theta_1 - \bar{\theta}_1) f'(\theta_1) + \tfrac{1}{2}(\theta_1 - \bar{\theta}_1)^2 f''(\bar{\theta}_1) + \ldots \\ &= \int_v \exp(\bar{\theta}_1 v) I_v \, dv + (\theta_1 - \bar{\theta}_1) \int_v v . \exp(\bar{\theta}_1 v) I_v \, dv + \ldots \\ &= [\bar{K}_t + (\theta_1 - \bar{\theta}_1) C_t] \end{aligned}$$

Then approximating $\ln[\bar{K}_t + (\theta_1 - \bar{\theta}_1)C_t]$ further, Wickens obtains

$$\begin{aligned} \ln J_t &= \ln[\bar{K}_t + (\theta_1 - \bar{\theta}_1) C_t] \\ &= \ln \bar{K}_t + \ln[1 + (\theta_1 - \bar{\theta}_1) C_t / \bar{K}_t] \\ &= \ln \bar{K}_t + (\theta_1 - \bar{\theta}_1) C_t / \bar{K}_t \end{aligned}$$

We get from 5.12a after incorporating the above

$$\begin{aligned} \ln(y_t/L_t) &= \ln A + \theta_2 t + \beta \ln(\bar{K}_t/L_t) \\ &\quad + \beta(\theta_1 - \bar{\theta}_1) C_t / \bar{K}_t + u_t' \end{aligned} \tag{5.12b}$$

The random term u'_t has now been added as usual. It contains, beside the pure random term that should be attached to 5.12 and 5.12a, the higher order terms of the Taylor series expansions which we have ignored. We can proceed to obtain FIML estimates by assuming u'_t to be normally independently distributed and maximising the joint likelihood function of u'_t. We have, however, four parameters α, δ, β, and λ but only three coefficients. Of these β is clearly identified but the other three have to be jointly determined by θ_1 and θ_2. While it is not possible to solve for them separately, we can test some hypotheses about them as we see below. Our assumptions for u'_t imply that we only need to use OLS on 5.12b initially and then iterate until two successive estimates of θ_1 converge.

Before proceeding with the estimation of 5.12b Wickens makes two further modifications. The summation over vintages in the integral for J_t goes from $-\infty$ to t. Instead of using this a base year is taken and $\bar{K}_t$ and C_t are evaluated from a base year. For this we need an initial value in year 0 for $\bar{K}(0)$ and $C(0)$. Wickens assumes several values for these and runs his regressions for each value of $\bar{K}(0)$ and $C(0)$. Thus,

$$\bar{K}_t^* = \bar{K}(0) + \int_0^t \exp(\bar{\theta}_1 v) I_v dv$$

$$C_t^* = C(0) + \int_0^t v. \exp(\bar{\theta}_1 v) I_v dv$$

and further

$$\bar{K}(0) = I(0)/\theta_1 + \gamma$$

$$C(0) = -I(0)/(\theta_1 + \gamma)^2$$

where γ is the annual rate of growth I in the years previous to year 0. 1900 was taken to be the base year.

A second modification was to introduce additional variables in 5.12b to take account of fluctuations in capacity utilisation. Following the practice in Solow's earlier work the rate of unemployment (U) was taken as the proxy and two terms were added to 5.12b in U and U^2. This done, Wickens proceeded to estimate 5.12b by OLS for 1900–1960 for three alternative values of $\bar{K}(0)$ and three alternative values of $C(0)$. Examining the residuals of these nine OLS equations, Wickens found that in every case the Durbin–Watson statistic indicated a positive serial correlation (all values of *DW* lay between 0.85 and 1.04). In order to remove the effect of serial correlation, Wickens derived an estimate of the autoregressive coefficient ρ from the asymptotic expression for the *DW* statistic and used this ρ to transform all his variables (see Chapter 2). Doing this he found that his estimate of θ_1, which was significant in OLS, was non-significant once the autoregressive transformation had been applied. The significance of θ_1 in OLS was thus traced to the downward bias in standard errors which is present when the errors are autoregressive. Solow's finding of embodied technical change is thus attributable more to time series properties than to economic behavioural phenomena.

Wickens' results for θ_2 were significant after the autoregressive transformation rather than before. Thus, θ_2 is positive and significantly different from zero, whereas θ_1 is positive and not significantly different from zero. Now $\theta_1 = (\lambda + \delta)$ by definition and δ is positive, so we can safely assume λ is unimportant. On the other hand $\theta_2 = \mu - \beta\delta$ which, if positive, is doubly reassuring about μ being notably positive but also larger than $\beta\delta$. Thus we use prior information about the non-negativity of δ to conclude that λ is unlikely to be positive and significant whereas μ is positive and significantly different from zero. We can go further and say that if δ is about 0.02, as is found in other studies, $\lambda + \delta$ ought to be significantly greater than (not just different from) 0.02. None of the values of θ_1 pass this test. For μ we can again say that if we let $\beta = 0.025$ then $\beta\delta = 0.005$, and if θ_2 is not significantly different from zero we cannot reject the hypothesis that $\mu = \beta\delta$. We may say that θ_2 being positive and significant is a confirmation of $\mu > 0.005$. Wickens' results show θ_2 being about 0.10. This confirms our earlier discussion about many hypotheses requiring one-tailed tests.

Wickens' results show the importance of appropriate stochastic specification for arriving at a valid economic interpretation of empirical phenomena. In a sense one can even say of Wickens' approach that he should have started with an error term in equation 5.12a. Then, when taking approximations for J_t and $\ln J_t$, the higher order terms will be clearly seen to be entering the error term u'_t in equation

5.12b. Since many of these higher order terms would be weighted sums of past investments, this would give us a fore-warning of the error behaving in a serially correlated fashion.

Solow's reason for specifying embodied technical change in the production function was to be able to provide an economic rationale for the 'residual'. It turns out, however, to be a statistical freak at least for one particular sample. This raises general questions about the sensitivity of technical change to measurement problems as well as estimation problems. We have already referred to the problems associated with the notion of an aggregate production function. Jorgensen and Grilliches (1965) have carried out a complete set of checks on the index number problems involved in measuring technical change as a residual from an aggregate production function. They also purport to seek an economic behavioural explanation for all observed changes in outputs, inputs, prices and incomes rather than just for 'technical change'.

The Jorgensen–Grilliches (JG) study is similar in spirit to those of Abramowitz and Solow. They wish to separate a pure shift of the production function from a movement along it. In doing so, however, they wish to avoid many of the errors of aggregation and measurement that we listed above. In the context of our equations 5.4a or 5.4b, they allow for a large number of inputs and a careful measurement of f_i or $w_i(t)$. In the original Abramowitz and Solow studies, technical change was falling from heaven, as it were, and could be called a costless shift of the production function. A motivation for the JG study was to check, with the help of a strictly neoclassical general equilibrium framework, the validity of such a finding. In a neoclassical world with perfect competition, any factor or product improvements would be transmitted through the price mechanism, and factor rewards as well as product prices would adjust as a result of profit maximising behaviour of producers and utility maximising behaviour of consumers to reflect any such improvement. There may still be left an overall neutral shift of the production function but this has to be correctly identified.

Jorgensen and Grilliches start with a social accounting framework of many outputs and many inputs where the total value of outputs equals the total sum paid to the inputs. Thus, if factor prices are p_i and output prices q_j, outputs labelled y_j and inputs x_i, we have a national income identity:

$$\sum_{j=1}^{m} q_j y_j = \sum_{i=1}^{n} p_i x_i \tag{5.14}$$

From this we can derive expressions for growth rates of output and inputs or, as an alternative (dual), growth rates of input prices and output prices.

$$\sum_j \mu_j(\dot{y}_j/y_j) = \sum_i w_i(\dot{x}_i/x_i) \tag{5.14a}$$

$$\Sigma\, \mu_j \left(\frac{\dot{q}_j}{q_j}\right) = \Sigma\, w_i \frac{\dot{p}_i}{p_i} \tag{5.14b}$$

where $\mu_j = q_j y_j/\Sigma q_j y_j$ and $w_i = p_i x_i/\Sigma p_i x_i$ and thus, since μ_j and w_i are weights of each output and input in the growth index, these weights are by definition non-negative and they sum to unity. Equations 5.14a and 5.14b are two alternative definitions/measurements of the growth rate over time. As before, if our observations are from time series, μ_j and w_i will be time dependent and 5.14a and 5.14b will have to be approximated in discrete time intervals (quarters, years, decades). In choosing a measure of w_{it}, we saw that Abramowitz took them as constants equal to base period w_i while Solow took observations as profit share for each year thus allowing for a better approximation. JG choose the Solow method.

To link 5.14 to 5.14b with the notion of a neoclassical production function, JG choose a generalised version of 5.1 to allow for many outputs and many inputs assuming constant returns to scale:

$$F(y_1, y_2, \ldots, y_m, x_1, x_2, \ldots, x_n) = 0 \tag{5.15}$$

A shift of the production function can then be defined as

$$GF = \Sigma\left(\frac{F_j y_j}{\Sigma F_j y_j} \cdot \frac{\dot{y}_j}{y_j}\right) - \Sigma\left(\frac{F_i x_i}{\Sigma F_i x_i} \cdot \frac{\dot{x}_i}{x_i}\right) \tag{5.15a}$$

where $1/G = \Sigma F_j y_j = -\Sigma F_i x_i$.

Now equation 5.15a is reminiscent of our equation 5.4a and the expressions on the r.h.s. involving $\dot{y}_j$ and $\dot{x}_i$ are also similar to 5.14a. If we now assume perfect competition in all output and factor markets and optimising behaviour on the part of all economic agents, we get the familiar conditions of general equilibrium that the price ratio of any output and/or input pair is proportional to the marginal rate of transformation or the ratio of partial derivatives of F in equation 5.15 with respect to the appropriate variables. Thus

$$\frac{q_j}{p_i} = \frac{F_j}{F_i}; \frac{p_i}{p_i'} = \frac{F_i}{F_i'}. \frac{q_j}{q_j'} = \frac{F_j}{F_j'}, \text{ etc.}$$

Given these neoclassical assumptions, we have now made a perfect link between our social accounting framework of 5.14 and 5.14a and the production function relationships of 5.15 and 5.15a. (A similar link can be made for 5.14b by considering the dual of 5.15 which is an equation in terms of output prices and input prices and would represent the zero abnormal profit-lowest average cost surface for all outputs and inputs.) Now we can establish a stronger correspondence by writing 5.14a to be commensurate with the definition of the shift in 5.15a.

$$\dot{y}/y = \sum_j \mu_j(\dot{y}_j/y_j); \qquad \dot{x}/x = \Sigma\, w_i(\dot{x}_i/x_i)$$

Total factor productivity is defined in the social framework as

$$\dot{p}/p = \dot{y}/y - \dot{x}/x$$

and is equal to $G\dot{F}$ above by our assumptions. $\dot{y}/y$ is an index of output such as an ideal GNP measure would try to capture and $\dot{x}/x$ is an index of input growth which, as we have seen above, Solow and Abramowitz were after.

What we have obtained up to now is a set of relationships. These relationships contain an innovation since many outputs and many inputs are being specified but we have not yet shown the advantages of doing this. We can now list a step by step improvement in measurement of total productivity (and therefore shift of the production function) by careful weeding out of aggregation and measurement errors. Jorgensen and Grilliches illustrate the results of their approach by studying US annual data between 1946 and 1965.

Stage 1: The Abramowitz measure. Taking conventional measures of GNP as output, capital and manhours, and combining capital and manhours with constant base-period weights, JG derive their first measure of technical change. Input growth explains 52.4% of the total growth in output. In terms of equation 5.5c, $(\dot{y}/y - \dot{A}/A)/(\dot{y}/y) = 52.4\%$.

Stage 2: The Solow measure with output disaggregation. Instead of using constant base-period weights, JG use each year's factor-share as weights to combine capital and manhours. This is what Solow did. JG show in their article that these changing weights correspond to a Divisia Index Number (w_{it} instead of w_i in our notation) which has several optimal properties, e.g. invariance of the index number as long as technology is unchanged. They disaggregate GNP into consumption goods and investment goods and combine them with their respective μ_{jt} to obtain a new index of output growth. Now input growth explains 54.3% of output growth.

Stage 3: Disaggregating the price index for capital. Capital appears as an input in the production function but investment goods appear as outputs. Inventories, for example, are part of capital inputs and correspond in terms of finished goods to consumer expenditure. JG obtain disaggregated price indices for structures, equipment and inventories and, by careful comparison of input prices with corresponding output price, indices for consumer durables, structures and private consumer expenditure obtain a better measure of capital input. This corrects for bias in input price indices as compared to output price indices. This raises the explanation of output growth to 61.1%.

Stage 4: Correcting for utilisation of input stocks. In his first investigation, Solow corrected his capital input for under-utilisation by multiplying the capital index with the employment rate. JG extend and refine this method for both inputs. To approximate the flow of input services from the stocks, they take an index of relative utilisation of power sources as an index of capital utilisation. They apply Denison's correction for variation in intensity of labour to their manhours. This correction places labour input below the minimum figure given by a number of men working. This correction for utilisation raises the explantion due to input change to 71.6%.

Stage 5: *Flow prices for capital services.* The prices of capital inputs used as yet are stock prices. For example, the price of a house is a stock price. A consumer of a house (dweller) gets from the house in any time period a service flow measured by an imputed rent. Imputed rent is thus a flow price corresponding to stock price of the house. In a world of no uncertainty, the price of a unit of capital goods is equal to the discounted value of the output stream. If P is the stock price, p is the flow price, r the rate of discount (equal to the market rate of interest under perfect competition) and δ the rate of depreciation, then in dynamic equilibrium

$$p = P(r + \delta)$$

Introduction of tax on profits or subsidies for faster replacement will modify this equation further (for a derivation see Chapter 6). For each category of capital input, land, residential and non-residential structures, equipment and inventories, a different depreciation rate and a different discount rate is appropriate. Tax rules also differ for different assets which have to be taken account of. Measuring flow prices this way improves the measurement of the weights considerably. This fivefold disaggregation of capital input and the correct flow prices raises the explanation to 82.7%.

Stage 6: *Flow prices for labour input.* Corresponding to the disaggregation of capital input, the labour input is disaggregated by educational achievement. Eight categories of education levels beginning from school level are distinguished and the reward to each category is measured for five cross section years. This allows for a better flow price for labour input by educational categories. Further disaggregation by skill, work experience, sex and age group is, of course, always possible. But by this time 96.7% of output growth is explained by input growth.

Technical change which originally was said to account for $\frac{7}{8}$ of observed growth of output can be seen to be a measurement error. In obtaining their more precise measure, JG assume constant returns to scale, perfect competition and a continuous state of dynamic equilibrium. These assumptions were implicit in Abramowitz's and Solow's work. The message of JG then is for a careful avoidance of aggregation and index number errors. They also imply that there is very little 'costless' shift of the production function. Every improvement in output and input gets paid for; every external economy is internalised by the market mechanism.

One major assumption throughout this chapter is that of an aggregate production function. Even equation 5.15 as adopted by JG, despite many output categories and many inputs, is an aggregate production function. On grounds of measurement of capital inputs as well as of internal consistency, this notion has been under increasing attack in recent years.[1]

Technical Change in a Microeconomic Context

As we said in the beginning of Chapter 4, as far as possible the notion of a production function should be confined to the firm or the plant level where it has a meaning as a *technological* relationship. We also cautioned then that the output and input variables should be *flow* variables. (In this sense, the attempts to measure technical change can be seen as several stages in the proper measurements of output and input flows.) There have been many attempts in recent years to measure technical change in a particular industry. Of these several efforts we shall discuss one to illustrate the problems that arise in a microeconomic context when measuring

1. See for a discussion and the main readings, G. C. Harcourt and N. F. Laing, *Capital and Growth*. In the context of our discussion of the Marschak–Andrews problem, the Cambridge (England) criticism of capital measurement and the aggregate production function can be seen as a further complication in the under-identification problem. We now have to add that both capital and labour prices also are endogenous in the aggregate model and their explanatory equations in turn involve other endogenous variables. A general lack of zero restrictions in each equation will then lead to under-identification.

technical change. This is a study by Ryutaro Komiya (1962) of technical progress in the industry producing electricity by means of steam power.

Komiya starts with the observation that between 1938 and 1956 average fuel requirement *per unit of electricity generated* (fuel input–output ratio) declined by 39% while labour and capital requirements *per unit of installed capacity* (input to capacity output ratio) declined by 51% and 11% respectively. There has therefore been some technical change in the steam power industry. The problem is to separate out the shift of the production function from the movement along the production function. In addition to this, unlike preceding authors, Komiya also allows for economies of scale rather than assume constant returns to scale. There are thus three aspects: (1) economies of scale, (2) factor substitution—movement along the production function, and (3) the shift in the production function. Unlike previous studies which are highly aggregative, Komiya's observations relate to plants.

The basic production function assumed by Komiya is also different from the standard neoclassical type. In the neoclassical p.f., the factor substitution possibility is always there. Even after a plant has been built, if relative factor prices change, the capital stock is assumed to be malleable and adaptable to a new capital labour ratio. Komiya allows for substitution possibilities *ex-ante* and not *ex-post*. When deciding to build a plant, the entrepreneur has a wide choice of techniques (input mixes): he may build a very automated capital intensive plant or a highly labour intensive one. Once a plant has been built, however, the input proportions cannot be changed. If factor prices change, the profitability of such a plant will change but no movement along the p.f. is possible to restore the original profitability.

Technical progress is allowed for by distinguishing the date of construction of a plant, a notion analogous to the Solow vintage capital model. Over time, technical knowledge improves and therefore the *ex ante* choice facing an entrepreneur is also different. A different production function has to be fitted for plants built at different times. One can, however, test for this assumption of technical change by testing whether production functions show any change over time. As we shall see, such a test can be devised in one of two different ways—by introducing dummy variables to allow for shifts over time or by an analysis of covariance. Komiya allows for a further distinction among plants according to the fuel they use—either coal or non-coal. The distribution of plants by age and type of fuel used is shown in Table 5.1.

Table 5.1. Number of new plants

Fuel type:	*Coal*($j = 1$)	*Non-coal*($j = 2$)	*Total*
1930–1945($i = 1$)	43	13	56
1946–1950($i = 2$)	48	14	62
1951–1953($i = 3$)	41	19	60
1954–1956($i = 4$)	44	13	57
	176	59	235

For each of the eight sub-groups in table 5.1, Komiya fitted a production function. He tried a Cobb–Douglas production function and a Leontieff production function (which he calls a limitational model). The results for the latter were better and hence we shall concentrate on that. The basic idea of the limitational model is that of all the inputs, one input acts as a constraint and, given the total availability of that constraint and the average output per unit of that input, total output is determined. Complementary inputs are then added in required proportions. Thus equation 5.1 can be rewritten for the limitational model as

$$y = \text{minimum}\ (a_1 x_1, a_2 x_2, \ldots, a_n x_n) \tag{5.17}$$

Implicitly, this production function allows for no substitution possibilities—the *ex ante* elasticity of substitution is therefore *zero* in this case. There are, therefore, only economies of scale and/or technical change remaining to be examined. Komiya fits log–linear input–output equations for each of the three inputs—capital (K), fuel (F) and labour (L). He measures capital in terms of the constant dollar cost of equipment per generating unit, neglecting costs of land and building. Fuel is measured in terms of B.t.u. per hour per generating unit when operated at capacity. Labour is measured in terms of number of employees per generating unit. It is recognised that any one plant may have more than one generating unit and this may lead to economies of scale. The measure of output (y) is the average size of generating unit in megawatts and the number of generating units per plant (N) is the scale variable. To each of the eight sub-groups listed in Table 5.1, the following three regressions are fitted

$$\ln F = \alpha_0 + \alpha_1 \ln y + \epsilon_1 \quad (5.18a)$$

$$\ln K = \beta_0 + \beta_1 \ln y + \beta_2 \ln N + \epsilon_2 \quad (5.18b)$$

$$\ln L = \gamma_0 + \gamma_1 \ln y + \gamma_2 \ln N + \epsilon_3 \quad (5.18c)$$

If β_1 (or γ_1) = 1 and β_2 (or γ_2) = 0 then we have constant returns to scale and taking either the plant or the generating unit as a measure of output makes no difference. By assumption there are no economies of scale in fuel consumption due to increasing the number of generating units. If the size of the average generating unit yields economies then α_1 or β_1 or γ_1 will be significantly less than one.

Technical change or shifts of the production function over time can now be checked for in two possible ways. Let us take for example equation 5.18a and write it out for each kth plant built in the ith time period and in the jth fuel group (suppressing for the time being the subscript on ϵ_1)

$$\ln F_{ijk} = \alpha_{0ij} + \alpha_{1ij} \ln y_{ijk} + \epsilon_{ijk} \quad (5.18a^{\mathrm{I}})$$

Now we can test whether the constant term α_{0ij} changes as i changes. If we observe that as i increases from 1 to 4, α_{0ij} goes down, then we have evidence of a downward shift in the input–output relationship over time. There is, of course, no reason either why $\alpha_{0i1} = \alpha_{0i2}$, i.e. coal and non-coal-using plants should have the same intercept. Similar remarks apply to the slope coefficient α_{1ij}. Changing parameters α_{0ij} and α_{1ij} as i and/or j change is then our evidence of technical change taking place over time (i) and at different rates for coal and non-coal-using plants (j).

We can now set up our two approaches for analysing such systematic changes in the intercept and slope. The first approach is the use of *dummy variables.* Dummy variables are artificial constructs and commonly though not always they take a value of either 1 or 0. Let us say that we want to distinguish plants by the type of fuel they use. We can then have for any one period (say $i = 1$) all the plants grouped together but add dummy variables indicating the type of plant, whether coal or non-coal using. With grouping of all observations for the period $i = 1$, we have

$$\ln F_{1k} = \alpha_{01} + \alpha_{11} \ln y_{1k} + \epsilon_{1k}. \tag{5.18a^{II}}$$

Now we have α_{01} instead of α_{011} and α_{012} and α_{11} instead of α_{111} and α_{112}. We are implying that neither the intercept nor the slope coefficient are different for coal-using plants as against non-coal-using plants. But we can allow for such difference by adding dummy variables. For the intercept difference we have a variable DJ_1 which takes a value of 1 for a coal-using plant (when $j = 1$) and 0 for a non-coal-using plant. We obtain

$$\ln F_{1k} = \alpha_{01} + \alpha_{11} \ln y_{1k} + \delta_{11} DJ_1 + \epsilon_{1k} \tag{5.18a^{III}}$$

Thus when $DJ_1 = 1$, i.e. for a coal-using plant, the intercept in fact is $\alpha_{01} + \delta_{11}$ while for a non-coal-using plant it is α_{01} only. For two types of plants we have only one dummy variable; why not have two? If we have a constant term α_{01} in the equation then adding on a second dummy variable DJ_2 taking on values of 1 for $j = 2$ and 0 for $j = 1$ with a coefficient of δ_{12} will violate the OLS assumption of full rank for our independent variable matrix, since $DJ_1 + DJ_2$ corresponds to the constant term variable X_0 which is a vector of 1's. This introduces linear dependence in our matrix of independent variables. In general therefore the rule is: If there is a constant term in an equation, the number of dummy variables for any particular classification should be one less than the number of separate classes. This holds for each type of classification.

Thus we can have one dummy variable for fuel type and three dummy variables for the age of plant to allow for variation of intercept along time and fuel type. We then obtain

$$\ln F_k = \alpha_0 + \alpha_1 \ln y_k + \delta_1 DJ_{1k} + \delta_2 DI_{1k} + \delta_3 DI_{2k} + \delta_4 DI_{3k} + \epsilon_k \tag{5.18a^{IV}}$$

Notice the changing subscript for the F, y and ϵ variables as we introduce the dummy variables. DI_1 analogously takes a value of 1 for plants built in the first time period and 0 everywhere else. Similarly for DI_2 and DI_3. α_0 is now the intercept for the non-coal-using plant built in the latest period ($j = 2, i = 4$). For a steady linear shift over time we expect

$$\alpha_0 < \alpha_0 + \delta_4 < \alpha_0 + \delta_3 < \alpha_0 + \delta_2$$

If we also want to let the slope change with fuel type or age of plant we can introduce a *multiplicative* dummy variable. It suffices to show this for the case of fuel type. Instead of 5.18a^{111} with DJ_1 we introduce a multiplicative dummy variable:

$$\ln F_{1k} = \alpha_{01} + \alpha_{11} \ln y_{1k} + \delta_{12}(DJ_1 . \ln y_{1k}) + \epsilon_{1k} \quad (5.18a^{V})$$

Now the intercepts are the same for $j = 1$, or 2 but the slope will be $\alpha_{11} + \delta_{12}$ for $j = 1$ and α_{11} for $j = 2$. We can therefore test for the presence of intercept shift or slope shift by fuel type or age of plant by (1) adding the appropriate number of dummy variables, (2) estimating the equation by OLS, and (3) checking the statistical significance of the coefficients of the dummy variable.

An alternative is covariance analysis. The intuitive idea behind it can be explained as follows. Let us compare equations 5.18a^{I} and 5.18a^{II}. Now 5.18a^{I} can be run for the two groups defined by $j = 1$ and $j = 2$ keeping $i = 1$. Equation 5.18a^{II} treats $j = 1$ and $j = 2$ alike. Do we lose anything by sacrificing this difference? If truly there is no difference in using coal ($j = 1$) or not using coal ($j = 2$) then equation 5.18a^{II} ought to perform just as well as the two equations using 5.18a^{I}. The only thing that remains is to compare their performance so as to allow for random differences. The method of covariance analysis is to take the residual sums of squares of the two equations of 5.18a^{I} say $\sum_k \hat{e}_{11k}^2$ and $\Sigma\, \hat{e}_{12k}^2$ with their appropriate degrees of freedom (DF_1) and compare that with the residual sum of squares of equation 5.18a^{II}, which is $\sum_k \hat{e}_{1k}^2$, with its appropriate degrees of freedom (DF_2) and then compute the F-statistic:

$$F = \frac{\Sigma\hat{e}_{1k}^2/(DF_2 - DF_1)}{(\Sigma\hat{e}_{11k}^2 + \Sigma\hat{e}_{12k}^2)/DF_1}$$

with $(DF_2 - DF_1)$ and DF_1 degrees of freedom. For each subset of assumptions about intercept and slope with respect to i and j, an appropriate test can be set up. If all plants are alike regardless of i and j with respect to intercept as well as slope then the residual sum of squares for 5.18a will not be statistically significantly higher than the sum for the eight separate residual sums of squares obtained by $5.18a^{I}$ being run for each i, j subgroup.

Komiya sets up ten separate models of this type for covariance analysis. A summary way of presenting his separate models is to look at the two parameters in 5.18a and present them with appropariate subscripts as we have done in $5.18a^{1}$ to $5.18a^{V}$. Thus he has,

1. $(\alpha_{0ij}, \alpha_{1ij})$
2. $(\alpha_{0ij}, \alpha_{1i})$
3. (α_{0ij}, α_1)
4. $[(\alpha_{0i} + \alpha_{0j}), \alpha_1]$
5. (α_{0i}, α_1)
6. (α_0, α_1)
7. $(\alpha_{0i}, \alpha_{1i})$
8. (α_{0j}, α_1)
9. $(\alpha_{0ij}, \alpha_{ij})$
10. $(\alpha_{0j}, \alpha_{1j})$

Model 6 (α_0, α_1) says, for example, that the intercept and slope are the same for all i, j groups while model 8 says, for example, that the intercept differs by fuel type but not by age of plant and the slope is the same for all plants. A chain of pairwise comparisons can be set up like the draw at Wimbledon. 1 can be tested against 2; if 1 performs better then we can try 1 against 9; if 1 wins again then there is no further work. We conclude that fuel type and age of plant are both important variables and production functions are different for each subgroup. If, however, 2 wins then we can match 2 with 3 or 2 with 7, and so on. A decision tree is set up by Komiya illustrating this 'match'.

If it turns out that 1 is the winner in this match, then we can conclude that for a dummy variable model we need four dummy variables for the intercept and four multiplicative variables for slope and their coefficients will all be statistically significant. If 6 is the winner then all the dummy variables will have non-significant coefficients.

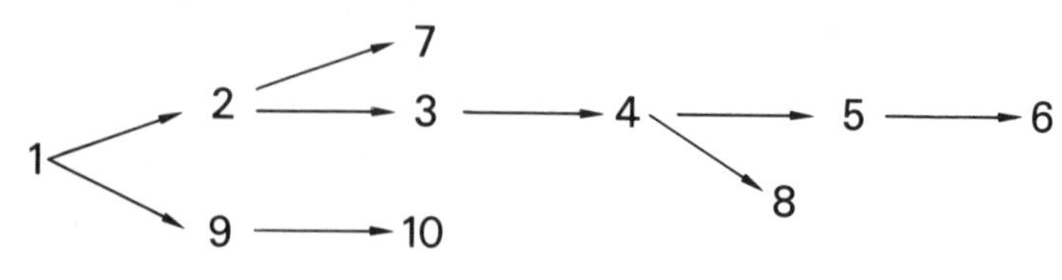

Fig. 5.2

Komiya's results show, for example, that for 5.18a for the entire sample model 4 is the winner, but for post-war observations ($i = 2, 3, 4$) model 8 is the best. The change over time is in the constant term, with a different constant term according to i and j (4) or only according to j. The slope is the same for all subgroups. Doing this for 5.18a to 5.18c for the ten models Komiya is able to arrive at the following explanation for observed input and output trends.

1. Fuel and capital input requirement changes between prewar years ($i = 1$) and postwar years ($i > 1$). Less fuel is used and more capital. The slope coefficients α_1 and β_1 are less than one indicating that it is the increase in size of the generating unit has led to input saving.
2. The slope coefficient for labour input γ_1 is even lower than α_1 or β_1 for most of the models showing even greater economies in use of labour input for larger generating units.
3. Thus even a fixed coefficient model indicates a substitution of capital for labour and fuel over the long run.
4. Coal and non-coal-using plants differ. Coal plants use less fuel but more capital and labour than non-coal plants. The difference is much greater in labour requirement than in capital or fuel.

5. On the whole, technological progress has occurred through change in size of generating plants (economies of scale effects) than through any pure shift of the production functions.

Komiya shows how in microeconomic work, if suitable data are available, a detailed analysis of the technological relationship can be carried out. The long-run substitution pattern as well as the importance of economies of scale is brought out by careful covariance analysis even when fixed coefficients are assumed; Komiya avoids the Marschak–Andrews problem by *a priori* assuming fixed coefficients. He has, however, come closer to measuring technological relationships than is the case in the more aggregative relationships. Further refinements can always be suggested, especially in his measure of labour input as well as a more disaggregated capital input, but his approach and method are worthy of follow up.

Bibliographical Notes

Most of the references are already given in the chapter. Abramowitz (1950), Solow (1957) and Solow (1959) are the basic references. The theoretical discussion of technical change in a two-input production function began with Hicks' Theory of Wages (1932) and continued in the 1930's. Also see Diamond (1965). Wickens' results have already been cited. Dennison has written extensively on this subject and also debated with Jorgensen–Grilliches in the *Survey of Current Business* (1971). For a survey of the theory of technical change see also Kennedy and Thirlwall (1972).

6
Dynamic single equation models: investment behaviour

In the previous three chapters, we have looked at a variety of equilibrium models. Demand and production theory yielded models of static equilibrium, and technical change entered as a shift variable in models of dynamic equilibrium. We now come to problems of specifying and estimating relationships describing dynamic disequilibrium behaviour. This leads us to the study of dynamic equations. In this chapter we confine ourselves to dynamic single equation models and hence to the behaviour of a single variable in dynamic disequilibrium. The theoretical basis for dynamic equations is not as firm and logically complete as that for static equilibrium situations such as demand theory. We shall find therefore that prior information on the specification of dynamic equations is much weaker, leaving a lot of room for *ad hoc* theorising.

We can develop the motivation for dynamic equations by questioning the realism of static specification. In demand analysis, factors such as habit formation, change in tastes, introduction of new goods and of durable goods would all point to the need for taking into account dynamic considerations. In production function studies, we not only encounter technical change but also the demand for capital services as one of the behavioural equations. The durability of capital goods, the problem of financing a purchase over time and the influence of expectations on investment behaviour indicate similar broadening of the static framework to include dynamic elements. In this chapter, we shall concentrate on that particular relationship—demand for capital services—as it manifests itself in terms of demand for capital goods or of investment expenditure.

The simplest way to illustrate the behaviour of a variable in dynamic disequilibrium is to specify a simple dynamic equation:

$$y_t = \alpha_0 + \alpha_1 x_t + \alpha_2 y_{t-1} + u_t \tag{6.1}$$

This is clearly a single equation version of the equation specified in Chapter 2 with $G = 1$, $K = 2$ and $\tau = 1$. This equation is said to have a first-order lag or a one-period lag since $\tau = 1$. Even this simple equation allows us to distinguish between the *short-run* influence of a change in x_t on y_t and its *long-run* influence. In evaluating the long-run influence, we use the notion of a dynamic equilibrium or steady-state relationship for y; by inference, the short-period relationship is then a disequilibrium one.

A unit increase in x_t has an immediate, contemporaneous effect on y_t equal to α_1. This increase in y_t appears in the period $t + 1$ as an increase in the lagged value of y. This has, therefore, an impact on y_{t+1} equal to $(\alpha_2 \alpha_1)$. If we only study a one-shot increase in x_t (say in $t = 1$) and follow its impact on y_t through the whole time period t, the total (cumulative) effect of a change in x_t on y_t is

$$\alpha_1 + \alpha_1 \alpha_2 + \alpha_1 \alpha_2^2 + \alpha_1 \alpha_2^3 + \ldots = \alpha_1 \sum_{t=1}^{\infty} \alpha_2^{t-1} \tag{6.1a}$$

If the series $\Sigma \alpha_2^{t-1}$ converges (i.e. if $|\alpha_2| < 1$) we get a finite quantity on the r.h.s. of equation 6.1a. If α_2 is positive and less than one we have on the r.h.s. $\alpha_1/(1-\alpha_2)$. This is then the cumulative impact of a change in x_t on y_t. The analogy of this calculation and especially of t to the 'rounds' on Keynes' discussion of the multiplier should be obvious. The short-run effect is α_1 and the long-run effect is $\alpha_1/(1-\alpha_2)$.

Another way of evaluating a long-run effect is to use the notion of equilibrium. Let us begin by assuming that there is a stable long-run equilibrium relationship between y and x, and that in periods previous to $t = 1$ they were in a state of no change. Something, e.g. a stochastic shock, changes x_t in

$t = 1$ by one unit above its previous value. This causes a corresponding change in y_t of α_1 thus making y_t in $t = 1$ different from y_{t-1}. We follow the consequence of this single shock until we observe y again in a state of no change, x_t having already returned to its previous value in $t = 2$. This happens when $y_t = y_{t-1}$, i.e. y is again in equilibrium. Setting $y_t = y_{t-1}$ in equation 6.1 we will again get the impact of a change in x_t on y_t $(= y_{t-1})$ as $\alpha_1/(1 - \alpha_2)$. Until y_t converges to equilibrium (so that $y_t = y_{t-1}$), equation 6.1 describes the behaviour of y_t out of equilibrium *as it is adjusting to a new equilibrium*. In a static equation, no such adjustment need, or does, take place. The questions we have to ask are about the economic rationale behind the formulation of dynamic models. Why are there lags in economic relationships?

Lags

Lags may be present in economic relationships due to psychological or behavioural reasons, as well as institutional or technological constraints. Given a stimulus of, say, a change in the price of a good, the response of consumer demand is not instantaneous but spread out over time. This may be due to habit persistence, delay in gathering information and costs of making frequent changes. Demand will then adjust to a change in price with a lag. Lags may also be due to the durability of the good in question. An illustration of an institutional lag would be the time taken, for example, to translate a decision to cut income taxes into higher disposable incomes for individuals through the administrative machinery. The influence of previous experience on present and future decisions also occurs when, in the face of uncertainty, indivduals have to act on the basis of expected values of variables rather than actual values, and the best way to form expectations may be to look at past experience. Technological lags appear as processing or transportation delays, or as lags due to physical or biological constraints. For example, a coffee plant takes four years to mature and attains its peak output three years later. The lag between sowing and harvesting is about three months. The time between starting a building and finishing it may be up to three years.

Lags can be point lags or distributed lags. Thus for a crop, the lag between sowing and harvesting can be thought of as a point lag of, say, exactly three months. This means that output harvested in month t is a function of the amount sown in month $(t - 3)$. This is a *fixed* point lag. In economics, most often we have distributed lags, the lagged effect being distributed over time. Here again, we may have a fixed distributed lag, i.e. regardless of the timing of the initial change in the x variable, the shape and length of response of y is the same. Or the distributed lag may be variable. To give an example, we can consider the well-known accelerator relationship between net investment and change in output. In the crude version of the accelerator relationship, the lag is a point lag and it is fixed. Thus, if y is net investment and x is change in output we have

$$y_t = \alpha x_{t-1} + u_t \tag{6.2}$$

the lag being one time period. This, however, is rather a strict formulation. We may alternatively think of the response of investment to change in output as being spread out over time. Some change in output may be met immediately by change in investment but others may be postponed.

$$y_t = \alpha_1 x_{t-1} + \alpha_2 x_{t-2} + \alpha_3 x_{t-3} \ldots + \alpha_N x_{t-N} + u_t \tag{6.2a}$$

Once again in equation 6.2 if we think of α as a capital–output ratio then equation 6.2a in a condition of long-run equilibrium should give us

$$\alpha = \alpha_1 + \alpha_2 + \alpha_3 + \ldots = \sum_{i=1}^{N} \alpha_i$$

This, however, is invariant to whether y_t refers to a prosperous time period or to a depression, whether the firm is operating at full capacity or excess capacity, whether credit conditions are easy or severe—the lag distribution remains the same shape for all t. This is also not totally satisfactory though, as we shall see later, it makes estimation easy. We can think of the lag distribution being narrow (quick response) if there is full capacity and there is credit availability but quite spread out if there are supply delays or uneasy expectations about the persistence of prosperity. Then the lag distribution (all the α_i coefficients and even the length N) will be variable from one time period to another.

Lag Operators

It is necessary at this stage to make a short detour into the use of lag operators. This will enable us to put the discussion above in a general framework and extend it to many new concepts. We are all familiar with the use of operators such as Σ (summation), Δ (first difference) and Π (product). The lag operator is L and is very useful in discussing dynamic equations. The simplest way of defining L is

$$x_t = L^0 x_t \qquad (L^0 = 1)$$

$$x_{t-1} = L^1 x_t \qquad (L^1 = L)$$

$$x_{t-2} = L^2 x_t$$

in general then

$$x_{t-i} = L^i x_t \qquad i = 0, 1, \ldots$$

We can rewrite equations 6.2 and 6.2a

$$y_t = \alpha L x_t + u_t \tag{6.2}$$

$$y_t = \Sigma\, \alpha_i L^i x_t + u_t \tag{6.2a}$$

$\alpha(L)$ is then a polynomial in the lag operator L and in general has the form $\Sigma\, \alpha_i L^i$. In equation 6.2a, $\Sigma\, \alpha_i L^i$ has the additional conditions that $\alpha_0 = 0$ and $\alpha_{N+i} = 0$ for $i = 1, 2, \ldots$.

We can illustrate the use of the lag operator by rewriting equation 6.1 as

$$(1 - \alpha_2 L) y_t = \alpha_0 + \alpha_1 x_t + u_t \tag{6.1c}$$

or

$$y_t = \frac{\alpha_0}{(1 - \alpha_2 L)} + \frac{\alpha_1}{(1 - \alpha_2 L)} x_t + \frac{1}{(1 - \alpha_2 L)} u_t \tag{6.1d}$$

Using the lag operator allows us to divide across by $(1 - \alpha_2 L)$. What interpretation can we give to $(1 - \alpha_2 L)^{-1}$? If α_2 is positive and less than one, we can express $(1 - \alpha_2 L)^{-1}$ as the polynomial

$$1 + \alpha_2 L + \alpha_2^2 L^2 + \alpha_2^3 L^3 + \ldots, = \Sigma \alpha_2^i L^i$$

[To check this multiply both sides by $(1 - \alpha_2 L)$.] We have therefore

$$y_t = \alpha_0 \Sigma \alpha_2^i L^i + \alpha_1 \Sigma \alpha_2^i L^i x_t + \Sigma \alpha_2^i L^i u_t \quad (6.1e)$$

For the constant α_0 we have, of course, $L = 1$ and $\Sigma \alpha_2^i L^i = \Sigma \alpha_2^i$. Then

$$y_t = \alpha_0 \Sigma \alpha_2^i + \alpha_1 (x_t + \alpha_2 x_{t-1} + \alpha_2^2 x_{t-2} + \alpha_2^3 x_{t-3} + \alpha_2^4 x_{t-4} + \ldots) + (u_t + \alpha_2 u_{t-1} + \alpha_2^2 u_{t-2} + \ldots) \quad (6.1f)$$

The presence of the lagged y_t terms is thus transformed into the effect of all the previous values of x but with exponentially declining impact. If we have long-run equilibrium we assume $x_t = x_{t-i}$ for all i and this special case once again makes $L = 1$ and we get $\alpha_1 \sum_i \alpha_2^i L^i = \alpha_1/(1 - \alpha_2)$ as we saw at the beginning of this chapter (similarly, of course, for the constant term α_0). The presence of the lagged y_t term is therefore equivalent to assuming that y_t is influenced not only by the current value of x_t but by all the past values, though the influence of past values of x_t diminishes as you go further away into the past.

This case of a lag distribution with exponentially declining coefficients (known as Koyck or geometric lag distribution) is frequent in the literature but is a rather special case. We can discuss a more general class of lag distributions by using the notion of the polynomial $\alpha(L)$ further. For the special case where (a) all the coefficients of the polynomial are non-negative, i.e. zero or positive, and (b) if they sum to one, we can draw an analogy between the probability density function and the polynomial $\alpha(L)$ which can be called the lag generating function. (These two conditions seem innocuous but the first one needs to be carefully examined. If all the coefficients are non-negative, then we are not allowing for overshooting or echo effects. In most cases, a negative coefficient may be unreasonable but this has to be argued.) We can then take α_i to be the discrete probability of the event $Z = i$ or, in our terms, when the x-variable takes a value of x_{t-i}. It is easy to satisfy condition (b) if (a) is satisfied by a suitable normalisation. In equation 6.1 the coefficients of x_{t-i} are $\alpha_1 \ \Sigma\ \alpha_2^i x_{t-i}$. The term $\Sigma\ \alpha_2^i$ sums to $1/(1-\alpha_2)$ for α_2 satisfying condition (a). We can therefore rewrite the coefficients by dividing each α_2^i by $(1-\alpha_2)$; let us call them ω_i. Then we have

$$\begin{aligned} \alpha_1\ \Sigma\ \alpha_2^i x_{t-i} &= (1-\alpha_2)\alpha_1\ \Sigma\ \omega_i x_{t-i} \\ &= (1-\alpha_2)\alpha_1\ \Sigma\ \frac{\alpha_2^i}{(1-\alpha_2)} x_{t-i} \end{aligned} \tag{6.3}$$

Now $(1-\alpha_2)\ \Sigma\ \omega_i$ equals one by definition and any ith term is non-negative and therefore analogous to the discrete probability of the ith event. The advantage of doing all this is that we can now summarise the lag distribution by parameters which correspond to the parameters we know in probability theory, e.g. the mean, the variance, the mode or the median. This is because in most (but not all) cases the normalised lag distribution can be treated as a moment generating function and then the mean, etc., can be calculated using well known lag distributions. We shall follow a standard notation for the dynamic equation

$$\begin{aligned} y_t &= \alpha\ \Sigma\ \omega_i x_{t-i} + u_t \\ \omega_i \geqslant 0, &\qquad \Sigma\ \omega_i = 1 \end{aligned} \tag{6.4}$$

We begin with the *Koyck distribution* which we have discussed before. Its general normalised form is the polynomial

$$(1-\lambda) \sum_{i=0}^{\infty} \lambda^i L^i$$

and therefore it is a one-parameter (λ) distribution. The maximum lag is infinitely long. Its shape is one humped, the hump being in the very first period. The maximum impact is therefore immediate and declines monotonically afterwards. This is, therefore, a unimodal distribution and its mean is given by $\lambda/(1-\lambda)$ and its variance by $\lambda/(1-\lambda)^2$. Being a single parameter distribution it is much favoured by econometricians, although as we shall see later there are some estimation problems associated with it.

We have mentioned that the Koyck distribution is often called the geometric distribution. This name derives from the probability density function of that name from which the Koyck can be derived. Similarly, a lag distribution can be derived from *the Pascal distribution* which can be derived from the negative binomial p.d. function. Solow was the first to use this. The coefficients ω_i of x_{t-i} can be derived then as follows

$$\omega_i = (1-\lambda)^r \binom{r+i-1}{i} \lambda^i \qquad (6.5)$$

where λ is as usual between zero and one and r is positive. For $r = 1$, we get the Koyck and thus the Pascal can be seen as a series of r *independent* Koyck distributions each with parameter λ piled upon each other. Using this analogy, we can say that the mean of the Pascal is $\lambda r/(1-\lambda)$ and its variance $\lambda r/(1-\lambda)^2$. The Pascal is a two parameter distribution, λ and r, and the mode does not occur in the first time period unless $r = 1$. The mode depends on λ and r since the coefficients of ω_i increase as long as $i < \lambda r^{-1}/(1-\lambda)$ and decrease when the inequality is reversed. The longest lag is once again infinite.

A third lag distribution is associated with the name of Shirley Almon [1965] and is derived by the method of Lagrangean interpolation. The idea here is that the researcher specifies the *shape* of the distribution by denoting the degree of the polynomial, e.g. quadratic, cubic, quartic, etc. He also lists the initial and terminal periods for the series of lag coefficients and consequently the *length* of the lag. The method of Lagrangean interpolation then derives the best coefficients for the desired shape and then links this shape to the coefficients ω_i of the variables x_{t-i}. Given equation 6.4 we divide up the length of the lag, i.e. the interval between the initial and terminal points into smaller intervals by choosing K points to define the polynomial. These K points plus the initial point (or the terminal point) are sufficient to determine a polynomial of degree K. The height of the polynomial at any of $(K + 1)$ points is of interest to us, however, only if we can relate it to the coefficient ω_i of our variable x_{t-i}. Thus the length of the lag may be eight time periods but, if we want to fit a quadratic, three points are sufficient for that. We then have to define the coefficients ω_i in terms of the three points which define the quadratic shape. This is done by relating ω_i to the coefficients of the polynomial whose degree we have specified *a priori*. The steps in this process are technical and can be omitted by the reader who is not interested in such detail but they are as follows

$$\omega_i = P(i) \tag{6.6}$$

where P is a polynomial

$$P(t) = \sum_{i=0}^{k} b_i S_i(t) \tag{6.6b}$$

and

$$S_i(t) = \frac{\prod_{j \neq i} (t - t_j)}{\prod_{j \neq i} (t_i - t_j)} \qquad i = 0, 1, 2, \ldots, K \tag{6.6c}$$

Notice that

$$S_i(t_j) = 1 \text{ for } i = j$$
$$= 0 \text{ for } i \neq j$$

Each ω_i is then the sum of the terms in $P(t)$ in equation 6.6c by putting $t = i$. We estimate equation 6.4 by reweighting x_{t-i} by the formula in 6.6c and then estimate the b_i coefficients.

Such an elaborate procedure as above is necessary for the Almon lag because we really impose strong prior restrictions on the shape as well as the length of the lag distribution. The method of Lagrangean interpolation is then an efficient way of translating ω_i in terms of the polynomial whose shape we specify. Its flexibility lies in being able to provide us any shape that we think is likely to be appropriate. It also has the advantage that further generalisations can be carried out to provide variable lag coefficients as has been done by Tinsley (1967). The mean of the Almon lag can be defined by the formula $\Sigma\, \omega_i i$, using the analogy of ω_i to probabilities.

We come finally to the rational lag distribution which is much the most general of all (fixed) lag distributions. Its shape is left free to be decided by the sample as is the length of the maximum lag. The crucial property is that a rational polynomial can be expressed as a ratio of two polynomials and that a polynomial of a very high degree can be expressed as a ratio of two polynomials of much lower degree. The only requirement is that the polynomial in the denominator be at least one degree higher than that in the numerator. Thus if we express the coefficients in equation 6.4 as a polynomial $W(L)$, then

$$W(L) = \sum_{i=0}^{N} \omega_i L^i$$

$$B(L) = \sum_{i=0}^{M} \beta_i L^i$$

$$A(L) = \sum_{i=0}^{K} \alpha_i L^i$$

Then

$$W(L) = B(L)/A(L) \tag{6.7}$$

and $K \geqslant (M + 1)$ and both K, M are much smaller than N. We have already seen an example of this when we discussed the Koyck distribution. Here a polynomial of infinite degree could be expressed as a ratio of two polynomials of degrees zero and one respectively since

$$\sum_{i=0}^{\infty} \lambda^i L^i = 1/(1 - \lambda)$$

Thus $N = \infty$, $M = 0$ and $K = 1$ in the context of 6.7. Our purpose is then to estimate the $(K + M)$ coefficients α_i and β_i and derive from the formula in equation 6.7 the N parameters ω_i thus saving ourselves $N - (K + M)$ degrees of freedom. Let us show this by taking $M = 2$ and $K = 3$. Then

$$\frac{\beta_0 + \beta_i L + \beta_2 L^2}{\alpha_0 + \alpha_i L + \alpha_2 L^2 + \alpha_3 L^3} = \Sigma\, \omega_i L^i \tag{6.7a}$$

Multiplying across and equating terms in like powers of L, we have

$$\beta_0 = \alpha_0 \omega_0 \qquad \text{or} \qquad \omega_0 = \beta_0/\alpha_0$$

$$\beta_1 = \alpha_1 \omega_0 + \omega_1 \alpha_0$$

or

$$\omega_1 = \frac{\beta_1 - \alpha_1 \omega_0}{\alpha_0} = \frac{\beta_1 \alpha_0 - \alpha_1 \beta_0}{\alpha_0^2}$$

$$\beta_2 = \alpha_2 \omega_0 + \alpha_1 \omega_1 + \alpha_0 \omega_2$$

$$\text{or} \qquad \omega_2 = \frac{\beta_2 - \alpha_2 \omega_0 - \alpha_1 \omega_1}{\alpha_0}, \text{ etc.}$$

Thus each ω_i can be solved recursively knowing the α_i, β_i and the ω_{i-1}. Once we come to zero terms in the $B(L)$ and $A(L)$, e.g. β_3, α_4 and higher terms, we shall begin to feel their effects on the computed ω_i, and ω_i would therefore slowly decline to zero. After this detour, we can now return to our main theme.

Capital Theory

It has been recognised for a long time that a study of determinants of investment must be cast in a dynamic framework. The durability of capital stock, the long gestation period required between the initiation and completion of an investment project (a long 'period of production' in the Austrian sense), the phenomenon of compound growth rate in biological commodities such as trees and of maturity in wines —all these factors have pointed to the importance of dynamic specification in studying investment. An unresolved question, however, is whether the approach should be in terms of equilibrium dynamics as in a Fisherian neoclassical model or disequilibrium dynamics as in the theories of Wicksell or Keynes or in the accelerator relationship. We shall confine our attention to the determinants of demand for fixed investment, thus neglecting inventories (working capital) and, more important, the supply constraints which may exist, for example, in periods of boom in a developed economy or during early phases of growth in a less developed economy.

Measurement problems and conceptual problems of definition are closely interwoven in any study of capital accumulation. The most primary of these problems is that capital *stock* is measured at a point of time while the output of productive services from capital stock is a continuous *flow*. Investment is the addition to capital stock between two points of time, but it is necessary to distinguish between gross investment and net investment–the difference being depreciation. One thinks of depreciation of capital stock in physical terms but the statistical measures of gross and net investment are usually in money terms. One may regard the difference as being spent in the same time period to repair the depreciation which may have occurred and maintain the original piece of cpaital equipment at its normal level of performance. Alternatively, one may think of it as a reserve fund out of which a new machine is bought to replace the old one when 'its time is up'. In the case of one investor this may lead to two different time shapes of expenditure–one smoothly spread out over time and another bunched at the end of the life of equipment. At the level of many investors and many machines with differing life cycles, the distinction is between economic obsolescence and physical depreciation since technical change, or fiscal policy change (e.g. accelerated depreciation provision), may render it profitable to scrap an old machine before its time is up. On the other hand, the problem of separating net investment from the usually available data on gross investment disappears if, as in the case of Solow's vintage model, we regard gross investment as the economically more meaningful variable to study.

The conceptual problem in studying investment behaviour in so far as it can be separated from the measurement problem relates to the specificity or its opposite, the malleability, of capital stock. In the neoclassical production function both capital and labour inputs are assumed to be *malleable*. Thus starting from a high capital–labour ratio, an entrepreneur can slide down a smooth isoquant substituting labour for capital if relative factor prices so change. But how can one transform, say, a very automated factory into one using a lot of labour? How can, in other words, capital be realistically regarded as malleable into different forms as price changes warrant? This has been a point of debate and a large bibliography has been built upon the topic (see Harcourt and Laing, 1971). For our purposes, we only need to look at those aspects of the controversy which bear on the problem of specifying or identifying econometric investment functions.

One way in which capital can be malleable is through the existence of perfect markets for capital stock of every variety, vintage and age. Thus in our example above, the entrepreneur can sell the automated factory in the perfect market for second-hand automated factories and, with the money, buy a new factory. If there are no delays in buying and selling and if the financial market is also perfect, capital is malleable. If capital is only imperfectly malleable we have to specify the imperfect substitutability of capital either by introducing asymmetric effects of price change (ratchet effect) or by specifying separate investment functions for each type of capital equipment. The latter is, however, a Utopian alternative because data do not exist on the purchase and sale of every piece of equipment even broadly defined.

An alternative is to regard the demand for capital as a demand for capital services and define the price of capital services properly. A piece of physical capital equipment can then be seen to yield different rates of flow of capital services according to whether it is intensively utilised or whether excess capacity exists. An investment demand function is then not only a demand for net addition to stock but also a decision as to the appropriate level of utilisation. The translation of stock price into flow price, however, begs all the questions regarding perfect markets and above all abstracts from uncertainty and expectations. To many people, specificity or irreversibility, uncertainty and the over-riding importance of expectations is what makes investment demand dynamic and hence they prefer an alternative framework to the neoclassical one.

These several problems have meant that the guidance from economic theory about specification of the investment function is not unambiguous. Unlike demand theory where an agreed body of theoretical results can be used as prior restrictions on parameters in fitting investment demand functions, several conflicting theoretical schemes exist and there is as yet no consensus on the theoretical aspects. This has led to specifications being influenced by previous empirical results. Variables are introduced more because they have been found to have 'worked' in previous studies than on theoretical grounds. This tendency towards *ad hoc* specification is partly unavoidable since unique prior specifications are not available. Contending explanations of determinants of investment behaviour abound, each side claiming superiority for its own version in terms of predictive power. We shall study the main contending theories and the problems of specification and estimation they entail.

Specifications

One way to organise the discussion on different specifications is to concentrate on the economic theoretical aspects or on the purely estimation problems arising. Such a division is, however, false. In many discussions in the econometric. literature exclusive attention is often paid to one of the two aspects or it alternates between the two. The basic hypothesis is framed and argued in terms of a nonstochastic model. When discussing estimation problems or empirical results, the nature of the random error term in alternate models is discussed independently of the theoretical specification. We hope to show that such a division leads to many serious mistakes.

The two main strands of economic hypotheses are built round the neoclassical theory of investment behaviour and the accelerator relationship. The difference between these two theories is regarding assumptions about factor substitutability and malleability of capital. To start with, the accelerator principle posits a relationship between net investment and expected or actual change in output (or sales). Thus, if I_{nt} is net investment–addition to end of year capital stock K between last year and this year–and Q is output and Q^e is expected output, we have in a deterministic version

$$K_t - K_{t-1} = I_{nt} = f(\Delta Q_{t-i}) \tag{6.8}$$

$$= g(\Delta Q^e_{t-i}) \tag{6.8a}$$

The questions to ask are: (i) whether f (or g) is linear, (ii) whether other variables are involved, (iii) what is the nature of the lag between investment and change in output—is it fixed at i or is it distributed (iv) what is the underlying theoretical rationale and (v) what is the structure of error terms involved?

Let us begin by exploring the linear relationships for f and g. To begin with we can take up a Harrod model with an equilibrium capital output ratio β, and to capture the disequilibrium aspects of the investment process we combine it with a *partial adjustment* framework. Thus K_t^* is equilibrium or desired capital stock and actual investment is undertaken to adjust actual previous capital stock to equilibrium capital stock, but the adjustment is partial:

$$I_{nt} = \Delta K_t = \lambda(K_t^* - K_{t-1}) + u_{1t} \tag{6.9}$$

where $0 < \lambda < 1$ and u_{1t} is a random error term. K_t^* is in its turn given by the Harrod relationship but with an added error term v_{1t}:

$$K_t^* = \beta Q_{t-i} + v_{1t} \tag{6.9a}$$

In equilibrium, the expected value of I_{nt} is zero and, since $E(v_{1t}) = 0$ as usual, we have $E(K_t) = K_{t-1}$. But by the definition of equilibrium we also have $E(Q_t) = Q_{t-1}$. There is no reason to change capital stock. Putting 6.9 and 6.9a together we have

$$\begin{aligned} \Delta K_t &= \lambda\beta Q_{t-i} - \lambda K_{t-1} + \epsilon_{1t} \\ K_t &= \lambda\beta Q_{t-i} + (1-\lambda)K_{t-1} + \epsilon_{1t} \end{aligned} \tag{6.9b}$$

where $\epsilon_{1t} = u_{1t} + \lambda v_{1t}$. Equation 6.9b is a regression equation including a lagged dependent variable as in equation 6.1. It is not, however, like our equation 6.8 or 6.8a since the level of output rather than change is involved. The error term is composed of two separate terms u_1 and v_1 but if each of them can be assumed uncorrelated with its past value and with that of the other, no estimation problems arise with 6.9b. (Modifications of 6.9a have been proposed to introduce other variables such as profit levels, cost of borrowing and rate of return on alternative investment outlets.) Often attempts are made to cast 6.9b in the form of 6.8 partly due to lack of data on capital stocks. This however, causes problems since, taking the first difference of 6.9b, we have[1]

$$I_{nt} = \lambda\beta\Delta Q_{t-i} + (1-\lambda) I_{nt-1} + \Delta\epsilon_{1t} \quad (6.9c)$$

If originally u_{1t} and v_{1t} were uncorrelated with their own past values, the error in first difference will now show correlation since

$$E\{\Delta(\epsilon_{1t})\Delta(\epsilon_{1t-1})\}$$
$$= -E(u_{1t-1}^2) - \lambda E(v_{1t-1}^2)$$
$$\neq 0$$

assuming all other terms are zero. Also the error term will not therefore be independent of I_{nt-1} and inconsistent estimates would result.

The lag distribution in 6.9b should also be noticed. Unit change in Q_{t-i} has the immediate effect of $\lambda\beta$ but a delayed effect is felt due to the partial adjustment process and we have the coefficients $\lambda\beta$, $\lambda\beta(1-\lambda)$. $\lambda\beta(1-\lambda)^2, \ldots,$ $\lambda\beta(1-\lambda)^j$ after j periods. They sum, of course, to β which is the long-run impact and the average lag is $\beta(1-\lambda)/\lambda$. (Readers are advised to check this for themselves as an exercise.)

Two alternatives to (6.9) are an adaptive expectation process and what we may call a permanent income or moving average process. They both come to an almost identical estimating equation but embody different behavioural assumptions. We can study both as a modification of equation 6.9a or 6.8a. In the adaptive expectation model we hypothesise that net investment is related to change in expected output, ΔQ^e, rather than change in actual output. In a world of forward planning and long gestation lags, it is

1 Data are usually available only for *gross* investment. This leads to further problems. Define gross investment I_t as $I_t = I_{nt} + \delta K_{t-1}$, where δ is the rate of depreciation. We then have for 6.9b

$$I_t = \lambda\beta Q_{t-1} - (\lambda - \delta)K_{t-1} + \epsilon_{1t}$$

Then we proceed to eliminate K_{t-1} since by 6.9b

$$K_t = \frac{\lambda\beta}{[1-(1-\lambda-\delta)L]}(Q_{t-i} + \epsilon_{1t})$$

easy to see that today's actual (or desired) investment may be related to tomorrow's change in expected output. Then we set up a framework for deriving change in expected output from available information. This is necessary because expected output is unobservable while only actual output can be observed. If it is expected output at time t, we have for an adaptive expectation equation

$$Q^e_{t+1} - Q^e_t = \Delta Q^e_{t+1} = \gamma(Q_t - Q^e_t) + u_{2t}; \qquad 0<\gamma<1 \tag{6.10}$$

It is not usual to include an error term but we shall proceed with this more general case. Clearly, if in this period expected output equals actual output, there is no need to change expectations about output except for random influences. (If an upward trend is to be introduced in expected output we can add an intercept term to 6.10 or modify the l.h.s. by giving a coefficient to Q^e_t greater than one.) We can combine 6.10 with either a version of 6.8a relating actual net investment to change in expected output, or combine it with 6.9a giving desired net investment in terms of change in expected output and then adopt a partial adjustment process as in 6.9 to obtain actual net investment. These two models are different in their behavioural implications as well as their estimation requirements. Let us take actual net investment first. Equation 6.8a gives a nonlinear accelerator in terms of change in expected output. We linearise 6.8a and add an error term v_{2t}:

$$I_{nt} = \alpha \Delta Q^e_{t+1} + v_{2t} \tag{6.8b}$$

Now from equation 6.10 we have by a recursion relationship (since $0<\gamma<1$)

$$Q^e_{t+1} = \gamma \sum_{i=0}^{\infty} (1-\gamma)^i Q_{t-i} + \sum_{i=0}^{\infty} (1-\gamma)^i u_{2t-i} \tag{6.10a}$$

Equation 6.10a translates the process of adaptive expectations in terms of past history of actual output. By substituting 6.10a into 6.8b we get

$$I_{nt} = \alpha\gamma \sum_{i=0}^{\infty} (1-\gamma)^i \Delta Q_{t-i} + \epsilon_{2t} \tag{6.10b}$$

where

$$\epsilon_{2t} = v_{2t} + \alpha\,\Sigma(1-\gamma)^i \Delta u_{2t-i}$$

Equation 6.10b involves a polynomial with an infinite number of terms in the change in output variable. But by our discussion above we can translate this into a ratio of two polynomials of smaller order.
Since $\Sigma(1-\gamma)^i L^i = 1/[1-(1-\gamma)L]$

$$I_{nt} = \frac{\alpha\gamma}{[1-(1-\gamma)L]}\Delta Q_t + \epsilon_{2t'}$$

Multiplying across and rearranging, we have

$$I_{nt} = \alpha\gamma\Delta Q_t + (1-\gamma)I_{nt-1} + [\epsilon_{2t} - (1-\gamma)\epsilon_{2t-1}] \tag{6.10c}$$

Equation 6.10c is identical to equation 6.9c except for a modification in the random error term. In 6.9c we have $\epsilon_{1t} - \epsilon_{1t-1}$ and here we have $\epsilon_{2t} - (1-\gamma)\epsilon_{2t-1}$. Let us study the error term in 6.10c carefully. We introduced originally an error term in the adaptive expectation process. This error term appears in equation 6.10b in the form of a polynomial in Δu_{2t} but since we have multiplied across by $[1-(1-\gamma)L]$ we get for the error term

$$\begin{aligned}[1-(1-\gamma)L]\,\epsilon_{2t} &= \epsilon_{2t} - (1-\gamma)\epsilon_{2t-1} \\ &= [1-(1-\gamma)L]\,[v_{2t} + \alpha\Sigma(1-\gamma)^i \Delta u_{2t-i}] \\ &= v_{2t} - (1-\gamma)v_{2t-1} + \alpha\Delta u_{2t} \qquad (6.10\text{d})\end{aligned}$$

As we said before, taking the adaptive expectation process to be stochastic rather than deterministic has non-trivial consequences for the error term in the estimating equation. Even if u_{2t} is zero for all t, we have a moving average error term in equation 6.10c which is made up of v_{2t} and its past value. If u_{2t} is not zero but assumed to be so, we compound the mis-specification. In any case, the parameters α and γ appear in both the deterministic as well as the stochastic parts of the model.

In equations 6.9c and 6.10c once we derive consistent estimates of the coefficients of ΔQ_t (or ΔQ_{t-i}) and I_{nt-1}, we can separate out λ and β or α and γ. These parameters can thus be derived from our coefficients. We now come to the case where we combine the adaptive expectation process with the partial adjustment process. We have, along with equation 6.10, a modification of 6.9a:

$$K_t^* = \beta Q_{t+1}^e + v_{3t} \tag{6.11}$$

and equation 6.9, we have

$$K_t = \lambda\beta Q_{t+1}^e + (1-\lambda)K_{t-1} + u_{1t} + \lambda v_{3t} \tag{6.11a}$$

Using 6.10a we get

$$\begin{aligned}[1-(1-\gamma)L]K_t &= \lambda\beta\gamma Q_t + (1-\lambda)[1-(1-\gamma)L]K_{t-1} \\ &\quad + \{[1-(1-\gamma)L]u_{1t} + \lambda[1-(1-\gamma)L]v_{3t} + \lambda\beta u_{2t}\}\end{aligned} \tag{6.11b}$$

This can be rewritten as

$$\begin{aligned}K_t &= \lambda\beta\gamma Q_t + [(1-\lambda)+(1-\gamma)]K_{t-1} \\ &\quad - (1-\lambda)(1-\gamma)K_{t-2} + \epsilon_{3t}\end{aligned} \tag{6.11c}$$

where ϵ_{3t} is made up of the three error terms with appropriate coefficients as defined in 6.11b. If a researcher were first to differentiate 6.11c to get it in estimable form, we have

$$\begin{aligned}I_{nt} &= \lambda\beta\gamma\Delta Q_t + [(1-\lambda)+(1-\gamma)]I_{nt-1} \\ &\quad - (1-\lambda)(1-\gamma)I_{nt-2} + \Delta\epsilon_{3t}\end{aligned} \tag{6.11d}$$

Once again we may have to modify 6.11d further to get it in gross investment terms, but the problem is complicated enough at this stage. We have in 6.11d three parameters λ, β and γ and three coefficients, one each for ΔQ_t, I_{nt-1} and I_{nt-2}. There is, however, no simple relationship between the parameters and coefficients. Given the nature of the error term $\Delta\epsilon_{3t}$, the first important task is to ensure that *consistent* estimates of the coefficients can be obtained by using appropriate instruments. OLS will certainly not do this and conventional tests for autoregressive errors will give wrong answers as we have seen in Chapter 2. Provided we have consistent estimates of the coefficients, call them A_1, A_2 and A_3 respectively; we can solve for the parameters as follows.

Solve the two characteristic roots of the homogeneous part of the quadratic equation in I_{nt} since we have from 6.11d

$$I_{nt} - A_2 I_{nt-1} - A_3 I_{nt-2} = A_1 \Delta q_t + \Delta \epsilon_{3t}.$$

The two roots are given by

$$\frac{2-(\lambda+\gamma)+(\lambda-\gamma)}{2} \quad \text{and} \quad \frac{2-(\lambda+\gamma)-(\lambda-\gamma)}{2}$$

(Readers can check this for themselves.)

Given λ and γ from above it is straightforward to solve for β. A problem with the above procedure is to be able to separately identify λ and γ since they are both between 0 and 1, and also to derive appropriate standard errors for them so as to be able to test hypotheses about these parameters. Once again notice that the error term involves the same parameters as the deterministic part of the equation.

An alternative specification to the partial adjustment process is to relate actual net investment to desired net investment. This can now be quickly done. We have

$$\Delta K_t = I_{nt} = \mu(\Delta K_t^*) + u_{3t} \tag{6.12}$$

For K_t^* we can again either adopt 6.9a or 6.11. If we take 6.9a relating desired capital stock to actual output, we immediately get

$$I_{nt} = \beta\mu\Delta Q_{t-i} + \epsilon_{4t} \tag{6.12a}$$

$$\epsilon_{4t} = u_{3t} + \mu\Delta v_{1t}$$

choosing 6.11 and 6.10 with 6.12 we get

$$\Delta K_t = \beta\mu\Delta Q^e_{t+1} + u_{3t} + \mu\Delta v_{1t}$$

and

$$[1-(1-\gamma)L]\,\Delta K_t = \beta\mu\gamma\Delta Q_t + [1-(1-\gamma)L]\,(u_{3t} + \mu\Delta v_{1t}) + \beta\mu\Delta u_{2t} \tag{6.12b}$$

or

$$I_{nt} = \beta\mu\gamma\Delta Q_t + (1-\gamma)I_{nt-1} + \epsilon_{5t} \tag{6.12c}$$

Apart from any problems of estimation with the error term such as ϵ_{5t}, equation 6.12c has only two coefficients but three parameters. We cannot thus distinguish β and μ.[2]

Let us now bring together our discussion of the various specifications. We shall write them down in terms of coefficients or as they would appear at the estimation stage. For convenience we shall choose net investment rather than capital stock as our dependent variable: this brings us closer to empirical work in the field and heightens the problems of error specification. We have

$$I_{nt} = a_0 + a_1 \Delta Q_{t-i} + a_2 I_{nt-1} + \Delta\epsilon_{1t} \quad (6.9c)$$

$$I_{nt} = b_0 + b_1 \Delta Q_{t-i} + b_2 I_{nt-1} + \Delta\epsilon_{2t} \quad (6.10c)$$

$$I_{nt} = c_0 + c_1 \Delta Q_{t-i} + c_2 I_{nt-1} + c_3 I_{nt-2} + \Delta\epsilon_{3t} \quad (6.11c)$$

$$I_{nt} = d_0 + d_1 \Delta Q_{t-i} + \epsilon_{4t} \quad (6.12a)$$

$$I_{nt} = e_0 + e_1 \Delta Q_{t-i} + e_2 I_{nt-1} + \epsilon_{5t} \quad (6.12c)$$

We have generalised the notation and added an intercept term to each equation since it is usual to do so (often without justification) in empirical studies. At first glance, an investigator who proceeds without any preliminary theoretical work can distinguish only three different specifications: 6.12a, 6.9c, 6.10c and 6.12c or 6.11c depending on whether a lagged investment term appears or not and whether the lag is of first or second order. As we have seen, these models arise from different behavioural postulates. There is no way of distinguishing between them, however, except as to whether they involve one, two or three parameters. Since α and γ are both between 0 and 1 we cannot say whether an estimated equation comes from a partial adjustment or adaptive expection process by looking at the number unless we have strong *a priori* information about the likely size of α as against γ. Similarly for 6.11c when compared with 6.9c and

[2] For the sake of completeness, a word should be added about what we called a 'permanent income' or moving average process on p. 183 above. This would say, for example, that in equation 6.9a, we replace actual Q by permanent Q^P, i.e. a weighted average of its past values. $Q^P = (1 - \xi) \Sigma \xi Q_{t-i}$. The similarity with 6.9c should be noted.

6.10c except that now we get a product of two parameters rather than one parameter. It is when we combine partial adjustment and adaptive expectation and assume that the adaptive expectation process is of the Koyck type that we get a genuinely different specification enabling us to distinguish λ and γ.

This discussion explains partly perhaps why the field of investment behaviour is full of contending specifications. As between rival specifications, we do not have enough differences to be able to discriminate one hypothesis from another when we come to look at the estimated equation. Each person can obtain confirmation for his own view in such a situation. Only a more rigorous formulation with additional zero (or other) restrictions on the model can hope to render the situation less controversial.

The estimation problems of equations 6.9c, 6.10c, 6.11c, 6.12a and 6.12c must now be considered before we can look at some of the published studies in the field. It is customary for a researcher to ignore the question of how his error term comes to be and just add it at the estimation stage. Then he either assumes (wrongly) that the error term has all the OLS properties or (wrongly again) assumes some simple first-order autoregressive pattern. Both these procedures are mistaken since they neglect the information contained in the structure of the model (e.g. partial adjustment or adaptive expectations) but also because testing of either of these hypotheses about the error term is most likely to be faulty leading to inappropriate acceptance or rejection.

If we start by assuming that our errors follow the OLS assumptions and then cite the Durbin–Watson statistic computed from OLS residuals, we arrive at a wrong inference in all cases except 6.12a (neglecting the problem of simultaneity between I_{nt} and Q_t). This is because, as we saw in Chapter 2, OLS gives inconsistent estimates if our assumption is untrue and we have lagged dependent variables. The use of the *DW* statistic is hence inappropriate. If we assume that the errors follow a first-order autoregressive process with a coefficient of $\rho (0 < \rho < 1)$, we cannot fare much better. To begin with our model tells us that the process may be more complex (higher order). Secondly, the standard procedures such as the Durbin two-stage or the Hildreth–Lu iterative process described in Chapter 2 are inappropriate since, with the presence of lagged dependent variables, consistency of OLS estimates is not automatically assured and hence a criterion such as minimum sum of squared errors will by itself not help since error estimates will also be inconsistent. Both these procedures rely on a hypothesised first-order autoregressive structure which is not always true in these cases (once again excepting equation 6.12a).

What can we do then? As we have already indicated in Chapter 2, we have open to us the instrumental variable estimation procedure which will ensure consistency where OLS cannot, or we adopt the maximum likelihood approach. In searching for appropriate instruments, we need to take into account the structural relations from which our reduced form equation arises. Let us apply this procedure to the equations listed above. Take 6.9c first. We know that from our model we have $\epsilon_{1t} = u_{1t} + \lambda v_{1t}$ and that our error term in 6.9c is of the form $\Delta\epsilon_{1t}$. Even if u_{1t} and v_{1t} are independent of their own past values and those of each other, $\Delta\epsilon_{1t}$ will be autoregressive of the first order with ρ approximating to $\frac{1}{2}$. If both u_{1t} and v_{1t} are first-order autoregressive then a higher order autoregressive pattern in $\Delta\epsilon_{1t}$ will result. If, however, we know this or can hypothesise this, we can choose our instruments carefully. In each case ΔQ_{t-1} can be its own instrument and we only need an instrument for I_{nt-1}. If therefore we choose an instrument which is not correlated with $\Delta\epsilon_{1t}$ or $\Delta\epsilon_{1t-1}$ (i.e. $u_{1t}, u_{1t-1}, u_{1t-2}, v_{1t}, v_{1t-1}, v_{1t-2}$) we obtain consistent estimates. In equation 6.9c, the instrument that readily comes to mind is ΔQ_{t-i-1}. In 6.10c, however, this may not be appropriate since the error is the adaptive expectation process u_{2t} and its lagged value appears in the estimating equation itself, ΔQ_{t-i} may not be uncorrelated with the error term. We need, therefore, instruments for ΔQ_{t-i} as well as I_{nt-1} if 6.10c embodies our structural model.

The choicė of particular instruments will always depend on individual circumstances so we do not need to give here any uniform answer. We only need to point out that the choice of instruments is aided by rigorous specification of the structural equations including their stochastic properties and careful translation into the reduced form equation which is to be estimated. Once consistency has been assured by the proper choice of instruments, one can go on to ensure efficiency by a suitable GLS estimator.

Having discussed the inter-related issues of specification and estimation, we can now look at the published work in the field of investment behaviour. Unlike demand studies which have a long history of econometric work, lack of macroeconomic data delayed the work on investment for a long time. It started with Tinbergen's pioneering work on business cycle models for the UK and USA carried out in the 1930's for the League of Nations–since then, a considerable amount of empirical work has been carried out at firm level, industry level and at national level. The main points round which a survey of this literature can be grouped are

(i) the importance of profits as against output (or sales) as a major explanatory variable;
(ii) the significance of interest rates in particular and relative factor and product prices in general for investment demand and the interest elasticity of the investment demand schedule;
(iii) relevance of other *ceteris paribus* variables such as capacity utilisation, expectations, tax policy, liquidity position of firms, availability (as against cost) of credit, the phase of the business cycle, etc.;
(iv) the set of other relationships which are simultaneously dependent on investment–demands of other inputs especially labour, portfolio of other assets, etc.

The difficulty of deriving unambiguous results in investment behaviour was foreshadowed in Tinbergen's pioneering work. For aggregate data, Tinbergen (1951) found that lagged profits was the best explanatory variable for investment activity, but for railroads the accelerator principle was found to hold. The long-term rate of interest had a negative coefficient but was not very significant. In his work, Tinbergen also discovered the importance of lags because his profit variable was lagged between $1\frac{1}{2}$ years to $2\frac{1}{2}$ years. Klein (1952) in his work on the US economy as well as railroads found profits or non-wage income to be the significant variable but also discovered that lagged capital stock was a depressing influence.

Tinbergen–Klein studies were done with time series data. Problems of multicollinearity and of autoregressive errors with time series data render any particular specification subject to doubt because addition or removal of one variable can change the signs and significance of the remaining coefficients. Meyer and Kuh (1959) therefore made a sustained attempt at exploring five separate samples of cross-section data for US firms for each year between 1946 to 1950. For each year, they tried to explore specifications by *correlating* gross investment with many possible independent variables. Meyer and Kuh used correlation rather than multiple regression since they were concerned much more with qualitative results concerning signs of certain correlational persistence over time. By taking five years over which the US economy saw a postwar boom, recession and recovery, Meyer and Kuh were able without having to set up a simultaneous equation model to study the effect of macroeconomic business conditions on microeconomic investment decisions. They tried level of sales or profit as two alternatives along with a set of other common variables such as depreciation expense, depreciation reserve (to indicate age of capital equipment), change in sales, stock of net quick liquidity of the firm and 'needed capacity'. Needed capacity was similar to the notion of the capital stock to 'permanent' sales ratio, an adaptation of 6.9a with sales replacing output and a moving average of sales rather than any single term. They found that in postwar boom conditions the accelerator helped but in recession, profits and liquidity became more important. In recovery, the effect was mixed. Thus, the investment function shifted from boom to recession and clearly showed that macroeconomic variables need to be specified either as extra variables or as extra equations in investment studies. By deliberately eschewing a formal model either in economic or econometric terms, Meyer and Kuh emphasise the tentative and exploratory nature of their work and they also demonstrate its usefulness.

One important statistical problem MK tackled was that of heteroscedasticity. Since firms were of differing size, error variances tended to be related to firm size. This led MK to deflate all their variables—dependent as well as independent—by lagged capital stock as the indicator of firm size. This makes the implicit assumption that error variances in the original undeflated variable model is proportional to K_{t-1}^2. Such deflation in a regression equation such as 6.9c creates problems of mis-specification unless care is taken. Given 6.9c dividing by K_{t-1} gives

$$I_{nt}/K_{t-1} = a_0/K_{t-1} + a_1 \Delta Q_{t-i}/K_{t-1} + a_2 I_{nt-1}/K_{t-1} + \Delta\epsilon_{1t}/K_{t-1} \qquad (6.9\text{c}^{\text{I}})$$

Notice that 6.9c^{I} has no intercept but a new variable $1/K_{t-1}$ with coefficient a_0. Often this is neglected and a pure constant introduced implying that the original model had no intercept but a term in K_{t-1}.

Further problems are caused when, for example, researchers deflate I_{nt-1} by K_{t-2} or ΔQ_{t-i} by K_{t-i-1} since it seems intuitively plausible. Such a practice would mean a different structural model than the one which led to 6.9c as an estimating equation. For example, as another alternative we could treat I_{nt}/K_{t-1} as an approximation of $d\,(\ln K_t)/dt$ in discrete form. Symmetrically, now we could have on the right-hand side I_{nt-1}/K_{t-2} or $d \ln K_{t-1}/d_t$. If we treat our dependent variable as $d\,(\ln K_t)/dt$ and our lagged dependent variable in a similar fashion, we must be implicitly proposing an investment behaviour model in log–linear terms. This then means that ΔQ_{t-i} should really be $\Delta \ln Q_{t-i}$ or growth rate of output $\Delta Q_{t-i}/Q_{t-i-1}$. We have for 6.9c in a log–linear framework

$$I_{nt}/K_{t-1} = a_0 + a_1 \Delta Q_{t-i}/Q_{t-i-1} + a_2 I_{nt-1}/K_{t-2} + e_{1t} \qquad (6.9\text{c}^{\text{II}})$$

e_{1t} is then some appropriate random error term. Equations 6.9c^{II} or 6.9c^{I} look like some rearrangement of 6.9c but they in fact embody different structural models (especially if there is an intercept in 6.9c^{I}).

Further work on the accelerator relationship in cross-section work was done by Eisner (1960). Eisner took sales as an output measure and related net investment to change in sales as an output measure and related net investment to change in sales. The problem of heteroscedasticity that we mentioned above led Eisner to deflate his data by a measure of initial size of capital stock. Let us see what this means in terms of our discussion of equation 6.9c above. Eisner's data relate to about 200 non-financial corporations in the US for 1945–1955. For each year's investment by a firm he tried a distributed lag form in change in sales and profit levels and the estimating equation was as follows.

$$
\begin{aligned}
I_{jt}/K_{j0} = {} & b_0 + b_1(\Delta S_{jt}/S_{j0}) + b_2(\Delta S_{jt-1}/S_{j0}) \\
& + b_3(\Delta S_{jt-2}/S_{j0}) + b_4(\Delta S_{jt-3}/S_{j0}) \\
& + b_5(P_{jt}/K_{j0}) + b_6(P_{jt-1}/K_{j0}) + b_7(P_{jt-2}/K_{j0}) \\
& + b_8(P_{jt-3}/K_{j0}) + b_9(D_{j0}/K_{j0}) \\
& + b_{10}(N_{j0}/K_{j0}) + \epsilon_{6jt} \qquad (6.13)
\end{aligned}
$$

K_{j0} was gross fixed assets for the base year 1953, S_{j0} sales for the base year (each for jth firm), P was profits, D depreciation charges and N net fixed assets. I was gross investment expenditure. This equation was estimated for 1953, 1954 and 1955. On the whole Eisner's results demonstrated that the sales change terms were more important than profit levels indicating an accelerator principle at work. What interests us here, however, is not his detailed result but his specification of equation 6.13 and the sort of structural model from which it could be derived. In the light of our discussion above, equation 6.13 is neither of the form 6.9c^{I} or 6.9c^{II}. The sales change terms are deflated by base year sales while all other terms are deflated by base year gross fixed assets K_0. To rationalise 6.13 in the light of 6.9c^{I} we need additional assumptions that (i) in the base year, K was a constant multiple of S, an equilibrium gross fixed assets to sales ratio corresponding to a capital output ratio β of equation 6.9a, (ii) in the original equation in undeflated I_{jt} there was a term $b_0 K_{j0}$, (iii) the error term in the original equation was $\epsilon_{6jt} K_{j0}$ with variance proportional to K_{j0}^2. Given these assumptions we can treat 6.13 as a deflated version of 6.12a with the desired capital stock equation being

$$K_{jt}^* = \beta \sum_{i=0}^{3} \alpha_i S_{jt-i} + \delta_1 \sum_{i=0} P_{jt-i} + \delta_2 \sum_{i=0} P_{jt-i-1} + \delta_3 \sum_{i=0} P_{jt-i-2}$$
$$+ \delta_4 \sum_{i=0} P_{jt-i-3} + r_3 \widetilde{K}_{jt} + r_1 \widetilde{D}_{0j} + r_2 \widetilde{N}_{0j} + v_{4jt} \quad (6.13a)$$

First differencing 6.13a and using 6.12 and dividing by K_{j0} gives us 6.13. The error term in 6.13 is therefore made up of $(\mu \Delta v_{4jt} + \mu_{3jt})/K_{j0}$. We have to assume that (if Δv_{4jt} and μ_{3jt} are uncorrelated with each other) the variance of Δv_{4jt} and of u_{3jt} are each proportional to K_{j0}^2. Looking at 6.13a we see that desired capital stock is a function of level of sales and of sums of profits while $\widetilde{K}_{j0}$, $\widetilde{D}_{j0}$ and $\widetilde{N}_{j0}$ are some constructs whose first differences yield K_{j0}, D_{j0} and N_{j0}. Since P is total profit rather than undistributed profit, it is hard to see its justification in the summation form since it is neither an indicator of the liquidity position nor of the assets position. It must, therefore, be thought of as a sort of combination of expectations, liquidity and other effects. If some of these go in opposite directions, say in time periods which are at turning points of business cycles (e.g. when profit may be high due to a recent boom but expectations low due to anticipation of the oncoming slump), then the separate effects will be under-identified. In any case, the profits explanation and the accelerator are alternatives to be specified rather than to be put together. Also, in the final equation it would be difficult to separate out the equilibrium capital output ratio β of equation 6.13a from the adjustment coefficient μ of equation 6.12.

Kuh (1965) has tackled the question of relative importance of profit as against capacity levels with the help of panel data—a cross section of a set of 30 firms over 1935–1956. The advantage here is that one can observe many firms at a point of time and firms over time. The use of covariance analysis technique which we discussed in the context of Komiya's study is made by Kuh. He explores various specifications of the form

$$I = f(C, K, S, P) \quad (6.14)$$

where I is investment, K capital stock, S sales, P profits and

C an index of capital intensity or the inverse of capital–sales ratio such as β discussed before. Therefore $C = 1/\beta = \overline{S}/\overline{K}$, where bars indicate permanent values. He then forms different estimating equations from the following four alternatives:

$$I_{jt} = \alpha_0 + \alpha_1 C_{j0} + \alpha_2 K_{jt-1} + \alpha_3 S_{jt-1} + \alpha_4 P_{jt-1} + \epsilon_{7jt} \tag{6.15}$$

$$\ln I_{jt} = \alpha_0 + \alpha_1 \ln C_{j0} + \alpha_2 \ln K_{jt-1} + \alpha_3 \ln S_{jt-1} + \epsilon_{8jt} \tag{6.16}$$

$$\frac{I_{jt}}{K_{jt-1}} = \alpha_0 + \alpha_1 \left(\frac{P_{jt} + P_{jt-1}}{2K_{jt-1}} \right) + \alpha_2 \left(\frac{S_{jt-1}}{C_{j0} K_{jt-2}} \right) + \alpha_3 \left(\frac{S_{jt}}{C_{j0} K_{jt-1}} \right) + \epsilon_{9jt} \tag{6.17}$$

$$I_{jt} = \alpha_0 + \alpha_1 (\beta S_{jt} - K_{jt-1}) + \alpha_2 (\beta S_{jt-1} - K_{jt-2}) + \epsilon_{10jt} \tag{6.18}$$

K_{jt} is the end of year capital stock of the jth firm; β is treated as a known variable being the inverse of C. Equation 6.17 is closest to equation 6.13 which was Eisner's basic equation. Here the deflation is by K_{jt-1} except for S_{jt-1}, but the deflation by base year capital intensity index means that we have $(S_{jt-1}/\overline{S}_{j0})(\overline{K}_{j0}/K_{jt-2})$ and a similar term in S_{jt}. The Eisner equation is thus modified by an appropriate term in the relative ratio of base year capital stock to recent capital stock. Equation 6.18 on the other hand is an adaptation of the partial adjustment model with $K_j^* = \beta S_{jt}$ and then we have instead (6.9):

$$\Delta K_t = \alpha_0 + \alpha_1 (K_t^* - K_{t-1}) + \alpha_2 (K_{t-1}^* - K_{t-2}) + u_{1t} \tag{6.9^{I}}$$

$(\alpha_1 + \alpha_2)$ can therefore be treated as estimations of λ since the equilibrium capital–output ratio β is taken as an already known parameter. Equation 6.15 is similar to 6.9b except that the desired capital stock equation is now in terms of *level* of sales and profits and a capacity variable. Equation 6.16 purports to be a log–linear version of 6.15 with profits omitted, since profits can be negative. Notice, however, that specifying 6.16 is not the same as specifying 6.9c^{II} which was in growth rates. The estimation was by OLS combined with covariance analysis. Given our discussion of the instrumental variable, we can easily work out the appropriate instruments since Kuh's equations correspond closely to the equation 6.9b except for deflation by lagged capital stock or logarithmic transformation.

The neoclassical theory of investment behaviour has been most extensively specified and tested in the work of Jorgensen and his associates. Jorgensen begins by specifying the objective function of a firm in terms of maximising net worth. Net worth is by definition the discounted sum of revenue in excess of outlay, the discounting factor being assumed to be the market rate of interest. Outlay is specified in terms of current labour costs and investment expenditure and the tax payable is deducted. The different rates of taxation applied to different parts of a firm's account, e.g. depreciation, capital gains or profits, are all specified. The presence of taxation and of capital gains modifies the flow price of capital which, as we saw in the previous chapter, is given by the formula $p = P(r + \delta)$(see Chapter 5).

The entrepreneur decides on a dynamic path of capital accumulation which maximises his net worth at each point of time by equating the marginal product of capital to the suitably calculated flow price deflated by the price of output. This then yields the desired capital stock which combined with 6.12 yields estimable investment equations. Since Jorgensen has formally specified his model and then used rational distributed lag transformations, his estimated equations need to be formally derived. We shall first proceed using his notation and then draw the analogy with the equations above at appropriate moments. Net worth (NW) is maximised in a non-stochastic framework with perfect certainty by considering the integral of net revenue after tax. Denote gross revenue minus current outlay by R and total tax deductions by D and the rate of discount (assumed to be equal to the market rate of interest) by r. We have then

$$\mathrm{NW} = \int_0^\infty [R(t) - D(t)]\, e^{-rt} dt \tag{6.19}$$

where

$$R = pQ - sL - qI \tag{6.20}$$

and

$$D = u[pQ - sL - (v\delta q + wrq - x\dot{q})K] \qquad (6.21)$$

p, s and q are the prices respectively of output (Q), labour (L) and investment goods (I). Notice that q is the stock price of an investment good not a flow price and that $sL + qI$ is the total outgoings (not the sum of factor rewards). u is the overall rate of taxation on profits, v, w and x are the proportions respectively of depreciation expenditure, interest charges and capital gains (all per unit of capital) deductible from profits before tax. These parameters $[u, v, w, x]$ are taken to be known and would, of course, change with changes in fiscal policy over time and be different for different countries. Substituting 6.20 and 6.21 into 6.19 the entrepreneur is assumed to be maximising subject to two constraints, the neoclassical production function

$$Q = F(K, L) \qquad (6.22)$$

and an identity relating net investment to capital stock

$$I = (dK/dt) + \delta K \qquad (6.23)$$

where δ in 6.21 as well as 6.23 is the rate of depreciation and I in 6.20 as well as 6.23 is gross investment. Equation 6.23 therefore defines net investment (dK/dt) plus depreciation (δK) as gross investment. Forming the Lagrangean and maximising with respect to Q, K, L we get the usual first-order condition. [The only exception to the static case is that K as well as $\dot{K}$ (dK/dt) is involved in both the objective function and the constraints. The Euler condition for this case is to equate the derivative of the Lagrangean with respect to K to the rate of change of the derivative with respect to $\dot{K}$. Thus if G is the Lagrangean formed by taking 6.19 after substituting 6.20 and 6.21 subject to 6.22 and 6.23 the condition is

$$\partial G/\partial K = d/dt(\partial G/d\dot{K})$$

This is a standard result in the calculus of variations, see R.G.D. Allen, *Mathematical Analysis for Economists*, ch 20.]

We obtain thus three first-order conditions of which we shall concentrate on that relating to K, neglecting as does

Jorgensen the other two. We have then

$$\frac{\partial Q}{\partial K} = \frac{c}{p} = \frac{q}{p}\left[\frac{1-uv}{1-u}\delta + \frac{1-uw}{1-u}r - \frac{1-ux}{1-u}\frac{\dot{q}}{q}\right] \tag{6.24}$$

It is easy to check that for $u = 0$ (no tax on profits) this formula reduces to $q[\delta + r - (\dot{q}/q)]/p$ which is the relevant formula for translating the stock price q of capital to the flow price c and then deflate it by p to obtain real flow price of capital services. Different rates of deduction and taxation thus modify the basic neoclassical formulation of flow price in terms of stock price. If we then assume that the production function in 6.22 is Cobb–Douglas we get an explicit expression for $\partial Q/\partial K$ and we have

$$\frac{\alpha Q}{K} = \frac{c}{p} \tag{6.24a}$$

α being the elasticity of output with respect to capital. (We retain the notation α though we have used it before in 6.8b as in both cases the interpretations turn out to be not too far apart, as we show below.) Equation 6.24a is then the basic one for deriving the desired capital stock in the dynamic non-stochastic equilibrium world. We get

$$K_t^* = \alpha\left[\frac{pQ}{c}\right]_t \tag{6.24b}$$

(pQ/c) is indeed the purchasing power of total revenue in terms of capital. Notice, however, that c/p is the purchase price of a unit of capital services and q is the price of a unit of stock of capital. Equation 6.24a is then similar to our equation 6.9a or equation 6.11 (if we think of Q as Q^e) except that (i) we modify the Q term by relative price (p/c), and (ii) equation 6.24a is non-stochastic. If the maximisation process is not perfect or if any of the parameters of 6.19–6.23 are not known with certainty we shall get errors in equations 6.24 and/or 6.24a. Given the nonlinear nature of the dynamic maximisation process, this will be a complex error term and may involve its own past or future values. We shall, however, add an error term to 6.24a corresponding to equation 6.9a and see the consequences of specifying 6.24a as deterministic rather than as stochastic. *Notice that in a one-commodity world p/c would be unity given u = 0 and 6.24a will be 6.9a with i = 0.* We have therefore

$$K_t^* = \alpha\left(\frac{pQ}{c}\right)_t + v_{1t} \tag{6.24b}$$

The adjustment of actual investment to desired investment follows a rational distributed lag pattern. The justification for such a pattern as provided by Jorgensen depends partly on behavioural grounds and partly on delays between orders and deliveries. Equation 6.24b can help generate orders for new investment but an order placed in a particular time period is delivered not instantaneously but over a period of time. Actual investment expenditure at t (I_t^E in Jorgensen's notation), is therefore a weighted sum of previous orders a fraction of each of which is being delivered in the present time period. At t, new orders I_t^N are equal to the difference between K_t^* and K_{t-1}^*. So we have

$$I_t^N = \Delta K_t^* \tag{6.25}$$

$$I_t^E = \mu(L)\Delta K_t^* + u_{3t} \tag{6.25a}$$

We have added an error term u_{3t} since 6.25a is similar to 6.12. We then transform the problem to explain gross investment expenditure (I_t) rather than net and we have

$$I_t = I_t^E + \delta K_{t-1} = \mu(L)\Delta K_t^* + \delta K_{t-1} + u_{3t} \tag{6.26}$$

$\mu(L)$ is a rational lag polynomial and as such can be approximated by a ratio of two polynomials say $\lambda(L)/\gamma(L)$. Substituting 6.24b into 6.25 and 6.25a, we get

$$\gamma(L)I_t = \alpha\lambda(L)\Delta\left(\frac{PQ}{c}\right)_t + \gamma(L)\delta K_{t-1} + \lambda(L)\Delta v_{1t} + \gamma(L)u_{3t} \tag{6.27}$$

We have to choose the appropriate degrees for $\lambda(L)$ and $\gamma(L)$. We could try out several alternatives in an *ad hoc* fashion and choose the best one on the R^2 criterion. We could alternatively impose the restrictions that some of the terms of the polynomial are set equal to zero *a priori*. Given the fact that the terms in $\mu(L)$ signify as delivery lag, Jorgensen makes an *a priori* assumption of $\mu_0 = 0$ and $\mu_1 = 0$. This implies (as can be checked by the reader) that $\lambda_0 = 0$ and $\lambda_1 = 0$. Then Jorgensen chose in the earliest of his studies the simplest specifications for $\lambda(L)$ and $\gamma(L)$ so that

$$\lambda(L) = \lambda_2 L^2$$

$$\gamma(L) = 1 + \gamma_1 L + \gamma_2 L^2$$

Since the coefficients of I_t and K_{t-1} are the common polynomial coefficients $\gamma(L)$, using the normalisation rule that $\gamma_0 = 1$, we rearrange 6.27 as

$$I_t = \alpha\lambda_2 \Delta \left(\frac{pQ}{c}\right)_{t-2} + \delta K_{t-1} - \gamma_1 (I_{t-1} - \delta K_{t-2}) - \gamma_2 (I_{t-2} - \delta K_{t-3}) + \epsilon_{11t} \quad (6.28)$$

Equation 6.28 looks similar to 6.11c above except for two problems: (i) the coefficient δ has to be assumed to be known in terms of $I_{t-i} - \delta K_{t-1-i}$ to reduce over-identification; the assumed value of δ can then be compared to the estimated value of δ, the coefficient of K_{t-1} (Jorgensen finds a value 0.025 optimal); (ii) whereas Jorgensen estimated 6.28 by OLS in his first study we can show that ϵ_{11t} is not likely to satisfy OLS properties since it is a moving average error term as

$$\epsilon_{11t} = \lambda_2 \Delta v_{1t-2} + u_{3t} + \gamma_1 u_{3t-1} + \gamma_2 u_{3t-2} \quad (6.28a)$$

Jorgensen estimated 6.28 by OLS and then could theoretically obtain the coefficients of $\mu(L)$ by computing $\lambda_2 L^2/(1 + \gamma_1 L + \gamma_2 L^2)$. His coefficient of $\Delta(pQ/c)_{t-2}$ is $\alpha\lambda_2$ not λ_2. We can estimate α by imposing the restriction that $\Sigma\mu_i = 1$ and hence the sum of the coefficients derived by dividing $\alpha\lambda_2 L^2/(1 + \gamma_1 L + \gamma_2 L^2)$ is $\alpha\mu(L)$, and summing $\alpha\mu_i$ we get an estimate of α. His studies have been criticised on the grounds that the implied estimate of α was too low (Eisner and Nadiri, 1967). The value of α is around 0.2 and it was suggested that a more general approach would be to assume a CES form for the production function in equation 6.22 rather than a Cobb–Douglas. This, however, changes the specification of the model to a log–linear one for equations

6.25 and 6.23a. This is analogous to our discussion above on pages 192–193. This controversy regarding the appropriate production function produced a lot of conflicting results but no clear agreement. Eisner and Nadiri's approach was criticised by Bischoff (1968) as ignoring the autoregressive properties of the error terms. We have already seen above that a similar argument can be made against Jorgensen's study. The need is for a rigorous error specification which in turn can suggest appropriate instruments which can help us obtain consistent estimates for the coefficients. In the case of 6.28, γ_1 and γ_2 are likely to be biased and hence the estimates of μ_i and therefore of α is also likely to be biased. In any case ϵ_{11} cannot be satisfactorily approximated as a first-order autoregressive error. Thus Bischoff's attempt also falls short of using all the available information.

A much more serious problem arises in combining a dynamic equilibrium model such as the neoclassical one with assumptions of distributed lag adjustment such as equations 6.25 and 6.25a. Once K_t is below K_t^*, all the maximising equations are similarly affected since K_t enters the production function and not K_t^*. We cannot thus derive desired capital stock by assuming the firm to be continuously in equilibrium and then assume it to be adjusting actual to desired capital stock. The adjustment process has to be integrated with the maximising procedure which, we must add, is not an easy task.

The problem in investment demand studies at present is that we have no agreed theory of how and why the firm adjusts its capital stock when in disequilibrium. The need for an endogenous adjustment equation which can generate its own consequent (endogenous) lag distribution is patent. But while Jorgensen's work does not incorporate these elements, it must also be said that in the absence of his studies, such questions could not have been adequately framed. In contrast with earlier studies, his approach is explicitly formal and based on a coherent theory of investment, for some, perhaps the only theory of investment. It is only in the course of its econometric application that we become clear about the many gaps that have to be filled before an economic theory can serve as a useful bedrock on which to base our applied studies.

What we lack, in short, is a theory of disequilibrium.

Another strand of criticism against investment studies is their frequent neglect of the problem of simultaneity. For example, if in the accelerator model one were to take change in sales rather than in output as the basic motive force then the gap between output and sales, i.e. inventory accumulation, has to be brought into the act. On the financial side, the firm has a choice between buying productive equipment, holding liquid assets or distributing higher dividends. All these choices indicate a simultaneous model. The problems of specifying and estimating dynamic multi-equation models are the topic of the next chapter.

Bibliographical Notes

The discussion of distributed lags here should be supplemented by Jorgensen's (1966) article on rational lags, Grilliches' (1967) survey of distributed lags and, above all, the fully rigorous if somewhat detailed treatment by Dhrymes (1971) in his book. Koyck's contribution was contained in his monograph in the 'Contributions to Economic Analysis' series (Koyck, 1954). Early discussion of the estimation problem for Koyck lags caused by a moving average term are in Klein (1958), Malinvaud (1961) and Liviatan (1963). Solow's specification of Pascal lags is in the volume of studies published by the Commission of Money and Credit (Kareken and Solow, 1963). Almon lags have been examined from the point of view of estimation by Trivedi (1970) and Schmidt and Waud (1973). The latter article brings out clearly the nature of restrictions imposed by the Almon lag procedure; see also Godfrey and Poskit (1975).

The capital theory controversy is surveyed by Harcourt in an article (1969) and a recent book (1972). A book of readings edited by Harcourt and Laing (1971) also gives the views of the main protagonists. It has had very little impact on applied econometric work so far.

The main investment studies are cited in the text already. A forthcoming book in the Cambridge Economic Handbooks series by S. Nickel provides a clear exposition of all the issues in the theory of investment behaviour (Nickel, 1976).

K. Wallis in his *Topics in Applied Econometrics* (1973) gives a clear and comprehensive account of Jorgensen's work on investment. Jorgensen's work with his associates on this topic are partially listed in the bibliography. For a critique of his model, the best single reference is Nerlove (1972) and the bibliography therein.

Most of the empirical studies cited here are concerned with US experience. For the UK, see Rowley (1972) and Boatwright and Eaton (1972). A simultaneous equations approach to the firm's financial decisions concerning investment, inventories and dividends has been attempted by Dhrymes and Kurz (1967). This has been extended to Indian data by Krishnamurty and Sastry (1975).

7
Dynamic simultaneous equation models: wages and prices

In the previous chapter, we discussed dynamic single equation models in the context of investment behaviour. We now come to discuss cases where dynamic effects are spread out over a system of equations. This case is the dynamic analogue of Chapter 4 where we had systems of simultaneous static equations. As in that case, simultaneous interaction can occur through the presence of jointly dependent variables in an equation but more so and equally importantly also through the interaction of the error terms. But since we now have a dynamic specification, such simultaneous interaction can occur through lagged values as well as through current values of variables *and* of the random error terms. Given the context of simultaneity, problems of causality and identification once again come up. We hope to relate these to the narrower problems of estimation as well as the broader problems of metatheory broached in our discussion of Herman Wold's position on causality and recursiveness in Chapter 1.

The particular example we shall take to discuss dynamic simultaneous equation models is that of wages and prices. Unlike demand theory, here we do not have an agreed body of theory which can give us *a priori* restrictions. Nor is this case strictly analogous to that of investment behaviour studies, where many explanations contend. We have instead an instance of beginning with a dramatic empirical regularity discovered by examining historical data with only an intuitive theoretical background. The problem is partly one of explaining this empirical regularity by means of our received theoretical framework but partly it is also of checking and verifying its very existence. In the latter process new and interesting relationships have been added to elaborate upon the original one and problems of estimation and specification inherent in the original study have also been brought up.

The empirical regularity we have been referring to is now well known as the Phillips curve or the Phillips relationship. This is a nonlinear relationship between percentage change in money wages and the level of unemployment as measured by the percent unemployed. Examining UK data for 1861-1913, Phillips discovered a relationship between money wage rates (W) and percentage unemployed (U) of the following form. (Phillips labelled his dependent variable $\dot{W}$, but in keeping with the notation of Chapter 1 we shall label it $\dot{W}/W$ since it corresponds to $d(\ln W)/dt$)

$$\frac{\dot{W}}{W} + a = bU^c \tag{7.1}$$

U is a measure of excess supply of labour in the labour market and $\dot{W}/W$ is the rate of change of price of labour. This price adjusts so as to bring demand and supply in equilibrium but what we observe is a time series of disequilibrium positions since the market is not cleared in every time period. We expect c to be negative and b to be positive. As U gets larger, bU^c tends to zero and $\dot{W}/W$ tends to $-a$. If we plot $\dot{W}/W$ on the y-axis and U on the x-axis we have $-a$ as the lower asymptote of $\dot{W}/W$ and when $\dot{W}/W = 0$ we get an 'equilibrium' value of U equal to $(a/b)^{1/c}$.

Phillips adopted an ingenious method of estimating a, b and c. He also examined the possibility of introducing additional variables by examining the residuals computed after estimating the parameters. Since Phillips' study is central to all subsequent discussion and since it contains many innovations in econometric technique which are only now being followed up we shall discuss it in some detail.

Let us rewrite equation 7.1 in three alternative stochastic

forms: we may have either an additive or a multiplicative error term or a combination of both. We have

$$(\dot{W}/W)_t + a = bU_t^c + \epsilon_t \quad (7.2a)$$

$$(\dot{W}/W)_t + a = bU_t^c \exp(\epsilon_{2t}) \quad (7.2b)$$

$$(\dot{W}/W)_t + a = bU_t^c \exp(\epsilon_{2t}) + \epsilon_{1t} \quad (7.2c)$$

Both 7.2a and 7.2b are nonlinear in parameters. If $c = 1$ then 7.2a is linear in a and b; if $a = 0$ then 7.2 is log–linear. If these two assumptions are not fulfilled then if we proceed to minimize $\Sigma\epsilon_{1t}^2$ in 7.2a or $\Sigma\epsilon_{2t}^2$ in 7.2b, we end up with nonlinear rather than linear normal equations and OLS is not suitable. We need, therefore, another estimation method. Phillips chooses an iterative method (which he calls a trial and error procedure) to estimate 7.2c in two stages. Imagine that we start with a log–linear version of 7.2b

$$\ln[(\dot{W}/W)_t + a] = \ln b + c \ln U_t + \epsilon_{2t} \quad (7.2d)$$

Given equation 7.2d one straightforward method is to choose different values for a and for each value estimate $\ln b$ and c by OLS and choose a value of a that minimizes $\Sigma\epsilon_{2t}^2$. There is no guarantee, however, that $(\dot{W}/W)_t + a$ will always be strictly positive. In fact, Phillips encountered instances where it was not positive and hence taking logarithms was no longer a valid operation: Phillips chose to divide up his observations from 1861–1913 into different groups by the size of unemployment observed. He had six size-classes with U between 0 and 2, 2 and 3, 3 and 4, 4 and 5, 5 and 7 and 7 and 11. For each size-class, he took an average of values of U and a corresponding average of $(\dot{W}/W)$. With six size-class averages he obviated the problem of negative values of $(\dot{W}/W + a)$. He obtained values of a, b and c by a two-step procedure. First he confined himself to those four observations where $\dot{W}/W$ was positive (i.e. minimizing $\Sigma\epsilon_{2t}^2$ with $a = 0$) which corresponded to values of U less than 5%. From these he obtained $\ln b = 0{\cdot}984$ and $c = -1{\cdot}394$. He then adjusted the curve obtained by these values to fit the remaining two observations where $\dot{W}/W$ was negative, since a was that value which would (i) exceed the smallest value of $\dot{W}/W$ and give a positive $(\dot{W}/W) + a$ and (ii) satisfy the values for b and c obtained previously (i.e. minimize $\Sigma\epsilon_{1t}^2$ for given b and c). This value was then found to be 0·900.

Phillips thus estimates three parameters from six observations by using a two-step procedure which gives him an extra restriction on the size of a. His method is closer to exact curve fitting rather than least squares since in estimating ln b and c he only has two degrees of freedom but this enables him to get over any lengthy iterative method. His grouping of observations also has another advantage. He observed $6\frac{1}{2}$ cycles of eight years each over the time period 1861–1913. By taking the average over common values of U rather than over successive years, he avoids the problem of a moving average error term. By taking the average over size-classes, he also avoids the effect of a likely mis-specification. This mis-specification may arise due to the omission of a term in $(\dot{U}/U)$. Phillips argues that the nonlinearity of the relationship is reinforced by the fact that when unemployment is falling $(\dot{U}/U < 0)$, the rate of increase of money wages would be even higher than that predicted by equation 7.1 and when unemployment is rising, the downward rigidity of money wages will make the money wages fall less rapidly than predicted by equation 7.1. The omission of this variable would cause the familiar problems of autoregressive errors and inconsistent estimates but his method of averaging avoids this. In each size-class average he has a value of U which corresponds to some years of rising unemployment and some of falling unemployment. Thus a value of U between 0 and 2% will include some observations when U is falling from a higher value (upswing) and some where it is rising from even lower values (post-peak). These will tend to cancel out and in general the average U-value will be uncorrelated with $(\dot{U}/U)$. This would not be true, for example, if we had a three or five year moving average of actual annual values. The omitted variable is thus unlikely to be correlated with the independent variable and there is no inconsistency in estimates resulting from this omission.

Given the estimated equation, Phillips studies the residuals from the fitted equation for each of $6\frac{1}{2}$ cycles. Looking at the time pattern of residuals, Phillips finds confirmation for his hypothesis that the omitted variable

($\dot{U}/U$) has an important effect. For years when U is falling, residuals are positive and for those years when it is rising, they are negative. If one thinks of starting from a high value of U (trough) the first few residuals will lie above the curve since U is falling (up to peak) and then they will lie below, coming back to somewhere near the original high U value at the trough again. This will mean that if successive observations were joined together they would form a counter-clockwise loop with the fitted curve corresponding to a sort of 'stationary' or equilibrium relationship between $\dot{W}/W$ and U when $\dot{U} = 0$ (see figure 7.1).

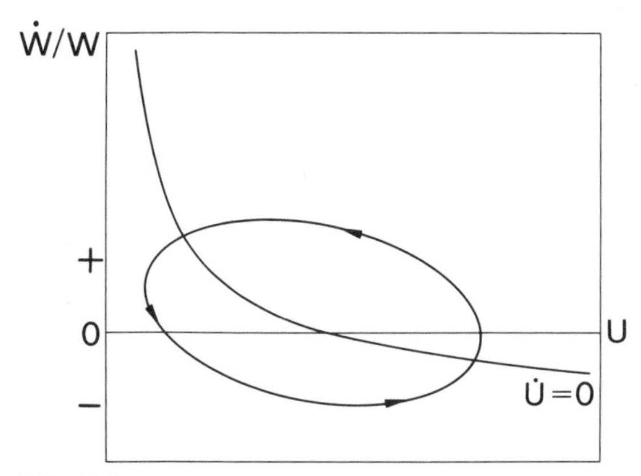

Fig. 7.1

A notable feature of Phillips' article was his measurement of the dependent variable. Such theory as we have of price adjustments in conditions of excess demand is in terms of continuous adjustment with demand and supply being also continuous functions of price. The data are, however, annual and hence in discrete form. In particular, money wage is a flow variable like income and Phillips needed to approximate the growth rate of this flow variable. Thus W_t is the average monthly money wage for *year t* obtained by taking a simple average of the twelve monthly observations. The change in money wage for any year t, ΔW_t (as an approximation for dW_t/dt), is then measured by Phillips as $(W_{t+1} - W_{t-1})/2$. Change in money wage in the year t is thus approximated by the difference in the money wage rate in year $t+1$ from that in the year $t-1$ divided by two. Another way of thinking about this measure is to take $\Delta W_t = W_t - W_{t-1}$ and then the Phillips measure is $(\Delta W_{t+1} + \Delta W_t)/2$. If we think of the average monthly wage rate for year t as being centred in mid year, ΔW_t is centred at the end of $t-1$ and ΔW_{t+1} at the end of t. An average of these two, once again centres the change in the middle of year t. We have already alluded to this measurement problem in Chapter 1 and again in Chapter 5. In our previous notation Phillips approximates $d(\ln W)/dt$ as

$$\frac{d \ln W}{dt} = \frac{1}{W}\frac{dW}{dt} = \frac{1 \Delta W_t}{W_t} \propto \frac{W_{t+1} - W_{t-1}}{2W_t} \qquad (7.3)$$

We shall come back to this aspect of Phillips' curve later in this chapter but here we note that he helped pioneer the method of approximating continuous variables by discrete variables systematically.

In the course of studying the residuals from his fitted equations, Phillips mentions a number of variables that could be added to the relationship. These are the rate of change of cost of living (especially the import price component of it for an open economy that he is studying), and collective action on the part of trade unions and employers' federations. Much of the subsequent discussion has centred on this question of improving the specification of the original Phillips relationship by adding such variables and/or other equations. There has also been a move towards linearising the Phillips relationship to make it amenable to the usual estimation techniques. In linearising equation 7.1 the term bU^c has been approximated by terms in U^{-1} and U^{-2}, the estimating equation then being

$$(\dot{W}/W)_t = \alpha_0 + \alpha_1 U^{-1} + \alpha_2 U^{-2} + \epsilon'_t \qquad (7.4)$$

To this equation, subsequent additions have been made of variables such as $(\dot{U}/U)_t$ (by Lipsey), percentage change in cost of living index $(\dot{P}/P)$ (also by Lipsey), number of trade union members (T) and change in this number (ΔT) (by Hines). Others (such as Bodkin and Perry) have introduced simultaneous equations models explaining $(\dot{W}/W)$ and $(\dot{P}/P)$

simultaneously adding productivity growth, profit levels, etc., in some cases. There has also been another strand (due to Klein and Ball) which seeks to explain the *level* of wages and prices or the absolute difference in them rather than the percentage change thus reducing the nonlinear nature of the model. The importance of expectations about the likely rate of inflation has been brought out (by Phelps and Friedman). Sargan and Kuh have modified the Phillips relationship by adding a term in real wage rate thus giving an equilibrium relationship in real wage rate rather than money wage rate. We shall not go into the details of these studies. We shall concentrate on the estimation problems in the wage–price equations. We begin with Sargan's study estimating the wage–price equation model in both absolute (Klein, Ball) and percentage change (Phillips, Lipsey) terms, especially his treatment of the problem of autoregressive errors. We shall then generalise this to a simultaneous equation model and take as one of our examples Lipsey and Parkin's study which has inspired much methodological debate.

Sargan (1964) studies the course of wages and prices in the UK economy for quarterly data between 1948–1960. His starting point is a study by Klein and Ball (1960) where they estimate a two-equation model of changes in level of wages and prices, with wage change being a function of price change and unemployment and price change being a function of wage change, change in import prices and productivity. Sargan particularly concentrates on two questions. The first is about the specification of the error term, especially assuming a first-order autoregressive process in the errors. Second is a question regarding the relative merits of linear as against log–linear specification of the wage–price model. In each case, he proposes an appropriate likelihood ratio test for choosing among alternative specifications. Since we have already outlined the problem of estimating equations with autoregressive errors in Chapter 2 we shall use it as background throughout.

Let us begin the discussion of estimation with autoregressive errors in general terms. Using Sargan's notation, we may write a single equation as

$$Ax = u \tag{7.5}$$

in matrix terms or equivalently

$$\sum_{i=0}^{n} \alpha_i x_{it} = u_t \tag{7.5a}$$

We designate x_{nt} as the dependent (endogenous) variable and set its coefficient $\alpha_n = -1$. This means that equation 7.5a can be written again, more conventionally, as

$$x_{nt} = y_t = \sum_{i=0}^{n-1} \alpha_i x_{it} + u_t \tag{7.5b}$$

Given an equation such as 7.5, we further assume that the error term u_t follows a first-order autoregressive process which in two equivalent representations is

$$u = \rho u_{-1} + e \tag{7.6}$$

$$u_t = \rho u_{t-1} + e_t \tag{7.6a}$$

where $-1 < \rho < 1$. Since the error term in 7.5 no longer satisfies OLS assumptions we transform it using 7.6. In the conventional notation, we have:

$$(y_t - \rho y_{t-1}) = \sum_{i=0}^{n-1} \alpha_i (x_{it} - \rho x_{it-1}) + e_t \tag{7.7}$$

Equation 7.7. now implies the restriction for each x_i variable that the ratio of the coefficient of the variable to its lagged value is $-1/\rho$. Thus, while equation 7.7 is a reduced form equation derived from the two structural form equations 7.5b and 7.6a, it has to satisfy this restriction on the coefficients. We have in 7.7, $(2n + 1)$ $(\alpha_i, \rho\alpha_i, \rho)$ coefficients but only $(n + 1)$ parameters (α_i, ρ). The n restrictions on each pair $(\alpha_i, \rho\alpha_i)$ make the parameters uniquely identifiable from the coefficients. Corresponding to 7.7, we can write down an *unrestricted* reduced form with $(2n + 1)$ coefficients (which could themselves be parameters) as

$$y_t = \sum_{i=0}^{n-1} a_{1i} x_{it} + \sum_{i=0}^{n-1} a_{2i} x_{it-1} + a_3 + \epsilon_t \qquad (7.8)$$

(If x_{0t} is a constant term then $x_{0t} = x_{0t-1}$ and we will have $2n$ coefficients.)

Equation 7.8 is an unrestricted reduced form where ϵ_t is assumed to satisfy all the OLS properties. A test for the validity of our structural form hypothesis about the error term and about the specification in 7.5 can be performed by computing a likelihood ratio test. This consists of comparing the maximum likelihood value obtained by estimating 7.7 and with that obtained by estimating 7.8 each time on the assumption that the relevant random error term is distributed normally independently with zero mean and a constant finite variance. If these assumptions are satisfied then in our case we can proceed with OLS estimates of 7.7 and 7.8 and compare the estimated residual variances. We have then a ratio of var $(\hat{e}_t)$ to var $(\hat{\epsilon}_t)$ which we can test by the χ^2 criterion for significance. If our restrictions hold then the ratio should be close to one otherwise it would be much higher than one. (Correspondingly the likelihood ratio would be less than or almost equal to one.) This is a test of the over-identifying restrictions on 7.7 as against 7.8 and not of the significance of ρ necessarily.

Sargan tests for ρ directly by running 7.5b and 7.7 and computing the likelihood ratio (var $\hat{u}_t$)/(var $\hat{e}_t$). Clearly if $\rho = 0$, 7.7 collapses to 7.5b. A rejection of 7.5b indicates a rejection of the null hypothesis $\rho = 0$. Thus while 7.8 is the unrestricted form corresponding to 7.7, 7.7 is the unrestricted form corresponding to 7.5b.

The main estimating problem with 7.7 is in obtaining consistent estimates of the parameters α_i and ρ. If among the variables on the right-hand side of 7.5b the lagged value of y_t does not appear, then we have no serious difficulty. We can use the Durbin two-stage procedure outlined in Chapter 2 and use the coefficient y_{t-1} in an OLS regression of 7.8 as our estimate of ρ and estimate equation 7.7 using that $\hat{\rho}$ to obtain consistent (and unbiased) estimates of α_i. The Hildreth–Lu procedure also outlined in Chapter 2 is another much more computer-intensive alternative. But in dynamic equations, we are bound to find that the original specification such as 7.5b will itself include a lagged dependent variable. If we use the Durbin two-stage procedure it may lead to under-identification of the parameters. Let us take a simple example such as equation 6.1.

$$y_t = \alpha_0 + \alpha_1 x_t + \alpha_2 y_{t-1} + u_t \tag{7.9}$$

$$u_t = \rho u_{t-1} + \epsilon_t \tag{7.6a}$$

Then

$$y_t = \alpha_0(1-\rho) + \alpha_1 x_t - \alpha_1 \rho x_{t-1} + (\alpha_2 + \rho) y_{t-1} + \alpha_2 \rho y_{t-2} + \epsilon_t \tag{7.10}$$

Sargan proposes two approaches both of which depend upon our ability to obtain consistent estimates. The first procedure is one that we mentioned in Chapter 2 – the instrumental variable approach. We can estimate 7.10 obtaining instrumental variables for y_{t-1} and y_{t-2} or just for y_{t-1} in 7.6a and estimate ρ from the computed residuals. This way we obtain consistent estimates of α_i and ρ. If we want asymptotic efficiency as well as consistency, we have to use a maximum likelihood approach. Forming the likelihood function of ϵ_t in equation 7.10 we obtain maximum likelihood estimates of the coefficients but not of the parameters. We can, however, start with an initial value of ρ and estimate by maximum likelihood method α_i and then use the $\hat{\alpha}_i$ thus obtained to estimate ρ again. We can iterate this way till we converge to stable values of α_i and ρ. This is a generalisation of the Durbin two-stage procedure except that we start with an arbitrary value of ρ (say $\rho = 0$). Other alternatives are: (1) use our instrumental variable estimate, (2) use the Hildreth–Lu procedure or (3) take the OLS estimate of equation 7.10 and instead of looking at the coefficient of y_{t-2}, compute the ratio of the coefficient of x_t to x_{t-1} (in general the ratio of any one x_{it} to its lagged value) to get $\hat{\rho}$. (This method lacks uniqueness if there is more than one x_{it} variable and has the added defect of loss of efficiency.)

If the χ^2 criterion rejects our restriction on the error term, what do we do then? Can we conclude that equation 7.5b is correctly specified but 7.6a is not and that the error is non-autoregressive? Unfortunately we cannot. We have to explore alternative specifications of 7.5b including higher order lags and/or alternative specifications of 7.6 including higher order lags in u_t. This makes the econometric exercise go on longer without a clear end but as we can see, the problem arises once more due to lack of clear prior specification.

Sargan then proceeds to check whether the specification should be linear or log–linear. Consider once again equation 7.9, and an alternative log–linear version:

$$\ln y_t = \alpha_0 + \alpha_1 \ln x_t + \alpha_2 \ln y_{t-1} + u_t' \qquad (7.9a)$$

We once again have to compare the variances of u_t and u'_t but they cannot be directly compared since the dependent variable is y_t in one case and $\ln y_t$ in the other. We compute therefore antilog $(\hat{u}_t')$ and compare the variance of $(\hat{u}_t)$ with variance of antilog $(\hat{u}'_t)$ and see whether the ratio is greater than one or less than one. If greater than one, we take the log–linear specification; if not we take the linear one. This is not a rigorous test but a criterion for choosing between 7.9 and 7.9a.

We can now take up Sargan's estimates of alternative specifications of the wage equation. The equation fitted by Klein and Ball in their study of UK quarterly data 1948–1956 was

$$(W_t - W_{t-4}) = a_0 + a_1 \left(\sum_{i=0}^{3} P_{t-i} - \sum_{i=0}^{3} P_{t-i-4} \right) + a_2 \sum_{i=0}^{3} (UN)_{t-i} + \epsilon_{3t} \qquad (7.11)$$

The dependent variable is change in money wages over four quarters. This is related to change in cost of living index (P) averaged over four quarters and the number unemployed (UN) over four quarters. In its form above it is not a dynamic equation in the sense we have defined it. It also has the appearance of a four-quarter moving average of an equation in $W_t - W_{t-1}$. Since a moving average error artificially reduces error variance and introduces autoregression even though the original errors are uncorrelated,

Sargan chooses an alternative form for 7.11:

$$(W_t - W_{t-1}) = a_0 + a_1(P_{t-1} - P_{t-4}) + a_2(UN)_{t-1} + a_3(W_{t-1} - P_{t-1}) + a_4 F_t + a_5 t + \epsilon_4 t \quad (7.12)$$

Equation 7.12 takes the quarterly change in money wage rate as a function of a lagged four-quarter change in price, number of unemployed lagged, the level of real wage rate approximated by the difference between money wages and price lagged one quarter, a dummy variable F_t taking as a value 0 during years of Labour Government and 1 during years of Conservative Government (first quarter 1952 on) and a trend variable. Equation 7.12 can arise from a partial adjustment framework or from an adaptive expectations framework. Contrasted to 7.11 equation 7.12 is now in dynamic form inasmuch as W_{t-1} appears on the r.h.s.

Given equation 7.12, Sargan assumes a first-order autoregressive process for the error term ϵ_{4t} and proceeds to estimate it by (i) the instrumental variable method choosing as the instruments an index of import prices lagged one quarter, an index of export prices lagged one quarter and a sum of exports, government expenditure and the previous quarter's consumption expenditure all lagged one quarter, F_t and t being their own instruments, (ii) a Durbin two-step procedure (OLS), and (iii) the iterative maximum likelihood procedure called by Sargan, autoregressive least squares. All the three procedures led to the rejection of the autoregressive hypothesis on the error term – the coefficients (with standard errors in parenthesis) were: IV 0.441 (0.597); OLS 0.178 (0.163); ALS 0.231 (0.159). There was some difference between the estimating procedures regarding signs of coefficients. We expect $a_1 > 0, a_2 < 0, a_3 < 0, a_4 > 0$ (from political–institutional facts known *ex post*) and $a_5 < 0$. ALS gave the wrong sign for a_1 though in all three cases it was non-significant. All the coefficients are given in table 7.1.

When it came to a choice between linear and log–linear specification of 7.12, the ratio of variance of $\hat{\epsilon}_{4t}$ in 7.12 to the variance of the antilog of the computed error term in the logarithmic version of 7.12 was found to be 0.987, the advantage being in favour of the linear form but so slight that the log–linear form was explored further. The log–linear form

Table 7.1

Method used	$\hat{a}_1$	$\hat{a}_2$	$\hat{a}_3$	$\hat{a}_4$	$\hat{a}_5$	$\hat{\rho}$	s^2	χ^2
Autoregressive least squares	−0·015 (0·090)	−0·017 (0·007)	−0·497 (0·148)	+0·391 (0·161)	+0·038 (0·056)	+0·231 (0·159)	0·846	9·17 4 D.F.
LS single stage iteration	+0·053 (0·102)	−0·015 (0·008)	−0·438 (0·137)	+0·231 (0·148)	+0·057 (0·061)	+0·178 (0·163)	0·921	8·76 4 D.F.
Inst. variables	+0·062 (0·262)	−0·289 (0·145)	−0·388 (0·512)	+0·283 (0·456)	+0·049 (0·110)	+0·441 (0·597)	1·022	0·51 2 D.F.

(not given here) had once again $\hat{\rho}$ non-significant, being 0.189 (0.157). The estimation was by OLS. The non-significance of $\hat{\rho}$ led to re-specification of the log–linear form of 7.12 including higher order lags. The particular form found most satisfactory was (estimated by ALS)

$$\Delta \ln W_t = \underset{(0.008)}{-0.018} \ln (UN)_{t-1} \underset{(0.119)}{-0.375} (\ln W_{t-1} - \ln P_{t-1})$$

$$+ \underset{(0\cdot064)}{0.106} \Delta \ln W_{t-1} \underset{(0.157)}{-0.524} \Delta \ln W_{t-2} + \underset{(0.0008)}{0.0019} t$$

$$\hat{\rho} = 0.441 (0.186) \; \chi^2 = 0.12 (4 \text{ DF})$$

$$s^2 = 0.353 \times 10^{-4} \qquad (7.13)$$

Notice that $\hat{\rho}$ is now significantly different from zero. The lag structure of 7.12 is much more complex than for earlier equations and the signs of the coefficients are all correct (although we have no clear prior expectations about the signs of $\Delta \ln W_{t-1}$ and $\Delta \ln W_{t-2}$). When we examine the dynamics and the steady state equilibrium of the equation we see that 7.12 is homogeneous *in terms of real wages rather than money wages*. This we can do by writing 7.13 either in terms of $\ln W_t$ or in terms of $\Delta \ln W_t$. Thus

$$\ln W_t = (1 - 0.731\,L + 0.630\,L^2 - 0.524L^3)^{-1} [-0.018 \ln (UN)_{t-4} + 0.375 \ln P_{t-1} + 0.0019t + \hat{\epsilon}_{4t}] \qquad (7.13a)$$

$$\ln W_t = (1 - 0.106L + 0.524L^2)^{-1} [-0.018 \ln (UN)_{t-4} - 0.375 (\ln W_{t-1} - \ln P_{t-1}) + 0.0019t + \hat{\epsilon}_{4t}] \qquad (7.13b)$$

As in Chapter 6, L is the lag operator. The dynamic of wages is given by the lag polynomial in each case and also, of course, the autoregressive process of the residuals $\hat{\epsilon}_{4t}$. We can solve for the stationary equilibrium equation by setting either $\ln W_t = \ln W_{t-1} = \ln W_{t-2}$, or equivalently by setting $\Delta \ln W_{t-1} = 0$ for all i. In the case of 7.13a, we put $L = 1$ for all the lag polynomial and also extend that assumption to our independent variables and the residual. We see then that the sum of the coefficients of L^i in 7.13a is 0.375, i.e. the same as $\ln P_{t-1}$ and we can rewrite 7.13a in its equilibrium form as

$$\ln W = \frac{[-0.018 \ln UN + 0.375 \ln P + 0.0019t + \hat{\epsilon}_4]}{0.375} \qquad (7.13c)$$

Putting $\ln W_{t-i} = 0$ in 7.13b we can multiply across by the lag polynomial, leaving us with the term in the square brackets which gives us

$$(\ln W - \ln P) = \frac{[-0.018 \ln UN + 0.0019t + \hat{\epsilon}_4]}{0.375} \qquad (7.13d)$$

Not surprisingly, we notice that 7.13c and 7.13d are two ways of writing the same equation. They make clear that the equilibrium process in Sargan's formulation is in terms of the *level of real wages* as a function of unemployment (in numbers) and a trend. This puts the model in the mould of a neoclassical excess demand model for a factor market. Notice, however, that even in the form 7.13c and 7.13d a residual is retained which follows its own autoregressive dynamic.

The next stage in Sargan's study is to introduce an

equation for price change thereby giving us a system of two simultaneous equations. Prices are a function of unit labour cost which is money wage deflated by labour productivity. But this is an equation for product prices while the price variable in the money wage equation is the cost of living index. (The contrast here is between output prices as against price of final demand goods, the two being different due to the nature of expenditure and product accounts.) Sargan takes as his dependent variable $\ln P_t - \ln W_t$ and his equation is

$$\begin{aligned}(\ln P_t - \ln W_t) = {} & \underset{(0.054)}{0.012} (\ln W_t - \ln \overline{W}_t) \\ & + \underset{(0.14)}{0.198} (\ln PM_{t-2} - \ln W_t) \\ & + \underset{(0.706)}{0.875} \ln T_t - \underset{(0.052)}{0.115} \ln R_t \\ & - \underset{(0.0008)}{0.0018\text{t}}\end{aligned}$$

$$\hat{\rho} = 0.587, \chi^2 = 0.55(4\text{DF}), s^2 = 0.705 \times 10^{-4} \qquad (7.14)$$

The estimation was by ALS and we notice that while $\hat{\rho}$ is significantly different, the specification is not dynamic. $\overline{W}_t$ is average weekly wage, *PM* is the price of imports, *T* is a measure of indirect taxes, *R* is a measure for labour productivity. Equation 7.14 is static in its above form. A corresponding static form for 7.13 can be obtained by setting $\Delta \ln W_t = \Delta \ln W_{t-1} = \Delta \ln W_{t-2} = 0$. We get from 7.13

$$\ln W - \ln P = 0.00491t - 0.0443UN \qquad (7.15a)$$

From equation 7.14 we have (taking $\ln \overline{W} = \ln W$)

$$\begin{aligned}\ln P - \ln W = {} & 0.198 (\ln PM - \ln W) + 0.875 \ln T \\ & - 0.115 \ln R - 0.0018t \qquad (7.15b)\end{aligned}$$

Here we have two static equations in two unknowns, $\ln P$ and $\ln W$. We can now get the static reduced forms for these two equations by solving $\ln P$ and $\ln W$ in terms of $\ln R$, $\ln T$,

$\ln UN$, $\ln PM$ and t and we get

$$\ln W = \ln PM + 5 \ln T - 0.22 \ln UN + 0.015t - 0.58 \ln R \tag{7.15c}$$

$$\ln P = \ln PM + 5 \ln T - 0.18 \ln UN + 0.010t - 0.58 \ln R \tag{7.15d}$$

These coefficients are now elasticities. We can see that import prices appear with unit elasticity while productivity has an elasticity of $\frac{1}{2}$. The high elasticity of T cannot be relied upon since the coefficient is non-significant in equation 7.14. The coefficient of UN is low compared to Phillips' coefficient c, though they are not directly comparable. A dynamic reduced form for $\ln W_t$ can be obtained by substituting equation 7.14 lagged one quarter in the $(\ln W_{t-1} - \ln P_{t-1})$ term in equation 7.13. Doing this we get

$$\begin{aligned} \Delta \ln W_t = & -0.018 \ln UN_{t-4} - 0.075 (\ln W_{t-1} - \ln PM_{t-3}) \\ & + 0.375 \ln T_{t-1} + 0.106 \Delta \ln W_{t-1} \\ & - 0.524 \Delta \ln W_{t-2} + 0.0012t - 0.042 \ln R_{t-1} \end{aligned} \tag{7.13e}$$

Once again we can compute the distributed lag $\mu(L)$ as in equation 7.13d and Sargan obtained an average lag of 18 quarters on doing this. A similar lag can be computed in terms of $\ln W_t$ using $\lambda(L)$. The important thing now is to look at the nature of this two-equation dynamic simultaneous equation model and its implicit static and dynamic reduced forms. In doing this, we can look at the specification of the error term and the estimation problem it causes.

We have now moved from a single equation situation of equation 6.1 to a two-equation model. We can write it in general matrix notation introduced in Chapter 2:

$$By'_t + \Gamma_1 x'_t + \Gamma_2 y'_{t-\tau} = u'_t \tag{7.16}$$

where B is a $G \times G$ matrix, Γ_1 is $G \times k$ and Γ_2 $G \times G\tau$ where τ is the longest lag on either of the endogenous variables. We have K exogenous variables and at most $G\tau$ lagged endogenous variables. In equations 7.13 and 7.14 we have two endogenous variables $(G = 2)$ $\ln P_t$ and $\ln W_t$. The longest lag (τ) is on $\ln W_t$ three and the actual number of lagged endogenous variables is four ($\ln W_{t-1}$, $\ln W_{t-2}$, $\ln W_{t-3}$, $\ln P_{t-1}$) instead of the maximum possible six. The total number of exogenous variables (K) is six ($\ln UN_{t-4}$, $\ln R_t$, $\ln T_t$, $\ln PM_{t-2}$, $\ln W_t$ and t). The B matrix can be checked to have the following form

$$\begin{bmatrix} 1 & 0 \\ -1 & 1 \end{bmatrix} \begin{bmatrix} \ln W_t \\ \ln P_t \end{bmatrix} \tag{7.16a}$$

The B matrix is triangular denoting that price depends upon wage but wage does not depend upon price. But this as we know is true only of the current values. The joint dependence comes from lagged values of the endogenous variables. Γ_2 has the form

$$\begin{bmatrix} \gamma_{2,11} & \gamma_{2,12} & \gamma_{2,13} & \gamma_{2,14} \\ \gamma_{2,21} & \gamma_{2,22} & \gamma_{2,23} & \gamma_{2,24} \end{bmatrix} \begin{bmatrix} \ln W_{t-1} \\ \ln W_{t-2} \\ \ln W_{t-3} \\ \ln P_{t-1} \end{bmatrix} =$$

$$\begin{bmatrix} 0.831 & -0.630 & 0.524 & 0.375 \\ 0 & 0 & 0 & 0 \end{bmatrix} \begin{bmatrix} \ln W_{t-1} \\ \ln W_{t-2} \\ \ln W_{t-3} \\ \ln P_{t-1} \end{bmatrix} \tag{7.16b}$$

So in fact our Γ_2 is not 2×4 but only 1×4 with the second row being zero. This arises from the static specification of equation 7.14. Notice, however, that if we followed the single equation definition of dynamic specification which we gave in Chapter 6, we could have the coefficients of $\ln W_{t-i}$ non-zero in the second row, but as long as $\ln P_{t-1}$ had a zero coefficient, we would call it a static equation. This would be clearly inappropriate since the influence of a lagged price variable will be felt indirectly on current price through its influence on current wages which in its turn influences price. In short, the dynamic reduced form equation for $\ln P_t$ will show a non-zero coefficient for $\ln P_{t-1}$. We also see that while the B matrix is triangular, $\ln W$ is not causally independent of log P since lagged values of $\ln P_t$ influence $\ln W_t$. We need to redefine in the context of a simultaneous equation model, the notion of causality (simultaneity) and that of dynamic specification. This has a bearing on the debate about simultaneity we alluded to in Chapter 1.

Wold has defined the notion of recursiveness – lack of simultaneity or the presence of unidirectional causality in terms of a triangular B matrix and a diagonal variance–covariance matrix of the error terms u and also the assumption that u is non-autocorrelated. In particular, we refer to Strotz's idea that simultaneity arises out of considering static equilibrium analogues of dynamic disequilibrium models. Recursiveness is much more the case if we are in disequilibrium situations. The Sargan model formed by equations 7.13 and 7.14 has already shown full simultaneity in its static equilibrium analogue as we see in equations 7.15a and 7.15b. In matrix notation when considering the equilibrium analogue we set $y_t = y_{t-\tau}$ for all τ for each endogenous variable and then simultaneity is shown by the following augmented B matrix, B^+ (when considering *static* equilibrium we set equal to zero any variable which is in change form – if some $y_t = x_t$ then we set $\dot{x}_t = 0$ as Sargan does):

$$B^+ = \begin{bmatrix} \beta_{ii} + \sum_i \gamma_{2ij} & \beta_{ij} + \sum_j \gamma_{2ij} \\ \beta_{ji} + \sum_i \gamma_{2ji} & \beta_{jj} + \sum_j \gamma_{2ji} \end{bmatrix} = \begin{bmatrix} 0.275 & 0.375 \\ -1.078 & 1.0 \end{bmatrix} \tag{7.16c}$$

On the r.h.s. we have given the coefficients of B^+ for the Sargan model; we see that while B is triangular, B^+ is now showing that the equilibrium analogue is indeed simultaneous.

While equilibrium analogues of recursive models are often simultaneous, we should still be wary of concluding that if a dynamic model shows recursiveness, it exhibits unidirectional causality. In order to do this we need to look more closely at the specification of lagged endogenous variables and the autoregressive nature of the error term. If lagged endogenous variables occur in the equations with non-zero coefficients, the pattern of autoregression in the error term is crucial. Up until now we have only considered autoregression in the error term of each equation taken separately. Now we need to look at all the error terms simultaneously. As we discussed towards the end of Chapter 2, we may have a general vector autoregressive process described by a matrix R:

$$u'_t = Ru'_{t-1} + e'_t \tag{7.17}$$

where u_{t-1} and e_t are $G \times 1$, and R is a $G \times G$ matrix. For the two-equation model we are considering, this becomes

$$\begin{bmatrix} u_{1t} \\ u_{2t} \end{bmatrix} = \begin{bmatrix} \rho_{11} & \rho_{12} \\ \rho_{21} & \rho_{22} \end{bmatrix} \begin{bmatrix} u_{1t-1} \\ u_{2t-1} \end{bmatrix} + \begin{bmatrix} e_{1t} \\ e_{2t} \end{bmatrix} \tag{7.17a}$$

One way to define full recursiveness (unidirectional causality) is to say that in a two-equation model if $E(y_{1t}u_{2t}) = 0$ but $E(y_{2t}u_{1t}) \neq 0$, then y_1 is independent of y_2 but not the other way around. Given the vector autoregressive nature of errors as in 7.17 above, we can see that the triangularity of the B matrix and the diagonality of Σ (variance–covariance of u) is no longer sufficient though necessary. *Even when there are no lagged endogenous variables present*, i.e. $\Gamma_2 = 0$ (static specification), *if R is a full matrix then $E(y_{1t}u_{2t})$ can be $\neq 0$ despite the triangularity of the B matrix.* In other words, in our equation 7.14, it will not be legitimate to use $\ln W_t$ as its own instrument if the error term in the two equations is vector autoregressive. Only if each error term is independent of the past values of the other error term (i.e. R is a diagonal matrix) will unidirectional causality be satisfied. Thus we need, even with a static specification, an additional condition that the off-diagonal elements of R be zero.

If we have a dynamic specification then the conditions of recursiveness are even more stringent. Let us consider in our general notation a partition of Γ_2 matrix into coefficients of y_{t-1} terms [Γ_{21} and coefficients of higher order lags $y_{t-\tau}$ $(\tau > 1)\Gamma_{22}$] Γ_{21} is now $G \times G$ or, in our particular case, 2×2. We then require for $E(y_{1t}u_{2t}) = 0$ that Γ_{21} *be triangular in just the same fashion as B and that R be* *diagonal.* In other words, either current or lagged values of y_2 must not appear in the y_1 equation *and* the error term u_{1t} must be independent of u_{2t-1}. In general, if the autoregressive process is of a higher order, even higher order Γ_2 matrices are similarly restricted. In our case we see that while the B matrix is triangular Γ_{21} is not similarly triangular since $\ln P_{t-1}$ appears in the $\ln W_t$ equation. We also have no information on the off-diagonal elements of R though we know that ρ_{11} and ρ_{22} are both non-zero. Therefore, once we move on to dynamic equations, the specification of the error term becomes an even more important part of our overall specification than before. Specifying only the structural equations and leaving out the error term specifications not only affects the consistency of estimates; it may affect the conclusions about causal inter-relationships we can derive from our structural model. The usual conditions for identifiability in terms of the number of zero restrictions on an equation can give a misleading answer. In extreme cases, we may find that while the deterministic part of the model is identified (by the rank conditions) and perhaps over-identified (by the order conditions), once we take into account the specification of the error term, our model may be under-identified. This brings us back to Liu's contention that identifiability criteria are satisfied only through mis-specification.

Let us see how this can arise. We may have a model such as described by equation 7.16. Now counting zero restrictions in 7.16, we ignore the error term. We may characterise certain variables as having zero coefficients in an equation. In the specific case of Sargan's two-equation model, the B and Γ matrices are as follows (arranging our variables as $\ln W_t$, $\ln P_t$, $\ln UN_{t-4}$, t, $\ln \overline{W}_t$, $\ln PM_{t-1}$, $\ln T$, $\ln R$, $\ln W_{t-i}$ and $\ln P_{t-1}$):

$$\begin{bmatrix} 1 & 0 & +0.018 & -0.0019 & 0 & 0 & 0 & 0 & 0.831 & -0.630 & 0.524 & 0.375 \\ -1 & 1 & 0 & +0.0018 & -0.012 & -0.198 & -0.875 & -0.115 & 0 & 0 & 0 & 0 \end{bmatrix} \tag{7.18}$$

In 7.18 we see that by order conditions both the equations are over-identified, there being five zero restrictions in each equation when one is sufficient. If, however, the error term follows the scheme of equation 7.17 we have to incorporate it into our model, we get instead of equation 7.16:

$$By_t' + \Gamma_1 x_t' + \Gamma_2 y_{t-\tau}' - RBy_{t-1}' - R\Gamma_1 x_{t-1}' - R\Gamma_2 y_{t-\tau-1}' = \epsilon_t' \tag{7.19}$$

We have to count zero restrictions in RB, and $R\Gamma_1$ and $R\Gamma_2$ as well as in B, Γ_1 and Γ_2. In Sargan's case, if we take the second equation, the incorporation of 7.17 means that now in the $\ln P_t$ equation, instead of the lagged endogenous variables having zero coefficients, every lagged endogenous variable in the original system has a non-zero coefficient and we have to add $\ln W_{t-4}$ and $\ln P_{t-2}$ with non-zero coefficients. Also the lagged value of every exogenous variable will appear in both the equations with non-zero coefficients.

We shall find if we carry out this calculation that the second equation will have only *one* zero coefficient (that of $\ln UN_{t-4}$) instead of the original five, while the first equation will continue to have five. This is so because with vector autoregressive errors the zero restrictions on lagged endogenous variables no longer count as identifying restrictions. In fact, they are mis-specified as zero. Only the restrictions on the B and Γ_1 matrix are valid. This also illustrates that, in general, counting the number of zero restrictions, i.e. the 'column' condition, is only sufficient. It is the rank condition which we discussed in Chapter 2 which is important. Notice in the case of equation 7.19 that the triangularity of the B matrix is additional, identifying information.

Let us now look at a study of wages and prices by Lipsey and Parkin (1970) which has invited some interesting methodological discussion, especially regarding the specification of the error terms and the resulting loss of identification. We shall first present the Lipsey–Parkin (LP) model and then examine its identifiability in the light of what we have said above. We shall present the original parameter estimates of the LP model by the authors and then the re-estimates when the error specification is modified that were discussed by K. Wallis (1971) in his comment.

Lipsey and Parkin seek to test whether 'incomes policy' in terms of a government policy of wage restraint was successful in containing wage and price inflation in the UK in the postwar years. They take as their time period of study 1948 (3rd quarter) to 1968 (2nd quarter). Following Phillips and Lipsey they specify their endogenous variables as percentage changes in money wages and prices and measure them by the method of centred first differences that Phillips used. Thus, for money wages (W)

$$(\dot{W}/W)_t = \left[\frac{W_{t+2} - W_{t-2}}{2(W_{t+2} + W_{t-2})}\right] \times 100 \tag{7.20}$$

Similarly for prices ($\dot{P}/P$), import price ($\dot{m}/m$), output ($\dot{q}/q$) and trade union membership ($\dot{N}/N$). Given these definitions, LP specify the following two equation model for estimation:

$$(\dot{P}/P)_t = a_1 + a_2\,(\dot{W}/W)_t + a_3\,(\dot{m}/m)_{t-1} + a_4\,(\dot{q}/q)_t + E_{1t} \tag{7.21a}$$

$$(\dot{W}/W) = a_5 + a_6 U_t + a_7\,(\dot{P}/P)_t + a_8\,(\dot{N}/N)_t + E_{2t} \tag{7.21b}$$

We have a system of two equations in two endogenous variables. The specification of 7.21a and 7.21b is not dynamic in the sense we have defined above. Lipsey and Parkin had originally specified the system to include the lagged value of the other endogenous variable in each equation but after experimenting with OLS estimates, they found that the above specification gave the best fit. We have in the system above a 2×2 B matrix and 2×4 Γ_1 matrix which are (excluding the intercepts)

$$By' = \begin{bmatrix} 1 & -a_2 \\ -a_7 & 1 \end{bmatrix} \begin{bmatrix} P/P \\ \dot{W}/W \end{bmatrix} \quad \Gamma_1 x' =$$

$$\begin{bmatrix} -a_3 & -a_4 & 0 & 0 \\ 0 & 0 & -a_6 & -a_8 \end{bmatrix} \begin{bmatrix} (\dot{m}/m)_{t-1} \\ (\dot{q}/q)_t \\ U_t \\ (\dot{N}/N)_t \end{bmatrix} \tag{7.22}$$

Each equation is over-identified by the order conditions and unless either a_3 and a_4 or a_6 and a_8 turn out to be zero, each equation is identified by rank condition as well. If both a_3 and a_4 are zero then the wage equation is under-identified by rank conditions and similarly for the price equations. The error terms are assumed to be non-autoregressive at the outset. An extra restriction which arose from the theoretical specification but which was rejected by the OLS estimates was that $a_2 = -a_4$. If this is so, price increase equals the difference between money wage increase and output increase plus an effect of import prices.

Lipsey and Parkin divide their sample period into two subsamples: 37 quarters of policy-on and the remaining 43 quarters of policy-off. The policy-on periods are in three groups: 1948(3)–1950(3), 1956(1)–1956(4), and 1961(3)–1967(2). They estimate 7.21a and 7.21b for the entire sample period and then separately for policy-on and policy-off periods. Once again since our interest is methodological we shall confine ourselves to the entire sample except when interesting estimation problems arise in the sub-periods. Estimates by OLS for the entire period were (t-ratios in parentheses):

$$
\begin{aligned}
(\dot{P}/P)_t &= \underset{(2.51)}{1.374} + \underset{(5.53)}{0.562}\,(\dot{W}/W)_t + \underset{(4.60)}{0.085}\,(\dot{m}/m)_{t-1} \\
&\quad - \underset{(3.48)}{0.145}(\dot{q}/q)_{t-1}
\end{aligned}
$$

$$R^2 = 0.697;\ DW = 0.946 \qquad (7.23a)$$

$$(\dot{W}/W)_t = \underset{(4.26)}{4.147} - \underset{(1.77)}{0.891}\,U_t + \underset{(5.76)}{0.482}\,(\dot{P}/P)_t + \underset{(2.09)}{3.315}\,(\dot{N}/N)_t$$

$$R^2 = 0.616;\ DW = 0.742 \qquad (7.23b)$$

All the coefficients have the expected *a priori* sign and the t-ratios are all reasonably high. Notice, however, that DW statistics indicate the presence of positive autoregression in the errors. Since, however, the estimating method is OLS, the coefficients of the endogenous variables are inconsistent estimates of the parameters a_2 and a_7 of the model. We need an instrumental variable estimate or some other simultaneous equations approach to obtain consistent estimates. The presence of positive autoregressive errors also leads us to suspect that the estimates are inefficient or that the equations are mis-specified and that the t-ratios are biased upwards. We need therefore a consistent as well as efficient method of estimation since OLS proves to be neither in this case.

In his comment on the LP article, Wallis takes up among other matters the problems of consistent estimation and of specification of the error term. He has indicated that if consistently estimated the model loses identifiability. While Wallis has not given his estimates in his comments, we shall use his estimates and those of David Hendry (which have been kindly made available to us by them) to illustrate the methodological problem. To begin with, we can obtain 2SLS estimates of 7.21a and 7.21b by using reduced form equation estimates of $(\dot{P}/P)$ and $(\dot{W}/W)$. Doing this we get

$$(\dot{P}/P)_t = \underset{(0.72)}{-1.0461} + \underset{(3.69)}{1.0462}\,(\dot{W}/W)_t + \underset{(1.71)}{0.0491}\,(\dot{m}/m)_{t-1} \underset{(0.48)}{-0.0364}\,(\dot{q}/q)$$

$$R^2 = 0.6067 \quad DW = 0.8594 \tag{7.24a}$$

$$(\dot{W}/W)_t = \underset{(2.56)}{3.564} - \underset{(1.08)}{0.6649}\,U + \underset{(3.88)}{0.5563}\,(\dot{P}/P) + \underset{(1.42)}{2.6737}\,(\dot{N}/N)_t \tag{7.24b}$$

$$R^2 = 0.6115; \quad DW = 0.735$$

(The R^2 statistic in 2SLS does not have the properties of the R^2 statistic of OLS but it is usually computed to indicate goodness of fit. We cannot however apply the F-test for significance.)

We notice that in the $(\dot{P}/P)$ equation our estimate a_2 changes quite drastically and now a_4 is no longer statistically significant. Similarly in the $(\dot{W}/W)$ equation, both a_6 and a_8 are not significantly different from zero. The t-ratios of all the coefficients are lower in the case of 2SLS than before. As we have indicated above, if a_6 and a_8 are zero, we have doubts about the identifiability of the $(\dot{P}/P)$ equation since the rank condition will not be satisfied. But we still do not have efficient estimates since the DW statistics continue to indicate positive autoregressive errors. To obtain consistent and asymptotically efficient estimates, we can use the maximum likelihood method with the assumption of vector autoregressive errors as in equation 7.17. As we have said in Chapter 2, David Hendry has derived the appropriate estimators in this case and using his method the estimates obtained are (with t-ratios in parentheses):

$$\begin{aligned}(\dot{P}/P)_t &= \underset{}{-15.7614} + \underset{(27.90)}{4.1496}\,(\dot{W}/W)_t + \underset{(0.63)}{0.1466}\,(\dot{m}/m)_{t-1} \\ &\quad \underset{(1.55)}{-0.0771}\,(\dot{q}/q)_t \qquad (7.25a)\end{aligned}$$

$$\begin{aligned}(\dot{W}/W)_t &= 2.1981 \underset{(1.75)}{-0.3921}\,U + \underset{(16.43)}{0.5081}\,(\dot{P}/P)_t \\ &\quad + \underset{(0.54)}{0.2456}\,(\dot{N}/N)_t \qquad (7.25b)\end{aligned}$$

With the estimated R-matrix (the figures in parentheses are standard errors rather than t-ratios):

$$\hat{R} = \begin{bmatrix} \underset{(0.279)}{0.544} & \underset{(0.0626)}{-0.0476} \\ \underset{(1.080)}{0.202} & \underset{(0.242)}{0.863} \end{bmatrix} \qquad (7.26)$$

Looking at (7.25a and 7.25b) we see that the t-ratios are once again very different from before; the estimates of the coefficients are also very different. Our new estimate of a_2 is nearly eight times the OLS estimate. Again a_4, a_6 and a_8

are statistically non-significant at the 5% level, raising doubts about the identifiability of the $(\dot{P}/P)$ equation. Looking at the R matrix we see that the off-diagonal elements are non-significant as well. Thus obtaining consistent and asymptotically efficient estimates, we see that the $(\dot{P}/P)$ equation may be under-identified while the R matrix is diagonal.

The problem of identifiability can be further explored by looking at the two subperiods. Following the LP division of the sample into two subsamples, Hendry estimated the model for the policy-off and policy-on period. For the policy-off period, he found that the B-matrix is singular, the product of a_2 and a_6 being exactly one. The singularity of the B matrix means that B^{-1} does not exist and that no reduced form can be derived from the model which incorporates the restrictions on structural equations. We cannot therefore separate out one structural form from another. No causal statement can be made about the price and wage variables – as Liu said, there is too much simultaneity. Even dropping the four observations for 1956 from the policy-on and adding them to the policy-off period, the B-matrix was singular as

$$B = \begin{bmatrix} 1 & -0.8755 \\ -1.1442 & 1 \end{bmatrix}$$

The coefficient of $(\dot{W}/W)$ in the $(\dot{P}/P)$ equation is the reciprocal of the coefficient of $(\dot{P}/P)$ in the $(\dot{W}/W)$ equation. Once again there are not two separate equations. We can only observe one mongrel relationship (or reduced form).

The lack of identifiability either due to singularity of the B matrix or to failure of rank condition to hold in an equation may, of course, mean that it is impossible to make any causal inference about the variables. On the other hand, we may try to respecify the system either with more complicated lags or with additional equations. This does not guarantee identifiability, but since we cannot regard any one specification (such as 7.21a and 7.21b) as unique, we cannot abandon the search for a stable structural model immediately. Our study of LP does indicate that while it is the most usual practice to choose among alternative specifications on the basis of OLS results, this is not a good guide. In relying on OLS results, especially regarding signs of coefficients and statistical significance, we deliberately impose a naive error specification which is most likely to be a mistake and which invalidates the basis on which we select among rival specifications. The most usual practice of specifying each equation, after first filtering many alternatives through OLS estimation and then proceeding to correct for simultaneous equation bias or autoregressive errors or multicollinearity, and to argue about the causal structure of the model should be by now discarded. It had advantages in the days of limited computer facilities and lack of computer programmes which could handle more complex estimating techniques. Even today in places where these circumstances hold one may be forgiven for showing healthy scepticism and sticking to OLS estimates. But if we believe that there are identifiable causal relationships which we can and should estimate, then only the most general specification of the error term and of the model is appropriate. This does make the task of econometric research more difficult but renders it less arbitrary. It is also desirable that in applied work we should employ the best available methods of estimation and inference. This is so not just because these techniques are available and more 'fancy' but, as we hope to have shown in this and previous chapters, we may reach meaningless conclusions otherwise.

One problem, however, does arise when we seek to apply a technique such as full information maximum likelihood with vector autoregressive errors. For a model of ten equations, this means one hundred additional parameters – the elements of the R matrix. For large models, therefore, this technique may quickly lead to lack of degrees of freedom. The specification and estimation of large models forms a separate topic in itself and we deal with this in our next chapter.

Bibliographical Notes

The literature on the Phillips curve is very large though much of it is of marginal quality. Phillips' original article (1958) is worth reading since it contains much besides the 'curve'; for a recent discussion see Desai (1975) and the bibliography therein. Sargan's (1964a) article is not easily accessible but worth the trouble of locating and reading. The methodology in Sargan has been subsequently used in Wallis (1971) as well as its extension to a simultaneous equations context in Hendry (1971). The original specification in Phillips' article was nonlinear in parameters as well as variables. In a recent article in *Economica*, Gilbert (1976) has tackled the nonlinear estimation problem and found the Phillips method very accurate.

8
Macroeconomic models: simulation and policy applications

In recent years, many large econometric models have been estimated. While most of these have been put together for pedagogic purposes, models are also coming into use for informing government economic policy. Forecasts from small and large models are now regularly published and used by many business corporations in making their investment plans. When studying the likely impact of a new set of government measures such as the price and wage control announced by President Nixon on 15 August 1971, models have proved an informative tool. These models are simulated to incorporate such policy measures and their likely impact is numerically estimated. This latter use can be best described as prediction. Prediction and forecasting are therefore two prominent uses to which models have been put. In addition, a government may use an econometric model formally or informally in policy formulation. Formally, an econometric model specifies the set of constraints a government must take account of in optimising its objective function. Informally, a government may use a model to generate alternative effects of various possible measures so as to be able to choose between them.

Macroeconomic models have grown in size (as indicated by the number of equations) and number very rapidly in recent years. At the beginning of the 1950's, the largest econometric model of the US was the Klein–Goldberger model. This was an annual model estimated for 1929–1952 with 22 simultaneous equations. This was itself an advance over Klein's model (known as Model I) published in 1950 which had only three stochastic equations. Today, the largest models are quarterly and run into two to three hundred equations. Similar examples can be cited for the UK econometric models where, once again, the transition was from small models to large models and from annual models to quarterly models. The larger size of these models enables the econometrician to explain many detailed components of economic activity, and sectors previously treated as exogenous can now be specified as endogenous. While these are clearly advantages, there is as yet no universal agreement on the desirability of larger models. As we shall see later, in forecasting smaller econometric models seem to perform just as well. The very size of the larger models also makes it difficult to use them quickly and flexibly without adequate computer and financial resources. In this chapter, for example, while we shall discuss large models, all our illustrations at the various stages will have to come from a small model due to limitation of space and ease of comprehension.

Macroeconomic models are the major but not the only example of large econometric models. Another type of model is the commodity model. Commodity models are also simultaneous equations models, often quite large, but they pertain to demand and supply of one or many commodities. Models of agricultural commodities such as watermelon, onions, coffee, tea and jute have been estimated as also those for minerals such as tin and copper and for manufactured goods such as automobiles or services such as railroad passenger travel, etc. The theoretical basis for commodity models is the microeconomic theory of markets with interactions of demand and supply curves. We shall, however, confine ourselves to macroeconomic models in this chapter.

The theoretical framework for macro models is provided by Keynesian economics. Except for Tinbergen's models of business cycles in the US and UK which predate the acceptance of Keynesian economics, all early macroeconometric models were Keynesian in their specification. This meant a concentration on expenditure equations, e.g. consumption, investment and imports, and on employment or income equations. Output equations suffered from comparative neglect as did monetary and financial relationships. These models were models of short-run fluctuations mainly designed to predict the course of business cycles and to estimate the size of government expenditure multipliers on income and employment. Thus we have comparatively few econometric growth models. Only recently have conscious attempts been made to redress this imbalance and greater care is taken to specify the supply constraints, money market equations and price equations. This new tendency has, of course, been helped by the synthesis of Keynesian and neo-classical economics which is embodied in most textbooks of macroeconomic theory.

Parallel with the rise of Keynesian economics was the compilation of national income statistics. As better and more detailed data on macroeconomic activity became available, econometricians were able to specify detailed relationships to study their inter-related structure. Availability of a long and continuous time series of annual and especially quarterly observations in the post-war period has been a major factor in econometric model building. To this we have to add the high speed computers as well as the sustained growth in the theoretical literature on estimation of simultaneous equations models. The confluence of these various forces in the 1930's and 1940's was crucial to the econometric revolution.

We have already seen above that econometric models derive from macroeconomic theory and national income statistics, the two bases for their growth in size. We can now illustrate this briefly by conjuring up a larger and larger model in successive stages. We begin with a model of the 'Keynesian cross'. We have here two equations—one stochastic and the second an identity. The stochastic equation is the consumption function expressing real consumption (C_t) as a function of total real income (Y)

$$C_t = \alpha_0 + \alpha_1 Y_t + u_t \tag{8.1}$$

The second relationship is the income identity

$$Y_t \equiv C_t + I_t \tag{8.2}$$

where I_t is real investment. We have two endogenous variables

C_t and Y_t and one exogenous variable I_t; admittedly, a very abstract and unrealistic picture of how the economy works. Is it, however, an adequate algebraic translation of the Keynesian cross? The 45° line in the Keynesian cross says that total expenditure equals total income. This is our identity (8.2). It hides the fact that there is no supply constraint in this model—all expenditure is translated into output and hence income. The exogeneity of investment in our model appears as the parallel shift of the total expenditure line above the consumption function.

In drawing our Keynesian cross, we have suppressed the output side while emphasising expenditure as the determinant of income. Our model neglects the labour market and the money market. We can start improving it by writing out a model of that other standard diagram in macroeconomics—the IS–LM curves. This makes investment dependent on the rate of interest and the state of expectations embodied in the marginal efficiency of investment. The latter is unobservable and in the diagram is normally suppressed. So we write

$$I_t = I(r_t) \tag{8.3}$$

We get the IS curve by combining 8.3 with the investment savings identity

$$I_t \equiv S_t \equiv Y_t - C_t \tag{8.4}$$

By virtue of 8.1, we combine equation 8.1 to 8.4 as the IS curve

$$I_t(r_t) = S(Y_t) \tag{8.5}$$

Notice that 8.5 is a compressed version of a four-equation model of 8.1 to 8.4. On the monetary side we have demand for money on transactions and speculative grounds

$$M_t^D = M_1(Y_t) + M_2(r_t) \tag{8.6}$$

and the identity of money demand with autonomous money supply, $\bar{M}$

$$M_t^D = \bar{M}_t \tag{8.7}$$

The LM curve is therefore

$$M_1(Y_t) + M_2(r_t) = \bar{M}_t \tag{8.8}$$

We have now, instead of a two-equation model, a six-equation model of 8.1 to 8.4 and 8.6 and 8.7. Geometrically we collapse this six-equation model into a two-equation model, 8.5 and 8.8. These two equations are not 'structural equations' nor are they reduced form equations. They will not help us in estimating α_1, for example, and the slope of 8.3, since both these are jumbled up in 8.5. If $I(r_t)$ is taken as linear, we may have

$$I_t = \beta_0 - \beta_1 r_t + v_t \tag{8.3a}$$

and then 8.5 is

$$r_t = \frac{(\alpha_0 + \beta_0)}{\beta_1} - \frac{(1-\alpha_1)}{\beta_1} Y_t + \left(\frac{v_t - u_t}{\beta_1}\right) \tag{8.5a}$$

It is clear by inspection that 8.5a will not give us estimates of our structural parameters α_0, α_1, β_0 and β_1. If we write 8.6 as a linear equation

$$M_t = \delta_0 + \delta_1 Y_t - \delta_2 r_t + e_t \tag{8.6a}$$

then equation 8.8 will become

$$r_t = (\delta_0/\delta_2) + (\delta_1/\delta_2)Y_t - (1/\delta_2)\bar{M}_t + (e_t/\delta_2) \tag{8.8a}$$

It looks as though equation 8.8a will help us in obtaining structural parameter estimates of δ_0, δ_1 and δ_2. When we take the two equations together we see, however, that we have only one exogenous variable, $\bar{M}_t$. This renders 8.8a under-identified by order conditions. We shall further discuss this problem later on.

Our progress from a two-equation model to a six-equation model still leaves us with an unrealistic model. Let us look again at our identity for total expenditure. For any modern economy, the components of total expenditure or of gross national product are much more varied. We can look at national income accounts and write instead of 8.2 or 8.4 a new identity.

$$C_t + I_t + G_t + E_t - F_t - T_t + S_t \equiv Y_t \tag{8.9}$$

where G is government expenditure, E exports and F imports of goods and services, T indirect taxes and S subsidies. Even further disaggregation can be carried out by breaking up investment into fixed investment and inventory investment. An alternative identity for GNP is to look at it from the point of view of income. Then income is the sum of factor shares—wages and salaries (W), retained profits (RP), dividends (DIV), rent and interest (RIN) payments and the amount collected by the government in taxes (TY) and social security payments (TP).

$$W_t + RP_t + DIV_t + RIN_t + TY_t + TP_t \equiv Y_t \tag{8.10}$$

A third relationship is the total output identity where total output is the sum of agricultural output (AG), mining and manufacturing (MG) transport and communications (TC) and other services (SV). We then have

$$AG_t + MG_t + TC_t + SV_t \equiv Y_t \tag{8.11}$$

These three identities for income, expenditure and output throw up a number of new explanatory variables. They also help us to frame more interesting hypotheses. We could, for example, specify the consumption function in terms of wages and salaries and non-wage income separately or in terms of personal disposable income (PDY) rather than income.

$$C_t = \alpha_0 + \alpha_1 W_t + \alpha_2 (DIV + RIN)_t + u_t \tag{8.12a}$$

or

$$C_t = \alpha_0 + \alpha_1 PDY_t + u_t \tag{8.12b}$$

$$PDY = Y - TY - RP - TP \tag{8.13}$$

We can generate equations for the wage component of the income equation by using the notion of production functions and the marginal product relationship to explain the wage rate and the total amount of labour employed. This will link the income and output sides. The output and expenditure sides can be brought together to see if there is demand–supply balance or prospect of a demand–pull inflation. Each of the sixteen components of the three identities can be made endogenous and they in turn will lead to additional equations. We cannot explain the split of total profits between retained profits and dividends without bringing in the yield on equities and return to capital. Very rapidly we find ourselves with a large collection of equations, all interlinked in the circular flow of income. Before, however, we go onto such a large model, we look at a small model in some detail.

The model we have chosen for detailed examination is a model for the US economy estimated for the inter-war period 1921–1941. It is a model with three stochastic equations and three identities. It is known in econometric literature as the Klein Model I. While it is a small model and the supply and monetary sides are totally neglected, as a model it has been used again and again as a touchstone for new estimating techniques and to illustrate the uses to which econometric models can be put. We can, therefore, take advantage of this and provide several alternative estimates of the parameters in the model as we go along.

The Klein Model I can be written as follows:

$$C_t = \alpha_0 + \alpha_1 P_t + \alpha_2 P_{t-1} + \alpha_3 (W_1 + W_2)_t + u_{1t} \qquad (8.14)$$

$$I_t = \beta_0 + \beta_1 P_t + \beta_2 P_{t-1} + \beta_3 K_{t-1} + u_{2t} \qquad (8.15)$$

$$W_{1t} = \gamma_0 + \gamma_1 (Y + T - W_2)_t + \gamma_2 (Y + T - W_2)_{t-1} + \gamma_3 (t - 1931) + u_{3t} \qquad (8.16)$$

$$Y = C + I + G - T \qquad (8.17)$$

$$Y = P + W_1 + W_2 \qquad (8.18)$$

$$K_t - K_{t-1} = I_t \qquad (8.19)$$

All the variables are in real terms.

Consumption (C) is related to the two components of income: profits (P), current and lagged, and the wage bill–private (W_1) and government (W_2). Thus, the original Keynesian specification of allowing MPC out of different incomes to be different is followed here. Investment (I) is a function of the current and lagged profit level and the previous level of capital stocks. Klein thus specifies a profits theory rather than an accelerator or a Fisherian neo-classical theory for net investment. The third equation relates the private wage bill (as an indicator of employment) to total private product measured as net national product (Y) plus business taxes (T) minus government wage and a trend (t). The first identity relates net national product to the sum of total expenditure net of taxes. The second expresses the income identity as the sum of factor incomes. The third says that net investment is the addition to capital stock.

We have, therefore, a small income–expenditure model which explains six economic variables (C, I, W_1, Y, P and K) treating as exogenous the government sector variables W_2, G and T and a trend. There are, in addition, lagged endogenous (P_{t-1}, K_{t-1}, Y_{t-1}) and lagged exogenous (T_{t-1}, W_{2t-1}) variables giving us six endogenous variables and nine predetermined variables. By order conditions, each stochastic equation is over-identified. We can add further identities for $W_1 + W_2 (W)$ or for $(Y + T - W_2)(E)$, etc., but these will not change anything essential.

The model above is stochastic, linear, simultaneous and dynamic. We can look at a variety of estimates provided. In table 8.1 we list estimates by OLS, 2SLS and FIML to indicate the relative merits of these methods. Looking at the OLS estimates in comparison with any other method, we can gauge the extent of the simultaneous equations bias present. Our estimate of β_1 drops from 0.48 in OLS to 0.15 in 2SLS and 0.231 in FIML. Correspondingly, β_2 estimates diverge in the opposite direction. The signs of most of the coefficients do not change under any of the estimation methods and they are all in line with *a priori* expectations. Taking the 2SLS estimates for the time being, we see that the sizes of the coefficients are also plausible though current profits has non-significant coefficients in both cases. In general, however, we would expect α_3 to exceed α_1 and/or α_2. The investment function shows a lag of investment behind profits while the reaction of the wage bill (employment) to changes in expenditure is much quicker since $\gamma_1 > \gamma_2$.

Apart from commenting on the sign, size and significance of individual coefficients (and, perhaps, remarks on goodness of fit) what else can we say about a model? In as much as we have a model, it embodies a hypothesis about a set of causal interactions among our endogenous variables themselves and between them and predetermined variables. The presence of simultaneity is indicated by the B-matrix (in our notation of Chapter 2) of the coefficient of endogenous variables. It is clear that the B-matrix as given below indicates simultaneity since there are non-zero coefficients both above and below the principal diagonal.

Table 8.1 Alternative Estimates of Klein Model I Parameters

Parameters	OLS	2SLS	3SLS	LIML	FIML(1)	FIML(2)
α_1	0.25	0.017	0.1249	0.02	0.02	−0.232
	(0.07)	(0.118)	(0.1086)	(0.07)		(0.312)
α_2	0 0	0.216	0.1631	0 0	0.23	0.395
		(0.107)	(0.1005)			(0.217)
α_3	0.80	0.810	0.7901	0.87	0.80	0.801
	(0.04)	(0.040)	(0.0379)	(0.04)		(0.035)
β_1	0.49	0.150	−0.0131	0.03	0.23	−0.801
	(0.10)	(0.173)	(0.1619)	(0.23)		(0.491)
β_2	0.33	0.616	0.7557	0.68	0.55	1.0519
	(0.10)	(0.162)	(0.1530)	(0.21)		(0.352)
β_3	−0.11	−0.158	−0.1948	−0.17	−0.15	−0.148
	(0.03)	(0.036)	(0.0326)	(0.04)		(0.030)
γ_1	0.44	0.439	0.4005	0.43	0.42	0.234
	(0.03)	(0.036)	(0.0318)	(0.03)		(0.0488)
γ_2	0.15	0.147	0.1813	0.15	0.16	0.235
	(0.04)	(0.039)	(0.0339)	(0.03)		(0.0345)
γ_3	0.13	0.130	0.1497	0.13	0.13	0.285
	(0.03)	(0.029)	(0.0279)	(0.02)		(0.045)
α_0	16.43	16.555	16.44	17.71	16.78	21.977
	(1.320)	(1.320)	(0.13)			(2.485)
β_0	10.13	20.278	28.18	22.59	17.79	10.135
		(7.523)	(0.68)			(7.938)
γ_0	1.50	1.500	1.80	1.53	1.60	10.729
		(1.147)	(0.12)			(1.650)

Sources: OLS, FIML(1)—Klein L. R., *Economic Fluctuations in the US, 1921–1941.*
2SLS, 3SLS from Zellner and Theil, 'Three-stage least squares: simultaneous estimation of simultaneous equations', *Econometrica*, Jan. 1962.
FIML(2)—from David Hendry FIML, *A User's Manual*, (available from LSE.)
FIML(1) assumes a diagonal Σ matrix while FIML(2) takes the full Σ matrix.

$$By' = \begin{bmatrix} 1 & 0 & -\alpha_3 & 0 & -\alpha_1 & 0 \\ 0 & 1 & 0 & 0 & -\beta_1 & -\beta_3 \\ 0 & 0 & 1 & -\gamma_1 & 0 & 0 \\ -1 & -1 & 0 & 1 & 0 & 0 \\ 0 & 0 & 1 & -1 & 1 & 0 \\ 0 & -1 & 0 & 0 & 0 & 1 \end{bmatrix} \begin{bmatrix} C \\ I \\ W_1 \\ Y \\ P \\ K \end{bmatrix} \tag{8.20}$$

The next question is, therefore, about the effect of the predetermined variables on the endogenous variables. This is made up of two components: the direct effect of a predetermined variable on the endogenous variable in question—the appropriate element of the Γ matrix of the coefficients of predetermined variables—and the indirect effect through the effect of the predetermined variable on another endogenous variable which in turn influences the endogenous variable in question. This total effect is captured by the reduced form which expresses each endogenous variable solely in terms of predetermined variables having solved out, as it were, the simultaneous interaction of the endogenous variables within themselves. In the familiar notation, we have

$$By' + \Gamma z' = u' \tag{8.21}$$

$$y' = -B^{-1}\Gamma z' + B^{-1}u' = \pi z' + v' \tag{8.22}$$

An appropriate coefficient of the π matrix now gives us the *total* effect—direct and indirect—of a predetermined variable on an endogenous variable. Having obtained $\hat{B}$ and $\hat{\Gamma}$, the estimates of our structural parameters, we can combine them to obtain $\hat{\pi}$. We give here the $\hat{\pi}$ obtained from the FIML estimates. Given nine predetermined variables and six endogenous variables our $\hat{\pi}$ matrix is 6 x 9. For convenience we shall partition our vector of nine variables into current exogenous (x), lagged exogenous (x_{t-1}) and lagged endogenous (y_{t-1}). Correspondingly, we partition our matrix into $\hat{\pi}_1$, $\hat{\pi}_2$ and $\hat{\pi}_3$. We have therefore

$$\hat{y}'_t = \hat{\pi}_1 x'_t + \hat{\pi}_2 x'_{t-1} + \hat{\pi}_3 y'_{t-1} \tag{8.23}$$

$$\begin{pmatrix} \hat{C} \\ \hat{I} \\ \hat{W}_1 \\ \hat{Y} \\ \hat{P} \\ \hat{K} \end{pmatrix} = \begin{bmatrix} 0.666 & -0.188 & 0.671 & 0.155 \\ -0.052 & -0.296 & 0.259 & -0.012 \\ -0.162 & -0.204 & 0.831 & 0.195 \\ 0.614 & -1.484 & 1.930 & 0.143 \\ -0.224 & -1.281 & 1.119 & -0.052 \\ -0.052 & -0.296 & 0.259 & -0.012 \end{bmatrix} \begin{pmatrix} W_2 \\ T \\ G \\ t \end{pmatrix}$$

$$
+ \begin{bmatrix} -0.189 & 0.189 \\ 0.015 & -0.015 \\ -0.237 & 0.237 \\ -0.174 & 0.174 \\ 0.063 & -0.063 \\ 0.015 & -0.015 \end{bmatrix} \begin{pmatrix} W_{2t-1} \\ T_{t-1} \end{pmatrix}
$$

$$
+ \begin{bmatrix} 0.743 & -0.098 & 0.189 \\ 0.746 & -0.746 & -0.015 \\ 0.626 & -0.119 & 0.237 \\ 1.489 & -0.283 & 0.174 \\ 0.863 & -0.164 & -0.063 \\ 0.746 & 0.816 & -0.015 \end{bmatrix} \begin{pmatrix} P_{t-1} \\ K_{t-1} \\ Y_{t-1} \end{pmatrix} \qquad (8.24)
$$

Having obtained our π matrix in the form we want, we can now begin to ask some questions. Let us look at π_1 matrix. What, for example, is the value of the income multiplier? If we look at the Y row and G column we see that the value is 1.930. The tax multiplier on the other hand is −1.484. A balanced budget with a matching unit increase in G and T will give us an income multiplier of $(1.930 - 1.484) = 0.446$ or about $\frac{1}{2}$. We can also see that a unit increase in G leads to a profit multiplier of 1.119 and a wages multiplier of only 0.811, though a balanced budget multiplier is mildly negative for profits, −0.162 (1.119 − 1.281), and positive on wages, 0.607 (0.311 − 0.204). The coefficients of the $\hat{\pi}_1$ matrix give us the multipliers called the *impact multipliers*, since they take effect in the same time period.

This is not the *total* effect of an exogenous variable on an endogenous variable but only the effect within the same time period. Since our specifications are dynamic, an increase in an endogenous variable keeps on having effect through time. We saw in Chapter 6 the short-run and the long-run impact of a change in x on y. We now extend the same idea to a model of many equations. We now obtain *dynamic multipliers.* We have in our model a set of simultaneous first-order difference equations. We obtain the dynamic long-run multiplier by substituting our equation recursively for values of $y_{t-1}, y_{t-2}, \ldots$. We get the *final form* of our model expressing each endogenous variable solely in terms of exogenous variables

$$y'_t = \hat{\pi}_1 x'_t + \hat{\pi}_2 x'_{t-1} + v'_t + \hat{\pi}_3 \{\hat{\pi}_1 x'_{t-1} + \hat{\pi}_2 x'_{t-2} + y'_{t-1} + \hat{\pi}_3 [\hat{\pi}_1 x'_{t-2} + \hat{\pi}_2 x'_{t-3} + y'_{t-2} + \hat{\pi}_3 (\ldots$$

$$y'_t = \hat{\pi}_1 x'_t + (\hat{\pi}_2 + \hat{\pi}_3 \hat{\pi}_2) x'_{t-1} + \hat{\pi}_3 (\hat{\pi}_2 + \hat{\pi}_3 \hat{\pi}_2) x'_{t-2} + \hat{\pi}_3^2 (\hat{\pi}_2 + \hat{\pi}_3 \hat{\pi}_2) x'_{t-3} + \ldots$$

$$y'_t = \hat{\pi}_1 x'_t + \sum_{i=1}^{\infty} \hat{\pi}_3^{i-1} (\hat{\pi}_2 + \hat{\pi}_3 \hat{\pi}_2) x'_{t-i} + \sum_{i=0}^{\infty} \hat{\pi}_3^i v'_{t-i} \tag{8.25}$$

Now a change in x_t has its effect spread out over a long time period. If, for example, we want to estimate the effect of a sustained one unit increase in one of our x_t over five years, we evaluate the first five terms π_1 and the four terms of the polynomial in x_{t-i}. Of greater interest to us is the long-run equilibrium multiplier which we can get if $\hat{\pi}_3^{i-1}$ converges. This implies that the implied dynamic process is not perpetually cyclical or even explosive but damped and hence convergent. If $\hat{\pi}_3^{i-1}$ is convergent then we get the long-run equilibrium equation for y

$$y'_t = [\pi_1 + (I - \pi_3)^{-1} (\pi_2 + \pi_3 \pi_1)] x'_t \tag{8.26}$$

Equation (8.26), therefore, gives the long-run impact of x_t on y_t. For the Klein Model I, Theil has calculated this set of multipliers (ignoring the trend variable)

	W_2	T	G
C	0.536	−0.569	1.323
P	−0.192	−1.237	0.965
W_1	−0.271	−0.333	1.358
I	0	0	0
Y	0.536	−1.569	2.323
K	−1.024	−6.564	5.123

Now we can compare the long-run equilibrium multiplier of government expenditure and income. This turns out to be 2.323 while the balanced budget multiplier is $(2.323 - 1.569) = 0.754$. The long-run multipliers for investment are zero because in equilibrium the capital stock remains unchanged and no net investment need take place. The balanced budget multiplier for W_1 is near unity $(1.358 - 0.333)$ while for π it is once again negative $(0.965 - 1.237)$.

From the reduced form we obtain impact multipliers and from the final form we obtain dynamic multipliers. The expression for dynamic multipliers can also be obtained straightaway from our reduced form equations 8.23 by putting $y_t = y_{t-1}$, i.e. assuming convergence to long-run equilibrium. The advantage of obtaining an expression such as the final form in 8.25 is that we can observe the time form of the distributed lag effect of x_t on y_t. Also if we do not want to assume damped fluctuations or cannot do so, then we may wish to evaluate the multiplier for two, three or five years—these are called interim multipliers. If convergence to long-run equilibrium takes too many years then long-run multipliers do not have any operational meaning and interim multipliers may be a better guide for policy making. We should also bear in mind that in going from 8.25 to 8.26 and 8.27 we have ignored the error terms. Equation 8.26 then only gives us the asymptotic value of y assuming all the v's are independent and equal to zero in the probability limit. As we shall see later, the fluctuations in the deterministic part of our system may be damped but the errors may themselves cause cyclical or explosive fluctuations.

Keynesian vs Monetary Explanation: Perspective on a Debate

While the Klein Model I is useful for pedagogic purposes, it has its limitations. Being small in size it allows for only very simple relationships. Many relationships are ignored, the most important one being the monetary ones. Apart from its equation for W_1, the Klein Model I can be said to be a simple extension of our two-equation model of the Keynesian cross. It respecifies the income identity to include the government sector and makes net investment endogenous. There is, however, no allowance for rate of interest effects on either consumption or investment. The Klein Model I equations imply a vertical IS curve stating that the level of income is independent of the rate of interest. This is a common criticism to be made of many recent macroeconomic models, i.e. their ignorance of the interaction of the monetary and real factors. This has led to a long and interesting debate on whether the 'monetarist' explanation performs better than the 'Keynesian' explanation in predicting income fluctuations. Our previous discussion enables us to put this controversy in perspective.

The controversy began when Milton Friedman and David Meiselman (1963) in a paper for the US Commission on Money and Credit presented regression results on two alternative hypotheses regarding income generation. They were

$$Y = a_0 + b_0 A + u \quad (8.28)$$

$$Y = a_1 + b_1 M + v \quad (8.29)$$

A is some measure of autonomous expenditure, M is money supply and Y is a measure of income. In their opinion, b_0 was the Keynesian multiplier and b_1 could be derived from a demand for money relationship as the measure of income velocity of money. Their regression results were run on US data for the twentieth century in various ways and they found that the monetary explanation equation 8.29 performed better in terms of R^2 than the Keynesian explanation.

This contention led to a long debate into the details of which we need not go. Modigliani and Ando (1965), for example, showed that the mis-specification implicit in the two equations biased the R^2 in favour of 8.29. For our purposes let us see if we can put Professor Friedman's equations in a broader context. For this we go back to our IS–LM equations. We remarked that, as a system of two-equations, 8.5a and 8.8a were under-identified since there were not enough zero restrictions: we had only $\bar{M}$ as an exogenous variable. Whenever such under-identification is possible, we are likely to find rival theories contending. One example was the work on investment behaviour we surveyed in Chapter 6. We saw that rival hypotheses about investment were indistinguishable from each other since insufficient restrictions were placed in the course of their specification. A similar situation arises here. We can deal with it by respecifying our income identity in equation 8.2 slightly:

$$Y_t = C_t + I_t + G_t \tag{8.2a}$$

This is but a slight modification. Now with equations 8.1, the consumption function, and (8.3a), the investment function, we can obtain the IS curve using the identity in 8.4. We have, after some manipulation

$$Y_t = \frac{(\alpha_0 + \beta_0)}{1-\alpha_1} - \frac{\beta_1}{1-\alpha_1} r_t + \frac{1}{1-\alpha_1} G_t + \frac{(u+v)}{1-\alpha_1} \tag{8.30}$$

Equation 8.30 is an IS curve of the type we had in 8.5a except that Y_t is the dependent variable rather than r_t. Now Friedman's Keynesian equation can be seen as the same as 8.30 with A replacing G and assuming $\beta_1 = 0$ *a priori*. Similarly, if we look at the demand for money equation 8.5a, we can set $\delta_2 = 0$ and derive a LM curve similar to Friedman's 8.28. The Friedman specifications therefore involve two extremes: (a) no impact of interest rates on real expenditure—a vertical IS curve; or (b) no impact of interest rates on the demand for money—a vertical LM curve. There are, however, several intermediate possibilities open. We may also be interested in *testing* whether $\beta_1 = 0$ and/or $\delta_2 = 0$, rather than imposing them *a priori*.

We should notice that adding an exogenous variable G to the IS relationship, we satisfy the order conditions for identification for the pair of equations 8.8a and 8.30. In fact our equations are just identified. Before only 8.5a was identified and 8.8a was not since the presence of $\overline{M}$ allowed the LM curve to shift, the observed points therefore lying along the IS curve. Now the G variable lets the IS curve shift thus identifying the LM curve. Now if we set $\beta_1 = 0$, the model becomes recursive since now the income level is determined by the IS relationship and the money market is dependent on the real equations but not the other way around. For this model of two equations 8.8a and 8.30 with $\beta_1 = 0$, the B matrix is triangular since

$$\begin{bmatrix} 1 & 0 \\ -\delta_1/\delta_2 & 1 \end{bmatrix} \begin{pmatrix} Y_t \\ r_t \end{pmatrix} \tag{8.31}$$

But if $\delta_2 = 0$ then the LM relationship determines the income level and the IS equation determines the rate of interest. The B matrix is (after some rewriting)

$$\begin{bmatrix} 1 & -(1-\alpha_1)/\beta_1 \\ 0 & 1 \end{bmatrix} \begin{pmatrix} r_t \\ Y_t \end{pmatrix} \tag{8.32}$$

We may, however, want to test whether β_1 and δ_2 are non-zero. If they are non-zero then setting them *a priori* equal to zero is a mis-specification and would lead to inconsistent as well as inefficient estimates. In testing these hypotheses, we may wish to expand the scope for the interaction of real and monetary sectors. Thus β_1 could be non-zero because savings are interest sensitive and/or because investment may be interest sensitive. We may prefer to estimate structural relations rather than equations which compound together two structural equations as is the case with 8.5a or 8.30. Modigliani and Ando provide in their article the smallest possible econometric model for testing IS–LM relationships with a realistic specification of national income identities. They start with the following model:

$$C_t = C(PDY, r, C_{t-1}) + u_{1t}$$ consumption function (8.33)

$$Z^a = f(r, C_{t-1}) + u_{2t}$$ 'investment' function (8.34)

$$M = L(Y, r, C_{t-1}) + u_{3t}$$ demand for money equation (8.35)

$$M = B(r, M^*) + u_{4t}$$ supply of money (8.36)

$$C^f = C + Z^i$$ induced expenditure identity (8.37)

$$Y = C^f + Z^a$$ net national product identity

$$PDY = Y - X$$ personal disposable income identity (8.39)

Z^a is 'autonomous' expenditure which is a sum of net investment, government expenditure and exports. X stands for the various items of tax deductions and business retention which account for the difference between NNP and disposable income. X can be further decomposed into induced items (X^i) and autonomous items (X^a). The predetermined variables in this system are C_{t-1}, M^* (maximum money supply possible) and X^a, while endogenous variables are C, PDY, r, Z^a, M, Y, Z^i, C^f, X^i. Z^i stands for induced expenditure items which equals inventory investment less imports. Notice that many 'autonomous' items are taken to be endogenous. We have above seven equations but nine endogenous variables. We specify two additional equations for X^i and Z^i in terms of themselves and their autonomous counterparts, C and PDY. These are just auxiliary equations to close the system. The system can be made larger by specifying individual items in Z^i and X^i separately with equations for each item. But we have already expanded to a nine-equation system. Now we can utilise our system including the two auxiliary equations: assume a linear specification for all the stochastic equations and reduce our nine equations to just four stochastic equations by solving out the identities. Doing this Modigliani and Ando get

$$C_t^f = \alpha_0 + \alpha_1 (Z^a + X^a)_t + \alpha_2 r_t + \alpha_3 C_{t-1} + u'_{1t} \quad (8.33a)$$

$$Z_t^a = \beta_0 + \beta_1 r_t + \beta_2 C_{t-1} + u'_{2t} \quad (8.34a)$$

$$r_t = \gamma_0 + \gamma_1 M_t + \gamma_2 (C^f + Z^a)_t + \gamma_3 C_{t-1} + u'_{3t} \quad (8.35a)$$

$$M_t = \delta_0 + \delta_1 M_t^* + \delta_2 r_t + u'_{4t} \quad (8.36a)$$

C_{t-1} stands as a surrogate for income level in the investment equation; M^* is the maximum money supply possible given the level of deposits and rules for required reserves, etc. M^* assumes zero excess reserves with commercial banks. We are allowing for money supply to be interest-sensitive as well as the other three variables, consumption, investment and demand for money. This is, therefore, a generalised version of the IS–LM system and we can see our equations such as 8.5a, 8.8a or 8.30 above as special versions of the above system. The B-matrix of endogenous variable coefficients can again be expressed as follows:

$$\begin{bmatrix} 1 & -\alpha_1 & -\alpha_2 & 0 \\ 0 & 1 & -\beta_1 & 0 \\ -\gamma_2 & -\gamma_2 & 1 & 0 \\ 0 & 0 & -\delta_2 & 1 \end{bmatrix} \begin{bmatrix} C^f \\ Z^a \\ r_t \\ M \end{bmatrix} \tag{8.40}$$

Our B-matrix shows full simultaneity since there are non-zero elements both above and below the diagonal. If, however, $\alpha_2 = \beta_1 = 0$, then the B-matrix becomes *block-triangular* or *block-recursive* since the block of the first two equations is independent of the block of last two equations but not the other way around. Thus we have

$$\begin{bmatrix} 1 & -\alpha_1 & 0 & 0 \\ 0 & 1 & 0 & 0 \\ -\gamma_2 & -\gamma_2 & 1 & 0 \\ 0 & 0 & -\delta_2 & 0 \end{bmatrix} \begin{pmatrix} C^f \\ Z^a \\ r \\ M \end{pmatrix} \tag{8.40a}$$

Similarly, if $\gamma_2 = 0$, then the last two equations form a block which is independent of the first two but not the other way round. We can recall that Friedman's specification of the Keynesian and monetary explanations involve block-triangular systems. In recent years, the larger models which have been fitted for quarterly data have frequently exhibited block recursiveness so that these models can be broken up into blocks forming a hierarchy of causal sequence with the first being independent of all lower blocks, the second block being dependent only on the first but not on the lower, and so on.

Expanding the Integrated Real and Monetary Model

Our detailed treatment of the IS–LM model was designed to show how quickly models can become large but also to bring into perspective the important debate about interactions of real and monetary equations. Our specifications above are still fairly simple and only a larger model will allow us to probe into greater detail of this interaction. Let us look at each of our four relationships and indicate how they can be expanded to allow for this interaction.

(a) C^f *equation.* Consumption of non-durables and durables can be separated. Since durables may be bought by hire purchase, mortgage, etc. interest payments and credit conditions can be specified in the consumer durable equations. On the other hand, consumers' stock of liquid assets such as cash and demand deposits and near liquid assets such as equity, time deposits, etc. can be introduced. Capital gains and losses through change in equity prices can then directly affect consumption. Other items in C^f, for example inventory investment and imports, also need separate treatment. Inventory investment decisions can be integrated with decisions regarding output (production function) and labour hiring decisions. Imports provide a link with capital movements and balance of payments constraints.

(b) Z^a *equation.* Appropriate interest rate for net investment and introduction of relevant tax and cost of borrowing should occur here. The choice between dividend payment and profit retention can be integrated here by introducing profits in the investment function. Other items such as government expenditure and exports can take up several equations. The links of government expenditure with taxation and interest payment on Public Debt also provide monetary links.

(c) *The demand for money equation.* This needs to be looked at in terms of separate behavioural equations of demand for demand deposits as against time deposits and demands by individual households as against corporations. The term structure of interests is important here since choice between demand deposits as compared to equity investment or building society deposits (savings and loan associations in US) will depend upon the complete pattern of yields. The rate of inflation is also an important variable in this set of equations.

(d) *The supply of money equations.* This is really a summary of many equations explaining the behaviour of commercial banks with relation to their portfolio of assets and liabilities. Institutional rules concerning reserves, costs of rediscounting, the maturity pattern of debt holdings come in here as exogenous rules subject to which banks optimise. Non-banking financial institutions have to be added as alternative suppliers of money substitutes.

Large Models: Pros and Cons

These hints make clear the scope for enlarging the simple IS–LM model into a large system. The advantages of building a large system are mainly in the predictive power of large models. By enabling us to get at the causal mechanism at work in the economic system, large models enable us to measure properly the separate effects of many variables. Detailed questions as to the alternative impact of, say, cutting the interest rate on hire purchase finance, a sales tax rebate on durable consumer goods and greater government expenditure in the form of military spending on income and employment can be studied by large models. Government policy measures are often very detailed and cannot be easily translated into changes in G or T or W_2 in a model such as the Klein Model I. If our model contains a well specified government sector then these many small policy changes can be readily translated in terms of their impact on the economy. To give a concrete example, the new policy announcement by President Nixon on 15 August 1971 included a cut in excise tax on US manufactured automobiles. While it is clear that this means a price reduction and increased sales depending on elasticity of demand, only a large model with an equation for consumer purchases of automobiles specifying price and excise taxes adequately will enable us to answer the question of the effect of such a move on income/employment immediately.

Not everyone concedes the superiority of larger models. It has been said that the degree of detail can only lead to a greater opportunity of mis-specification leading to inefficient estimates. Many equations are also only different in form; they do not add to the information content of the model. Thus, specifying ten investment demand functions for ten sectors does not add much if they are all functions of an identical set of variables and can easily be aggregated into one without much loss. Size should allow variety in specification and attention to individual equations. Otherwise, size for its own sake results. The most important criticism of large models has been in terms of their comparatively poor forecasting performance. Small models perform as well in forecasting if not better than large models. If short-run forecasting is our aim, we may do better by building small models. Small models often do not exhibit structural stability in the sense that their coefficients change upon addition of more observations. But then it is easier to keep a small model up to date by re-estimating with the latest available information. For a large model, this task may be very computer-intensive and time consuming. Many detailed series required in re-estimating a large model may not become available immediately. Thus we may have an estimate of total consumers' expenditure rapidly but expenditure on individual items such as automobiles may take some time to be released from government statistical offices. One may be forced to carry one small scale model for accurate forecasting while a large model may be used for predictive purposes and/or policy analysis.

Simulation of Econometric Models

The choice between large models and small models has been discussed mainly on grounds of predictive power and forecasting performance. A third dimension for judging the adequacy of a model is its performance *as a system*. Instead of criteria such as goodness of fit (R^2), forecasting error or the sign and size of multipliers, we now look at the system of equations as a whole and ask ourselves whether the system behaviour resembles the behaviour of the economic system which it purports to model. Thus one question may arise about the dynamics of the system—its stability or the pattern of growth and cycles it generates. One feature of a system may be its sensitivity to external shocks. We may ask whether a system returns to its dynamic equilibrium if it is subjected to a random shock and how long it takes the system to return to equilibrium. If the system can be written as a fairly small order difference equation then we can look at the characteristic roots of the system and check for stability and time taken for convergence to equilibrium. But for a large system this gets difficult. For a five-equation system with a longest lag of say five time periods, we have to examine twenty-five characteristic roots, and though some of these may be zero, we may not be much the wiser after obtaining these roots. To solve this problem and as an aid to evaluating a system as a whole, simulation techniques are increasingly being used in econometrics.

Simulation is a numerical technique made possible by high speed computers. For social sciences it also affords the nearest to an experimental situation. When simulating a model, we first of all solve it—trace out the time paths of our endogenous variables given our exogenous variables. This gives us then the freedom to alter the values of the exogenous variables or the size of some of our parameters to generate alternative time paths. Random shocks can be introduced by changing the specification of the error terms, for example arbitrarily increasing error variances. Counter-factual questions as to what would have happened if a certain action had not been taken can also be answered. Thus one may ask a question in the context of a model of the UK economy as to what would have happened if the Labour Government had devalued in the last quarter of 1964 instead of in 1967. If our model properly specifies the role of relative prices in imports and exports of goods as well as in capital flows, we may be able to answer that question. Such an answer is obviously subject to many limitations since we are only changing one event without allowing for a whole host of other consequences, but altering one thing at a time hypothetically is a methodological tool of great usefulness.

Since the technique of simulation has come into general use, let us look at it in some detail. Suppose we want to simulate the Klein Model I. How do we go about it? Without getting into problems of computer programming we can indicate what needs to be done. A simulation of the Klein Model I will yield us time paths of our endogenous variables C, I, P, Y, W_1 and K. We may want to study this time path for the sample period itself, 1921–1941, or for any future or past time period on the assumption that the model remains the same. Let us confine ourselves to the sample period. We already have values of the four exogenous variables W_2, G, T and t. Given these values and the initial values of the lagged endogenous variables, i.e. the value of P_{t-1}, K_{t-1} and Y_{t-1} for the first time period (actual values for the year 1920), we can solve our system. Thus for the first year, 1921, we take values for 1921 of W_2, T and t as well as values for 1920 for W_2 and T plus the value for 1920 of P, K and Y. These, together with the estimated coefficients, will give us values of C, I, Y, P, K and W_1 for 1921. We can do this by using the reduced form coefficients given in equation 8.24.

For the first year there is no difference between the simulated value of our endogenous variables and the values we have for computing residuals in the OLS case. In the next period (1922), however, we use not the actual values of the lagged endogenous variables, i.e. 1921 values of Y, P and K, but those that we obtain from our simulation calculations for 1921. For each successive year, we use actual values of exogenous variables but simulated values of lagged endogenous variables. If our simulated values differ very much from actual values then we pay the penalty in future time periods since we incorporate this error in our subsequent calculations. We can do this for all twenty-one observations and get simulated values of all the endogenous variables.

We have, however, only used the deterministic part of our model. We also have random error terms which stand for omitted variables or for purely random elements of the economic system. We calculate in the course of estimation the variance–covariance matrix (Σ) of the residuals. We can generate new values for our random errors instead of the computed residuals on the basis of which the variance–covariance matrix is calculated. One way is to pick the values out of a joint normal distribution with zero mean and $\hat{\Sigma}$—the estimated variance–covariance matrix. Simulations which use generated values of the error terms are called stochastic simulations.

Let us illustrate by taking our equation for GNP (Y) and see the simulation value for 1921 and 1922. The reduced form equation for Y_t based on FIML estimates is

$$\begin{aligned} Y_t = {} & 32.1117 + 0.8964P_{t-1} - 0.0923K_{t-1} \\ & + 0.3258(Y + T - W_2)_{t-1} - 0.3557T_t + 0.6235G_t \\ & + 0.8762W_{2t} + 0.2687t + v_{4t} \end{aligned} \tag{8.24a}$$

v_{4t} is the error term attached to the reduced form equation and therefore it is a linear combination of the error terms of all the three stochastic equations in the structural form. For 1921, we take 1921 values of $G(6.6)$, $W_2(2.7)$, $T(7.7)$ and t and the 1920 values of $P_t(12.7)$, $K_t(182.8)$, $Y(43.7)$ $T(3.4)$ and W_2. Doing this we get for 1921 the simulated value $\hat{Y}_t =$ \$45.25 billion. The actual value for 1921 was \$40.6 billion. For the next period we will use 45.25 rather than 40.6 as our value for Y_{t-1}. Similar simulated values for 1921 of $P(14.56)$, $K(184.69)$ can be combined with 1921 values of T, W_2 and 1922 values of G, T, W_2 and t to get Y for 1922. This turns out to be \$49.98 compared to the actual value of \$49.1 (all in billions). The actual and simulated values for Y_t are plotted in figure 8.1. These are non-stochastic simulations since we have ignored the v_{4t} term in our equation.

For the stochastic simulation we need $\hat{\Sigma}$, the variance–covariance matrix of structural form error terms. For the FIML estimates used in our simulation, this turns out to be of the following (symmetric) form:

$$\hat{\Sigma} = \begin{pmatrix} 2.1042 & & \\ 3.8790 & 12.7716 & \\ 0.4817 & 3.8575 & 1.8011 \end{pmatrix} \qquad (8.41)$$

From this information we generate simulated error terms, u_1, u_2, u_3 on the assumption that $u = N(0, \hat{\Sigma})$, or generate $v = N(0, \hat{B}^{-1}\hat{\Sigma}\hat{B}^{-1})$ for the reduced forms. Standard programmes are available for that. The stochastic simulation values for Y are also plotted in figure 8.4. What can we say from figure 8.1 about the Klein Model I as a system?

Comparing the actual GNP values with the two simulated paths, we notice that at the beginning and the end, these stay together. The non-stochastic path is smooth and shows almost no cyclical fluctuations. This indicates that the deterministic part of Klein Model I does not generate cycles. Cyclical fluctuations arise from the influence of the structural error terms since the stochastic simulation does generate cyclical fluctuations in Y. We can discern peaks at 1922, 1925, 1928, 1933 and troughs at 1923, 1927, 1930, 1938. We have therefore at least three complete cycles with average peak to peak length of $3\frac{2}{3}$ years and trough to trough length of 5 years. In the actual values we have only one complete cycle with peaks at 1929 and 1937 or troughs at 1932 and 1938.

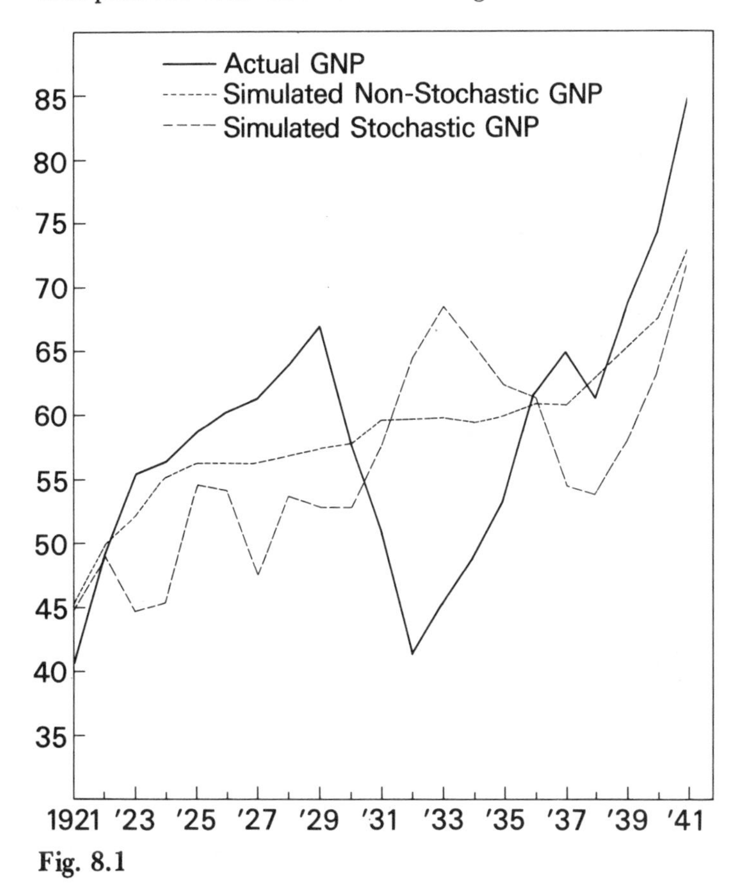

Fig. 8.1

The Klein Model I therefore generates cyclical fluctuations through stochastic shocks but the cycles are not very realistic since the simulated stochastic path cycles much more than the actual values. Except for timing the 1938 trough correctly, no other cyclical turning point is captured by Klein Model I. It misses out the Great Depression of 1929–1932 completely.

We need not be surprised at such a result, nor do we need to feel disheartened about the usefulness of econometric model building. For a complex modern economy such as the

USA at an untypical and rather cataclysmic period such as the inter-war years, it can be hardly expected that a three-equation model will capture the economy's working. The model reproduces the general upward trend of GNP by the end of the period but misses out on the cyclical fluctuations. For a similar analysis of the rather larger Klein–Goldberger model, Adelman and Adelman (1959) have shown that stochastic simulation paths of the *KG* model do exhibit cyclical fluctuations of the type observed in the US economy. In this case, larger and more disaggregated models do succeed in capturing the working of an economy better than small models and this is one strong reason for building them. Our simulation exercise with Klein Model I does reproduce one feature observed by Adelman and Adelman for the larger KG model; this is that the deterministic part of the econometric models, whether small or large, do not generate cycles but the stochastic parts do. In this way econometric models have been able to shed some light on the question asked in 1933 by Frisch as to whether it was the impulse given by the stochastic shock or the propagation mechanism (the endogenous dynamic) of the system which causes business cycles in a capitalist economy.

We can further use the Klein Model I (despite its limitations) to demonstrate the usefulness of simulation in answering counterfactual questions. The question we ask is about the impact of a larger amount of government expenditure on GNP—what would happen if $2 billion more had been spent by the government in 1933? We keep it to a one-shot increment in G in order to set up a *ceteris paribus* experiment. Figure 8.2 illustrates the two stochastic simulations with and without the change in G. The stochastic path without change in G is the same as that in figure 8.1. The difference in Y from 1933 is also plotted on an inset chart. We see that immediately the path with change in G goes above that without by about $1.25 billion and in the next period goes up further by about $1.3 billion but starts declining after that. The shape of the ΔY graph looks very much like a Koyck distributed lag except for the rise in period two. This is due to the presence of a first-order lag in the system. If we sum up all the ΔY terms we should approximate the long-run multiplier of G on Y. The increase from 1933 to 1941 is \$4.75 billion for a \$2 billion increase in G. The long-run multiplier is close to 2.38 which is quite close to the value 2.33 we show on page 244. We can also calculate a four-year multiplier of G by summing ΔY from 1933 to 1936 which is \$4.33/\$2 or 2.15, which is more than 90% of the long-run multiplier value. The modal lag can be seen to be two years, since by 1934 one half of the adjustment is finished.

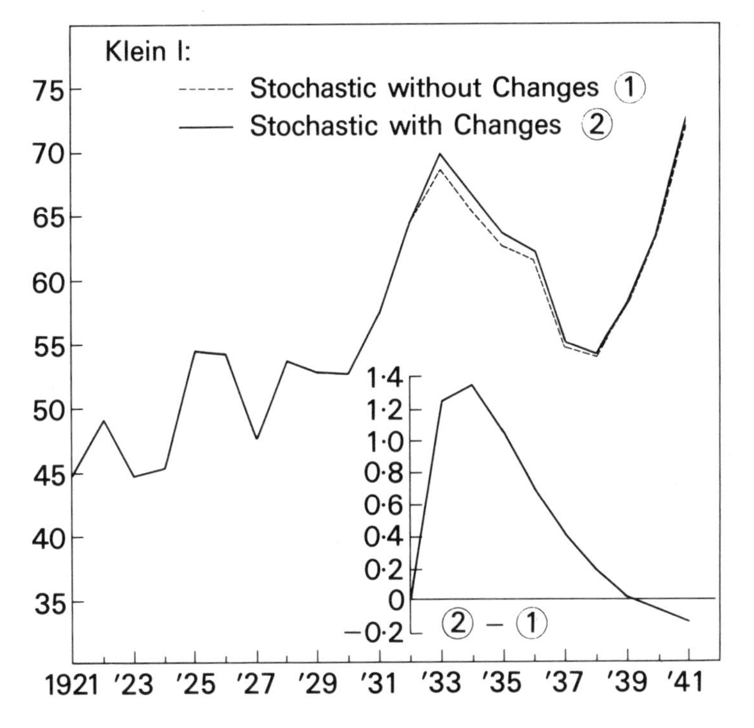

Fig. 8.2.

This example is kept deliberately simple. Much larger systems of equations can be subjected to a greater variety of complex policy simulations. But we only want to illustrate the method. Simulation is a heuristic or descriptive technique. We could run many different simulations changing our assumptions one at a time or many at a time. What, for

Table. 8.2. The Reduced Form of the Klein Model I used in Simultation Exercises

		P_{-1}	K_{-1}	E_{-1}	GT	G	W_2	t
	Equation 1							
C	21.97590	.39440	−.00090	.29760	.23865	.00605	.80060	.24544
	Equation 2							
I	10.13581	.50198	−.09145	.02818	.40570	−.38253	.07582	.02324
	Equation 3							
W_1	10.72845	.20984	−.02162	.36097	.15084	.14597	−.02893	.29770
	Equation 4							
Y	32.11171	.89638	−.09234	.32578	−.35565	.62353	.87642	.26868
	Equation 5							
P	21.38326	.68654	−.07073	−.03518	−.50649	.47756	−.09465	−.02902
	Equation 6							
K	10.13581	.50198	.90855	.02818	.40570	−.38253	.0782	.02324
	Equation 7							
W	10.72845	.20984	−.02162	.36097	.15084	.14597	.97107	.29770
	Equation 8							
E	32.11171	.89638	−.09234	.32578	.64435	.62353	−.12358	.26868

example, would be the effect of increasing G and cutting T and 'writing off' arbitrarily one tenth of the capital stock? It is difficult, however, to come to analytical conclusions from individual experiments since the number of possible alterations in the *ceteris paribus* conditions is infinitely large. As a validating method for systems of equations, as a numerical shortcut to calculating multipliers and for asking counterfactual questions, simulation is a useful method but it does not provide analytical answers to questions that we may ask. One such question is of optimal strategy for achieving the economic objectives that a government may want to pursue. How do we obtain optimising answers from an econometric model?

Models as Tools for Optimal Government Decisions

For the purposes of studying policy making, we have to frame the optimising problem in the usual terms–maximise (or minimise) an objective function subject to constraints. The decision-making agent in this case is a single entity called 'the Government'. The objective function has arguments and these are the target variables. In a simple case, a government objective function may have arguments such as national income or its growth rate, the percentage unemployed, the rate of inflation, the level of foreign exchange reserves, etc. These objectives will be framed in terms of these target variables–high growth rate of level of income, low unemployment, etc. For a formal exercise we must make sure that the arguments of our objective function are included variables in our model. We then divide our exogenous variables into those that are controllable by the policy maker–the instruments–and those that are given or *truly* exogenous. We then want to obtain optimal values of instruments that will maximise our objective function. The econometric model plays the role of the set of constraints by relating the target variables to the instruments. By maximising our objective function subject to the econometric model as constraint, we can solve for the optimal values of the instruments.

The analogy of such an optimising exercise with similar exercises in microeconomic theory (e.g. consumer's utility maximisation subject to budget constraint) is obvious but there are two differences. Our models are usually dynamic; the influence of previous achievements on our present and future actions is not zero. We have a set of dynamic constraints and the arguments in our objective functions are also related over time. We can frame the optimising problem as a dynamic or multi-period optimising one rather than as a static problem which occurs in the consumer behaviour case. A more suitable analogy would be the neo-classical theory of investment which we referred to in Chapter 6 in discussing Jorgensen's work. A second difference, however, is that our constraints now include a stochastic element. Our instruments relate to the targets in a stochastic rather than deterministic way. Achieving a target exactly is, therefore, impossible; we can only get close to it up to a random error. This is even on the assumption that our instruments are truly and completely controllable without any error or without any delay. The uncertainty due to the presence of the random error we cannot do away with; the best we can do is maximise *the expected value of our objective function* subject to our set of stochastic constraints.

We require of the objective function that it be convex and at least twice differentiable. The objective function's arguments can contain variables (y) as well as instruments (x_1) if we so wish, but not truly exogenous variables (x_2). The explicit form of the objective function then assigns relative weights to the different items in our objective function; we *do not* require for our purposes that the number of endogenous variables (y) entering our objective function be the same as the number of instruments (x_1). Implicitly we write our objective function as

$$W(y) \qquad \text{or} \qquad W(y, x_1)$$

For operating with linear constraints and deriving linear decision rules, the simplest convex objective function is quadratic. We can choose desired values y^*, x_1^* for our variables and then write our objective function in terms of the squared distance between actual and desired values. Say for one target variable y_1, we have

$$W = a_0(y_1 - y_1^*) + \tfrac{1}{2}a_1(y_1 - y_1^*)^2 \tag{8.42}$$

For many y and x_1 variables, we can write in matrix notation

$$\begin{aligned} W &= a'(x_1 - x_1^*) + b'(y - y^*) + \tfrac{1}{2}[(x_1 - x_1^*)'A(x_1 - x_1^*) \\ &\quad + (y - y^*)'B(y - y^*) + (x_1 - x_1^*)'C(y - y^*) \\ &\quad + (y - y^*)'C(x_1 - x_1^*)] \end{aligned} \tag{8.42a}$$

While the quadratic objective function is convenient, we should note the implied assumption of symmetry. Thus in equation (8.42), our objective function has a linear term which is negative when we are below the target and positive above the target, but the quadratic term has the same value whether actual values are above or below the target. When minimising our maximising W, only the quadratic term matters and hence symmetry is imposed. In real life, one may not mind being above the target, but only below the target, and we may wish to give different weights to positive and negative deviations. This would mean we should have an asymmetric objective function. We may also point out for the sake of generality that the weights assigned, e.g. a_1 in 8.42 or elements of A, B or C in 8.42a, *need not be* constant, but such varying weights make the optimising problem much more difficult to solve.

An additional element to specify in dynamic decision-making is the length of the horizon over which the policy is being made. We may introduce a discounting factor in our objective function for distant time periods but the length of the horizon is important for specifying the constraints as well. The length of the horizon makes for inter-dependence of policy decisions over time. From the point of view of constraints, if we have a horizon of length T, then the constraints have to be specified for all T periods. The endogenous variable value for y_T is then a function of x_{1T}, x_{2T} as well as previous values. Once again lagged endogenous variables have to be solved out for all the T periods. This is what we did before in evaluating the *final form* of the model. The appropriate specification for the constraints is then the final form of the model for all the T periods of the horizon. Thus for a model of G endogenous variables and T time horizon, using equation 8.25 above:

$$y_T' = \pi_{11}x_{1T}' + \sum_{i=1}^{T} \pi_3^{i-1}(\pi_{21} + \pi_3\pi_{21})x_{1T-i}' + \pi_3 y_0'$$
$$+ \pi_{12}x_{2T}' + \Sigma\pi_3^{i-1}(\pi_{22} + \pi_3\pi_{22})x_{2T-i}' + \Sigma\pi_3^{i-1}v_{t-i}' \tag{8.43}$$

We have separated x_1 and x_2 with appropriate subscripts to the π matrices. y_0 is the initial value of the lagged endogenous variables. We are interested only in x_1 variables and hence we treat all the other variables and the error term as given. A shorthand version of 8.43 is written as

$$\mathbf{y}' = \mathbf{R}\mathbf{x}_1' + \mathbf{s}' \tag{8.44}$$

For G variables and T time periods $\mathbf{y}'$ is a vector of $G.T$ elements. $\mathbf{R}$ is $GT \times K_1T$ matrix and $\mathbf{x}_1'$ is $K_1T \times 1$ vector and $\mathbf{s}'$ is a $GT \times 1$ vector of 'constants'. For each time period we have to compute $\mathbf{s}$ while $\mathbf{R}$ is given. The structure of the $\mathbf{R}$ matrix is also interesting since it gives us the effect of current and lagged instrument variables values. It is an asymmetric matrix, since future instruments do not influence current endogenous variables. Thus for $t = 1, \ldots T$, we can write out 8.44

$$\begin{bmatrix} y_1 \\ y_2 \\ \cdot \\ \cdot \\ \cdot \\ y_T \end{bmatrix} = \begin{bmatrix} R_{11} & & & \\ R_{21} & R_{22} & & \\ R_{31} & R_{32} & R_{33} & \\ & \cdot & & \\ & \cdot & & \\ & \cdot & & R_{TT} \end{bmatrix} \begin{bmatrix} x_{11} \\ x_{12} \\ \\ \\ \\ x_{1T} \end{bmatrix} + \begin{bmatrix} s_1 \\ s_2 \\ \\ \\ \\ s_T \end{bmatrix} \tag{8.45}$$

It is clear that the diagonal block in each case being the influence of current instruments on current endogenous variables, we have $R_{11} = R_{22} = \ldots = R_{TT}$ and for each R_{ii} matrix is the same as π_{11} matrix of 8.43. Similarly $R_{21} = R_{32} = R_{43} = R_{54} = \ldots R_{T,\,T-1}$, which is equal to $\pi_{21} + \pi_3\pi_{21}$ of equation 8.43 obtained by putting $i = 1$. Given the objective function W expressed in terms of T periods, we minimise it subject to the constraints 8.44 and obtain optimal values of x_1 which will minimise W. This can be done either by the Lagrangean method or by directly substituting 8.44 into

8.42a and minimising W with respect to x_1. For each time period from $t = 1$ to T we obtain an optimal x_1^* vector. Having implemented x_{11}^* in $t = 1$, in time period $t = 2$, we can solve the problem all over again treating x_{11}^* as given and defining the horizon from $t = 2$ to T. This way, while keeping our horizon long, we can act optimally in the short run and recompute in each time period.

Theil has used Klein Model I to illustrate optimal policy making with the help of an econometric model. Three targets and three instruments are chosen. Of the four exogenous variables, three (G, T, W_2) are taken as instruments and the fourth (t) is obviously a truly exogenous variable. The three endogenous variables chosen were C, I and D (defined as $W_1 - 2P$). D is a distributional variable specifying the share of wages in national product. The policy horizon is four years, 1933–1936, and this is an *ex-post* exercise. For each of the four years desired values of the endogenous variables C, I and D and the instruments W_2, G and T are specified and the objective function is then specified as follows:

$$W(x, y) = -\tfrac{1}{2}(xx' + yy') \tag{8.46}$$

where x' and y' are each 12×1 vectors and defined in terms of deviation from the desired values. Explicitly one could write the objective function as

$$W(x, y) = -\tfrac{1}{2}\left[\sum_{t=1}^{4}\sum_{j=1}^{3}(x_{1jt} - x_{1jt}^*)^2 + \sum_{t=1}^{4}\sum_{i=1}^{3}(y_{it} - y_{it}^*)^2\right] \tag{8.46a}$$

In specifying the constraints, the final form calculations for $T = 4$ are utilised. Given this information, optimal values of $x_{1t} - x_{1t}^*$ for 1933 are calculated as follows. For 1933 the actual values of the error terms are not assumed known, hence only the expected value of the objective function is maximised. We have, after some manipulation, optimal values of x_1, written as $\tilde{x}_1$

$$E(\tilde{x}_1') = -(I + R'R)^{-1}R'\sigma' \tag{8.47}$$

where I is the identity matrix and σ is the systematic (non-random) part of s, or $\sigma = E(s)$. Doing this for 1933, Theil gets

$$\tilde{x}_{11} = \begin{bmatrix} \tilde{W}_2 - W_2^* \\ \tilde{T} - T^* \\ \tilde{G} - G^* \end{bmatrix} = \begin{bmatrix} 1.10 \\ 1.22 \\ 3.83 \end{bmatrix}$$

Adding the desired values we have for the three instruments values of 6.13, 8.62 and 14.26 respectively while the actual values were 5.6, 5.4 and 9.3 respectively. This means that in terms of the GNP variable, implementation of the optimal instruments would mean a value of 50.42 compared to an actual value of 45.3 but quite close to the desired value of 49.63.

One way we can interpret the result is by comparing it with our one-shot increase in G in our simulation exercise. We increased G by 2 billion above the actual value which achieved an immediate increase in Y of around 1.25. A longer term strategy in terms of three instruments and three targets prescribes an increase in G of nearly 5 billion to achieve an equivalent 5 billion increase in Y. But what is more important is that we can now carry out the same exercise ahead. Our first calculations in 8.47 yield optimal x_1 values for all four years but we use only those for 1933. In 1934, we know $\tilde{x}_1$ values of 1933. We also assume that we know the value of the error terms for 1933. These two elements enter our s vector and once again we can maximise the expected value of our objective function. Now our R matrix is 9×9. Applying the same formula as 8.47 but with a new σ vector including $\tilde{x}_1$ for 1933 and v for 1933 we have $\tilde{W}_2$ (5.64), $\tilde{T}$ (8.34) and G (13.20) and we achieve a Y of 55.80 against a desired value of 57.02 but an actual value of only 48.9. Given these results we can see that the optimal policy decisions (although made *ex-post*) achieve a much better result than the actual policies did.

The Theil exercise can be easily adapted for *ex-ante* policy making. We need, of course, an estimated econometric model including in its specifications available instruments. Given a specific objective function, we can proceed with our exercise. We need, however, forecasts for our x_2 variables. Our optimal policy decision in the *ex-ante* case is based on more uncertainty than in the *ex-post* case. In real life there may also be delays in implementing policy even when one knows the optimal values. This is known as the *inside lag*. This will add a further adjustment lag of actual values of instruments to optimal values. In one sense, Theil's calculations assume an inside lag of length zero but in a more general exercise, the value of the inside lag can also be optimally calculated.

Our examples in this chapter have constantly made use of Klein Model I. Needless to say, models today are much larger and much more detailed in their specification. The reality they hope to reproduce is a match for them with its complexity. In a sense there is no perfect or ideal model which will work for all purposes; a search for such a model would be futile. Our task is constantly to improve our specifications, estimate our relationships better and make maximum use of our results for testing them against the real world. No doubt the real world will reject many models and make fools of econometric model builders. The only consolation we can claim is that we tried our best as best we knew. This is the challenge and the fascination of econometrics.

Bibliographical Notes

In recent years the literature on models has seen a very rapid growth. Klein's 1950 Cowles Commission monograph is much cited but seldom read. It carefully goes into the theoretical background of many specifications and has some refreshing insights to offer (e.g. an early formulation of vintage capital models). Ando and Modigliani's *AER* (1965) article gives the details concerning Friedman and Meiselman's (1963) article. Much has been written on the Friedman–Meiselman model but little of it raises any methodological issues. At the same time as Ando and Modigliani, D. Hester also attacked the FM model in *RE Statistics,* November 1964 which is also worth reading. For surveys of macroeconometric models, see Nerlove (1966) and Desai (1973).

Most models are income–expenditure models. For commodity models, see Labys (1973) for a survey and Desai (1966) for a specific example. Growth models have again been seldom estimated but Valavanis–Vail's early attempt (1955) is interesting. Morishima and Saito's model (1964, 1972) is one of the few log–linear macromodels where growth and stability considerations are explicitly analysed. This model also contains an imaginative treatment of the investment relationship treating it as a stochastic shock to the system.

For simulation studies of econometric models, see Duesenbery, Klein and Fromm (1963), Desai and Henry (1970), Henry and Desai (1975), Renton (1975). Forecasting performance of models is discussed in Hickman (1973).

Theil's work on optimal control is covered in his 1964 book and two of his articles with co-authors are reprinted in Zellner (1968). A recent book by Gregory Chow: *Analysis and Control of Dynamic Economic Systems*, (Wiley, 1975) came too late to our attention to cover in this book.

References

Abramowitz, M. (1950), Resources and output trends in the US since 1870, *American Economic Review*, Papers and Proceedings, Vol. XLVI, 5–23.

Adelman, I. and F.A. Adelman (1959), The dynamic properties of the Klein–Goldberger model, *Econometrica*, Vol. 27, 596–625.

Aitchison, J. and S.J. Prais (1954), The grouping of observations in regression analysis, *Review of International Institute of Statistics* Vol. 1, 1–22.

Allard, R.J. (1974). *An Approach to Econometrics*, Philip Allan.

Almon, Shirley (1965), The distributed lag between capital appropriations and expenditures, *Econometrica*, Vol. 33, 178–196.

Ando, A., F.M. Fisher and H. Simon (1963), *Essays on the Structure of Social Science Models*, MIT Press.

Ando, A. and F. Modigliani (1965), Velocity and the investment multiplier, *American Economic Review*, Vol. LV, 693–728.

Arrow, K., H.B. Chenery, B.S. Minhas and R.M. Solow (1961), Capital–labour substitution and economic efficiency, *RE Statistics*, Vol. 33, 225–50.

Barten, A.P. (1968), Estimating demand equations, *Econometrica*, Vol. 36, 213–51.

Barten, A.P. (1969), Maximum likelihood estimation of a complete system of demand equations, *European Economic Review*, Vol. 1, 7–73.

Bergstrom, A.R. (1966), Non-recursive models as discrete approximations to systems of stochastic difference equations, *Econometrica*, Vol. 34, 173–182.

Bischoff, C. (1969), Hypothesis testing and the demand for capital goods, *R.E. Statistics*, Vol. LI, 354–368.

Boatwright, B.D. and J.R. Eaton (1972), The estimation of investment functions for manufacturing industry in the UK, *Economica*, Vol. XXXIX, No. 156, 403–418.

Boyle, J.R., W.M. Gorman and S.E. Pudney (1975), *Demand for Related Goods: A Progress Report*, LSE Econometrics Programme Discussion Paper.

Brady, D.S. and H.A. Barber (1948), The pattern of food expenditures, *RE Statistics*, Vol. 30, 198–206.

Brown, J.A.C. and Angus Deaton (1972), Surveys in applied economics: models of consumer behaviour, *Economic Journal*, Vol. 82, 1145–1236.

Brown, M. (ed.) (1967), *The Theory and Empirical Analysis of Production: Conference on Research in Income and Wealth*. Vol. 32 (NBER), Columbia University Press.

Brown, M and D. Heien (1972), The S-branch utility tree: A generalization of the linear expenditure system, *Econometrica*, Vol. 40, 737–748.

Byron, R.P. (1970), A simple method of estimating demand systems under separable utility assumptions, *R.E. Studies*, Vol. 37, 261–274.

Chow, G.C. (1975), *Analysis and Control of Dynamic Economic Systems*, Wiley.

Christ, C.F. (1952), *A History of the Cowles Commission 1932–1952 in Economic Theory and Measurement*, a Twenty Year Research Report 1932–1952, Chicago, Cowles Commission.

Christ, C.F. (1966), *Econometric Models and Methods*, Wiley.

Cobb, C.W. and P. Douglas (1928), A theory of production, *American Economic Review*, Supplement Vol. 18, 139–165.

Cochrane, D. and G. Orcutt (1949), Application of least squares regression to relationships containing auto-correlated error terms, *JASA*, Vol. 44, 32–61.

Deaton, Angus (1974), The analysis of consumer demand in the UK 1900–1970, *Econometrica*, Vol. 42, 341–368.

Denison, E.F., D.W. Jorgensen and Z. Grilliches (1972), The measurement of productivity, *Survey of Current Business*, Vol. 52, 1–111.

Desai, M. (1966), An econometric model of the world tin economy 1948–1961, *Econometrica*, Vol. 34, 105–134.

Desai, M. (1968), Some issues in econometric history, *Economic History Review*, Vol. XXI, 1–16.

Desai, M. and S.G.B. Henry (1970), Fiscal policy simulations for the UK 1955–1966, in Hilton K. and D. Heathfield (1970).

Desai, M. (1973), Macroeconometric models for India: a survey, *Sankhya Series B*, Vol. 35, Part 2, 169–206.

Desai, M. (1974), Pooling as a specification error: a note, *Econometrica* Vol. 42, 389–91.

Desai, M. (1975), The Phillips curve: a revisionist interpretation, *Economica*, Vol. XXXXII, 1–19

Dhrymes, P. (1962), On devising unbiased estimators for the parameters of the Cobb–Douglas production function, *Econometrica*, Vol. 30, 297–304.

Dhrymes, P. (1965), Some extensions and tests for the CES class of production functions, *RE Statistics*, Vol. 37, 357–66.

Dhrymes, P. and M. Kurz (1967), Investment, dividend and external finance behaviour of firms, in R. Ferber (1967).

Dhrymes, P. (1970), *Econometrics*, Harper and Row.

Dhrymes, P. (1971), *Distributed Lags: Problems of Estimation and Formulation*, Holden Day.

Diamond, P. (1965), Disembodied technical change in a two-sector model, *RE Studies*, Vol. 32, 161–168.

Douglas, P. (1948), Are there laws of production? *American Economic Review*, Vol. 38, 1–41.

Duesenberry, J., L.R. Klein and G. Fromm (1963), *The Brookings Quarterly Econometric Model of the United States*, Rand McNally.

Durbin, J. (1970), Tests for serial correlation in least squares regression when some of the regressors are lagged dependent variables, *Econometrica*, Vol. 38, 410–421.

Durbin, J. and G.S. Watson (1950–51), Testing for serial correlation in least squares I and II, *Biometrica*, Vol. 37, 409–428 and Vol. 38, 159–178.

Eisner, R. (1960), A Distributed Lag Investment Function, *Econometrica*, Vol. 28, 1–29.

Eisner, R. and M. Nadiri (1968), Investment behaviour and the neoclassical theory, *RE Statistics*, Vol. L, 329–351.

Ferber, R. (ed.) (1967), *The Determinants of Investment Behaviour* (Universities – NBER Committee on Economic Research Conference No. 18), Columbia University Press.

Fisher, F.M. (1961a), The cost of approximate specification in simultaneous equation estimation, *Econometrica*, Vol. 29, 139–170.

Fisher, F.M. (1961b), Identifiability criteria in nonlinear systems, *Econometrica*, Vol. 29, 574–590.

Fisher, F.M. (1962), The place of least squares in econometrics: comment, *Econometrica*, Vol. 30, 565–567.

Fisher, F.M. (1963), Uncorrelated disturbances and identifiability criteria, *International Economic Review*, Vol. 4, 134–152.

Fisher, F.M. (1965), Near identifiability and the variances of the disturbance terms,

Econometrica, Vol. 33, 409–419.

Fisher, F.M. (1966), *The Identification Problem in Econometrics*, McGraw-Hill.

Fisher, F.M. (1970a), *Simultaneous Equations Estimation: The State of the Art*, IDA Economic Paper, Institute of Defence Analysis, Arlington, Virginia.

Fisher, F.M. (1970b), A correspondence principle for simultaneous equation models, *Econometrica*, Vol. 38, 73–92.

Fisher, F.M. (1971), Aggregate production functions and the explanation of wages: a simulation experiment, *RE Statistics*, Vol. LIII, 305–325.

Friedman, M. and D. Meiselman (1963), The relative stability of monetary velocity and the investment multiplier in the US 1897–1958, in *Commission on Money and Credit: Stabilization Policies*, Prentice-Hall.

Frisch, R. (1959), A complete system for computing all direct and cross demand elasticities in a model with many sectors, *Econometrica*, Vol. 27, 177–196.

Geary, R.C. (1948–49), A note on 'a constant utility index of the cost of living', *RE Studies*. Vol. 18, 65–66.

Gilbert, C.L. (1976), The original Phillips curve estimates, *Economica*, Vol. 43, 51–58.

Godfrey L. and D. Poskitt (1975), Testing the restrictions of the Almon lag techniques, *JASA*, Vol. 70, 105–108.

Goldberger, A. (1964), *Econometric Theory*, Wiley.

Goldberger, A. (1967), *Functional Form and Utility: A Review of Consumer Demand Theory*, University of Wisconsin Social Systems Research Institute Working Paper No. 6703.

Goldberger, A. and H. Theil (1961), On pure and mixed statistical estimation in economics, *International Economic Review*, Vol. 2, 65–78.

Goldberger, A. and T. Gamalestos (1970), A cross-country comparison of consumer expenditure patterns, *European Economic Review*, Vol. 1, 357–400.

Goldfield, S and R. Quandt (1972), *Nonlinear Methods in Econometrics*, North Holland.

Gorman, W.M. (1956), *Demand for Related Goods, Journal Paper J3129*, Iowa Agricultural Experiment Station, Ames, Iowa.

Gorman, W.M. (1959), *Demand for Fish: An Application of Factor Analysis*, University of Birmingham Discussion Paper A6.

Grilliches, Z. (1967), Distributed lags: a survey, *Econometrica*, Vol. 35, 16–49.

Harcourt, G.C. (1969), Some Cambridge controversies in the theory of capital, *Journal of Economic Literature*, Vol. 7, 369–405.

Harcourt, G.C. (1972), *Some Cambridge Controversies in the Theory of Capital*, Cambridge University Press.

Harcourt, G.C. and N.F. Laing (eds) (1971), *Capital and Growth*, Penguin.

Hendry, D.F. (1971), Maximum likelihood estimation of systems of simultaneous regression equations with errors generated by a vector autogressive process, *International Economic Review*, Vol. 12, 257–272.

Hendry, D.F. (1974), Stochastic specifications in an aggregate demand model of the United Kingdom, *Econometrica*, Vol. 42, 559–578.

Hendry, D.F. (1975), The consequences of mis-specification of dynamic structure, autocorrelation and simultaneity in a simple model with an application to the demand for imports, in G. Renton (1975), Heinemann.

Hendry, S.G.B. and M. Desai (1975), Fiscal policy simulations and stabilization policy, *RE Studies*, Vol. XLII, 347–359.

Hester, D. (1964), Keynes and quantity theory: a comment on the Friedman Meiselman CMC paper, *RE Statistics*, Vol. 46, 364–68.

Hickman, B. (ed.) (1973), *Econometric Models of Cyclical Behaviour*, Vols. 1 and 2, Columbia University Press.

Hicks, J.R. (1932), *Theory of Wages*, Cambridge University Press.

Hicks, J.R. (1939), *Value and Capital*, Oxford University Press.

Hicks, J.R., and R.G.D. Allen (1934), A reconsideration of the theory of value, Parts I and II, *Econometrica*, Vol. 1, 52–76 and 196–219.

Hildreth, C. and J. Lu (1960), *Demand Relations with Autocorrelated Disturbances*, Technical Bulletin No. 276, Michigan State University Agricultural Experiment Station, East Lansing, Michigan.

Hilton, K., and D. Heathfield (1970), *The Econometric Study of the United Kingdom*, Macmillan.

Hoch, I.J. (1958), Simultaneous equations bias in the context of the Cobb–Douglas production function, *Econometrica*, Vol. 26, 566–578.

Hoch, I.J. and Y. Mundlak (1965), Consequence of alternative specification in estimates of Cobb–Douglas production functions, *Econometrica*, Vol. 33, 814–628.

Hood, W.C. and T.C. Koopmans (eds.) (1953), *Studies in Econometric Method*, Cowles Commission Monograph No. 14, Wiley.

Houthakker, H. (1957), An international comparison of household expenditure patterns commemorating the centenary of Engel's law, *Econometrica*, Vol. 25, 532–551.

Houthakker, H., and S. Prais (1955), *The Analysis of Family Budgets*, Cambridge University Press. [Reissued in abridged version 1973]

Johansen, L. (1959), Substitution versus fixed production coefficients in the theory of economic growth, *Econometrica*, Vol. 27, No. 2, 157–176.

Johnston, J. (1963), 1972), *Econometric Methods*, 1st and 2nd edns, McGraw–Hill.

Jorgensen, D. (1963), Capital theory and investment behaviour, *American Economic Review*, Papers and Proceedings, Vol. 53, 247–59.

Jorgensen, D. (1966), Rational distributed lag functions, *Econometrica*, Vol. 34, 135–49.

Jorgensen, D. and Z. Grilliches (1967), The explanation of productivity change, *RE Studies*, Vol. 34, 249–83.

Jorgensen, D., L.R. Christiansen and L.J. Lau (1975), Transcendental logarithmic production frontiers, *RE Statistics*, Vol. LV, 28–45.

Jorgensen, D., L.R. Christiansen and L.J. Lau (1975), Transcendental logarithmic utility functions, *American Economic Review*, Vol. LXV, 367–383.

Kareken, J. and R.M, Solow (1963), Lags in monetary policy, in *Commission on Money and Credit: Stabilization Policies*, Prentice-Hall.

Kemp, M. (1962), Errors of measurement and bias in estimates of import demand parameters, *Economic Record*, Vol. 38, 369–372.

Kennedy, C. and A.P. Thirlwall (1972), Technical change: a survey, *Economic Journal*. Vol. 82, 11–73.

Klein, L.R. (1950a), *Economic Fluctuations in the United States 1921–1941*, Cowles Commission Monograph No. 11, Wiley.

Klein, L.R. (1950b), *The Keynesian Revolution*, Macmillan.

Klein, L.R. (1958), The estimation of distributed lags, *Econometrica*, Vol. 26, 553–65.

Klein, L.R. (1952, 1974), *A Textbook of Econometrics*, 1st edn., Row Peterson; 2nd edn., Pentice-Hall.

Klein, L.R. (1962), *An Introduction to Econometrics*, Prentice-Hall.

Klein, L.R. and H. Rubin (1947–48). A constant utility index of the cost of living, *RE Studies*, 84–87.

Klein, L.R. and A. Goldberger (1955), *An Econometric Model of the United States, 1929–1932*, North Holland.

Klein, L.R. and R.G. Bodkin, (1967), Nonlinear estimation of aggregate production function, *RE Statistics*, Vol. 49, 28–44.

Klein, L.R., R.J. Ball, A. Hazelwood and P. Vandome (1960), *An Econometric Model of the UK Economy*, Oxford University Press.

Kmenta, J. (1967), On estimation of the CES production function, *International Economic Review*, Vol. 8, 180–189.

Komiya, R. (1962), Technological progress and the production function in the US steam power industry, *RE Statistics*, Vol. 44, 156–66.

Koopmans, T.C. (1950), *Statistical Inference in Dynamic Economic Models*, Cowles Commission Monograph No. 10, Wiley.

Koyck, L.M. (1954), *Distributed Lags and Investment Analysis*, North Holland.

Krishnamurty K. and D.U. Sastry (1975), *Investment and Financing in the Corporate Sector in India*, Institute of Economic Growth, Delhi.

Kuh, E. (1965), *Capital Stock Growth: A Microeconometric Approach*, North Holland.

Labys, W. (1973), *Dynamic Commodity Models: Specification, Estimation and Simulation*, D.C. Heath.

Lancaster, K. (1966), A new approach to consumer theory, *JPE*, Vol. 74, 132–157.

Lipsey, R.G. and M. Parkin (1970), Incomes policy: a reappraisal, *Economica*, Vol. XXXVII, 115–38.

Liu, T.C. (1960), Under-identification, structural estimation and forecasting, *Econometrica*, Vol. 28, 858–865.

Liviatan, N. (1963), Consistent estimation of distributed lags, *International Economic Review*, Vol. 4, 44–52.

Maddala, G.S. (1971), The likelihood approach to pooling cross section and time series data, *Econometrica*, Vol. 39, 939–953.

Maddals, G.S. and J.B. Kadane (1966), Some notes on the estimation of the CES production function, *RE Statistics*, Vol. 48, 340–44.

Makower, H. (1957), *Activity Analysis and the Theory of Economic Equilibrium*, Macmillan.

Malinvaud, E. (1961), The estimation of distributed lags: a comment, *Econometrica*, Vol. 29, 430–33.

Malinvaud, E. (1966, 1972), *Statistical Methods of Econometrics*, North Holland.

Mann H.B. and A. Wald (1943), On the statistical treatment of linear stochastic difference equations, *Econometrica*, Vol. 11, 173–220.

Marschak, J. (1950), Statistical inference in economics: an introduction, in Koopmans (1950), 1–50.

Marschak, J. (1953), Economic measurement for policy and prediction, in Hood and Koopmans (1953), 1–26.

Marschak, J. and W.H. Andrews (1944). Random simultaneous equations and the theory of production, *Econometrica*, Vol. 12, 143–205.

Meyer, J.P. and E. Kuh, (1959), *The Investment Decision*, Harvard University Press.

Mood, A., F. Graybill and D. Boes (1950, 1963, 1974), *Introduction to the Theory of Statistics*, 1st, 2nd and 3rd edns, McGraw-Hill.

Morishima, M. *et al.* (1972), *The Working of Econometric Models*, Cambridge University Press.

Morishima, M. and M. Saito (1964), A dynamic analysis of the American economy, *International Economic Review*, Vol. 5, 125–164. Revised version in Morishima, M. (1972).

Nerlove, M. (1966a), A tabular survey of macroeconometric models, *International Economic Review*, Vol. 7, 127–75.

Nerlove, M. (1967), Recent empirical studies of the CES and related production functions, in Brown, M. (ed.) (1967).

Nerlove, M. (1972), Lags in economic behaviour, *Econometrica*, Vol. 40, 221–252.

Nerlove, M. and K. Wallis (1966b), Use of the Durbin–Watson statistic in inappropriate situations, *Econometrica*, Vol. 34, 235–38.

Nickell, S. (1976), *The Investment Decisions of Firms*, Cambridge University Press.

Pearce, I.F. (1964), *A Contribution to Demand Analysis*, Oxford University Press.

Phillips, A.W.H. (1958), The relation between unemployment and the rate of change of money wage rates in the United Kingdom 1861–1957, *Economica*, Vol. XXV, 283–299.

Phillips, A.W.H. (1959), The estimation of parameters in systems of stochastic differential equations, *Biometrica*, Vol. 46, 67–76.

Phillips, P.C.B. (1972), The structural estimation of a stochastic differential equation system, *Econometrica*, Vol. 40, 1021–1042.

Pollak, R.A. and T.J. Wales (1969), Estimation of the linear expenditure system, *Econometrica*, Vol. 37, 611–628.

Renton, G.A. (1975), *Modelling the Economy*, Heinemann.

Rowley, J.C.R. (1972), Fixed capital formation in the British economy 1956–1965, *Economica*, Vol. XXXIX, No. 154, 177–189.

Sargan, J.D. (1958), Estimation of economic relationships using instrumental variables, *Econometrica*, Vol. 26, 393–415.

Sargan, J.D. (1961), The maximum likelihood estimation of economic relationship with autoregressive residuals, *Econometrica*, Vol. 29, 414–26.

Sargan, J.D. (1964a), Wages and prices in the United Kingdom: a study in econometric methodology, in Hart, P. *et al.* (eds.) *Econometric Analysis for National Planning*, Butterfield.

Sargan, J.D. (1964b), Three stage least squares and full maximum likelihood estimates, *Econometrica*, Vol. 32, 77–81.

Sargan, J.D. (1974), Some discrete approximations to continuous time stochastic models, *Journal of the Royal Statistical Society, Series B.*, Vol. 36, 74–90.

Schmidt, P. and R. Waud (1973), Almon lag techniques and the monetary versus fiscal policy debate, *JASA*, Vol. 68, 11–19.

Schultz, H. (1938), *The Theory and Measurement of Demand*, University of Chicago Press.

Silvey, S.D. (1970), *Statistical Inference,* Penguin.

Simmons, P.J. (1974), *Choice and Demand*, Macmillan.

Simon, H. (1953), Causal ordering and identifiability, in Hood and Koopmans (1953).

Slutsky, E. (1915), On the theory of the budget of the consumer, in *Giornale Degli Economisti*, reprinted in Boulding K. and G. Stigler, *AEA Readings in Price Theory*, Irwin.

Solow, R.M. (1956), A contribution to the theory of economic growth, *Quarterly Journal of Economics*, Vol. 70, 65–94.

Solow, R.M. (1957), Technical change and the aggregate production function, *RE Statistics*, Vol. 39, 312–30.

Solow, R.M. (1959), Investment and technical progress, in K. Arrow *et al.* (eds.), *Mathematical Methods in the Social Sciences*, Stanford University Press.

Stigler, G. (1954), The early history of empirical studies of consumer behaviour, *JPE*, Vol. 62, 95–113, also reprinted in Stigler, G. (1965).

Stigler, G. (1965), *Essays in the History of Economics,* University of Chicago Press.

Stone, J.R.N. (1954), *The Measurement of Consumers' Expenditure and Behaviour in the United Kingdom 1920–1938*, Cambridge University Press.

Strotz, R. and H. Wold (1960), A triptych on causal systems, *Econometrica*, Vol. 28, 417–463.

Theil, H. (1964), *Optimal Linear Decision Rules for Government and Industry*, North Holland.

Theil, H. (1973), *Principles of Econometrics*, North Holland.

Thomas, J.J. (1974), *An Introduction to Statistical Analysis for Economists*, Weidenfeld and Nicolson.

Tinbergen, J. (1951), *Business Cycles in the United Kingdom*, North Holland.

Tinsley, P. (1967), An application of variable weighted distributed lags, *JASA*, Vol. 62, 1277–1299.

Tobin, J. (1956), A statistical demand function for food in the USA, *Journal of the Royal Statistical Society, Series A*, 113–141.

Trivedi, P. (1970), A note on the application of Almon's method of calculating distributed lag coefficients, *Metroeconomica*, Vol. 22, 281–6.

Valavanis-Vail, S. (1955), An econometric model of growth, USA 1869–1953, *American Economic Review, Papers and Proceedings*, Vol. XLV, 208–21.

Wallis, K.F. (1971), Wages, prices and incomes policies: some comments, *Economica*, Vol. XXXVIII, 304–310.

Wallis, K.F. (1972), *An Introduction to Econometrics*, Blackwell.

Wallis, K.F. (1973), *Topics in Applied Econometrics*, Blackwell.

Wickens, M.R. (1970), Estimation of vintage Cobb–Douglas production functions for the United States 1900–1960, *RE Statistics*, Vol. 52, 187–193.

Wold, H. and L. Jureen, (1963), *Demand Analysis: A Study in Econometrics*, Wiley.

Working, E.J. (1927), What do statistical demand curves show? *Quarterly Journal of Economics*, Vol. 41, 212–235. Reprinted in Boulding K. and G. Stigler, *AEA Readings in Price Theory*, Irwin.

Wymer, C. (1972), Econometric estimation of stochastic differential equation systems, *Econometrica*. Vol. 40, 565–578.

Zellner, A. (1972), An efficient method of estimating seemingly unrelated regressions and tests for aggregation bias, *JASA*, Vol. 57, 348–368.

Zellner, A. (1968), *Readings in Econometrics and Economic Statistics*, Little Brown.

Zellner, A. and H. Theil (1962), Three stage least squares: simultaneous estimation of simultaneous equations, *Econometrica*, Vol. 30, 54–78.

Index

(Only econometric topics are listed in this index)

Accelerator relationship, 181, 193, 194
Adaptive expectations (partial adjustment; permanent income), 50, 183–189, 216
Aggregation problem, 139–142, 154–158
ALS, 216, 217, 219
Autoregressive errors (Autocorrelation), ix, 46–53, 56–61, 68–70, 89–90, 183, 186, 189, 190, 192, 202, 208, 211–230; Moving average 46, 47, 185, 202, 208, 215

Continuous time, 15–16, 41, 139, 209–210
Correlation, 17, 192
Covariance analysis, 162–167, 195, 197

Demand analysis, ix, 56, 65–68, 71–104
Distributed lags, 13, 170–178, 218, 220; distributed lag polynomial, 172–178; rational lag distribution (polynomial), 177–178, 200; Almon lags (Lagrange interpolation method), 175–176; Pascal lags 175; Koyck lags 173–175, 177, 189; Point lags, 171
Dummy variables, 162–167, 216
Durbin-Watson statistic (DW), 1, 2, 3, 47, 50, 51, 89, 152–153, 189, 227–229
Dynamic models, ix, 43, 50–53, 56

Engel curves, 80–84, 90, 94, 96; Engel aggregation 91, 92, 99, 105
Estimation; estimators, 4, 32–37, 39–70; BLUE 45, 60, 63, 68; efficient, 32, 36, 41, 42; asymptotic, 42, 44, 45, 46, 50, 51, 52, 53, 191, 214, 229, 248; consistent, 36, 42, 43, 44, 45, 50, 52, 53, 59, 60, 63, 186, 190, 202, 208, 213, 214, 224, 227, 228, 248; unbiased/biased, 41; asymptotic unbiasedness, (42, 43), 44, 45, 46; linear 41; MSE 41

Forecasting, 4, 5, 6, 252–253

GLS, 46, 49, 53, 55, 56, 66, 67, 191

Heteroscedasticity, 45, 194
Homoscedasticity, 44, 45

Identifiability; identification, 4, 16–30, 54, 58–61, 107, 113–131, 138, 205, 224–225, 227–228, 230–231, 237, 246–247
Instrumental variables; instruments; IV estimation, 31, 57–61, 115, 190, 202, 214, 216, 228
Investment functions, 45, 168–204; neoclassical theory, 181, 197–204; capital theory, 178–181; Fisherian capital theory, 178
ICO, 3; Unstat Yearbook, 3

Linear expenditure system, 93–96, 99–101, 104

Marschak-Andrews problem, 113–125, 159, 167
Macroeconomic models, ix, 233–268; IS-LM, 26–30, 236–237, 246–250, 252; Keynesian economics 234, 235, 239, 245–250; Keynesian cross 235–6; monetarism 235–236, 246–250; demand for money, supply of money 236–237, 248, 251; optimal policy 261–268; Klein model I, 239–245, 252, 254–261, 265–268; impact multiplier, 243–245; dynamic multiplier, 243, 245, 259; final form 244, 245, 263; balanced budget multiplier, 245; targets (instruments) 262–268

Maximum likelihood (FIML), ix, 32, 44, 49, 62–77, 100, 151–152, 190, 213, 216, 229, 240–241, 242, 255–256
Mis-specification, 46, 54, 193
Models, 8; static models 43; structural form, 9, 18, 20, 23, 24, 53, 190, 212–213, 224, 237, 240; reduced form, 9, 20, 23, 24, 53, 54, 57, 62, 212, 213, 220, 221, 230, 237, 242, 245, 255, 256
Multicollinearity, 80, 86, 90, 192

OLS, 11, 12, 30, 31, 32, 33, 35, 36, 44–45, 47, 48, 49, 51, 52, 53, 56, 57, 60, 61, 62, 63, 66, 68, 88, 113, 115–117, 120–122, 125, 131, 134, 152, 153, 163–164, 186, 189, 190, 197, 201, 207, 212, 213, 214, 216, 217, 226, 227, 230, 231, 240, 241, 255

Phillips curve, vii, 206–211
Prediction, 5, 6
Production function, ix, 105–136, 137–167; neoclassical 198–199; Cobb-Douglas, 76, 199, 201 (CD form for demand), 94 (CD form for utility), 111–113, 115–136, 146, 148, 161; CES, 67, 112–113, 125–136, 150, 201; Leontieff (limitational/fixed coefficients) 102, 112–161; translog, 104; translog utility 104; returns to scale, 106, 110–111, 151, 143; elasticity of substitution, 106, 109–111, 132–134

R^2, vii, viii, 1, 2, 3, 11, 30, 36, 200, 228, 246, 253
Recursive models (block recursive), 34–37, 59–61, 205, 222–224, 250
Restrictions, testing of, viii, ix, 4, 5, 61–70, 88–89, 99–103, 227, 246–247; identifying R, 16–30, 58, 212, 213; Lagrange multiplier test, 44, 65, 66, 69–70; Wald test, 44, 65, 69–70; *LR* test, 44, 62, 64–65, 66, 67, 69–70, 92, 211
Rotterdam system, 98–101, 104

SURE, 56
Simulation, ix, 253–261
Slutsky effect, 74; equation 76, 91, 92; symmetry, 105
Specification, ix, 4, 11, 12, 13, 32–38, 131–134, 137

Test statistics (t, F), 2, 11, 31, 61, 62, 64, 164–165, 228–229; χ^2, 64, 65, 66, 88–89, 92, 100, 213, 214, 217, 219
Technical change, ix, 137–167; disembodied 143–154; neutral, 142; Hicks neutral, 145–147; Harrod neutral, 145–147; embodied (vintage model), 147–154, 179
3SLS, 55, 56, 61, 63, 241
2SLS, 53, 54, 55, 56, 131, 228, 240–241; ILS, 130

von Neumann Ratio, 89